RISE AND RISE OF RABINDRA NATH TAGORE

RISE AND RISE OF RABINDRA NATH TAGORE

R. Subramanayan

CYBER TECH PUBLICATIONS
4264/3, Ansari Road, Daryaganj, New Delhi-110002 (India)
Ph.: 011-23244078, 011-43559448 Fax: 011-23280028
E-Mail: cyberpublicationsdelhi@yahoo.com
Website: www.cybertechpublications.com

RISE AND RISE OF RABINDRA NATH TAGORE

R. Subramanayan

First Edition 2010

Published by : Asian Offset Printers

G.S. Rawat for **Cyber Tech Publications**

4264/3, Ansari Road, Daryaganj, New Delhi-110002 (India)

Ph.: 011-23244078, 011-43559448 Fax: 011-23280028

E-Mail: cyberpublicationsdelhi@yahoo.com

Website: www.cybertechpublications.com

Preface

The creative genius of Rabindranath was almost universal in expression and temper. Literature, music, arts and thoughts, activities, education or the cooperatives, etc., all were touched and turned into gold. Yet the same genius was rooted in our very soil again. India of the ages spoke through him, he was the finest exponent of vedic lore of composite culture of Hindus, of the universal message of the medieval saints like Kabir, Nanak, etc., right up to Rammohan Roy, of the modern times. Whatever is true in our tradition has its voice in Rabindranath.In Rabindranath a comprehensive view of life and reality emerged. How far this comprehensive view is unique and novel and how far adds new dimensions to our life will be discerned in the study. Study of Rabindranath and Upanishads is certainly a saviour of degenerated culture and civilization. This will bring again the integrated view of the reality.

The Upanishads acted as a perennial source of inspiration for Rabindranath. 'Realisation of the supreme being in each and all' is the pivot of the philosophy of Rabindranath. The quintessence of the Upanishadic teaching forms the edifice of Indian culture. Rabindra Nath Tagore achieved international fame on account of his superb academic qualities of a poet. In his writings, speeches and correspondence with learned persons, he showed his remarkable scholarly worth while dealing with socio-economic, cultural, educational and political problems. He wrote about the common man and his theme were simple in language to be easily understood by one and all. The foundation of Santiniketan in the rural surroundings and its international academic stature greatly enhanced Tagore's prestige all over the globe.

Although Tagore wrote successfully in all literary genres, he was first of all a poet. Among his fifty and odd volumes of poetry are Manasi (1890) [The Ideal One], Sonar Tari (1894) [The Golden

Boat], Gitanjali (1910) [Song Offerings], Gitimalya (1914) [Wreath of Songs], and Balaka (1916) [The Flight of Cranes]. The English renderings of his poetry, which include The Gardener (1913), Fruit-Gathering (1916), and The Fugitive (1921), do not generally correspond to particular volumes in the original Bengali; and in spite of its title, Gitanjali: Song Offerings (1912), the most acclaimed of them, contains poems from other works besides its namesake. Tagore's major plays are Raja (1910) [The King of the Dark Chamber], Dakghar (1912) [The Post Office], Achalayatan (1912) [The Immovable], Muktadhara (1922) [The Waterfall], and Raktakaravi (1926) [Red Oleanders]. He is the author of several volumes of short stories and a number of novels, among them Gora (1910), Ghare-Baire (1916) [The Home and the World], and Yogayog (1929) [Crosscurrents]. Besides these, he wrote musical dramas, dance dramas, essays of all types, travel diaries, and two autobiographies, one in his middle years and the other shortly before his death in 1941. Tagore also left numerous drawings and paintings, and songs for which he wrote the music himself.

The book also aims at an appraisal of Tagore's novels in English translations. It highlights his thematic concerns and novelistic technique. The book also provides a comprehensive and authentic account of his literary genius and his vision of the human predicament. It contains a faithful profile of his age marked by profound convulsions in individual and collective consciousness. This specific study of Tagore's novels based on the themes of humanism and nationalism has shown his position and achievement in the domain of Indian fiction.

— *Author*

CONTENTS

1

INTRODUCTION

Rabindranath Tagore (7 May 1861 – 7 August 1941), also known by the sobriquet Gurudev, was a Bengali poet, Brahmo Samaj philosopher, visual artist, playwright, novelist, and composer whose works reshaped Bengali literature and music in the late 19th and early 20th centuries. He became Asia's first Nobel laureate when he won the 1913 Nobel Prize in Literature. A Pirali Bengali Brahmin from Calcutta, Tagore first wrote poems at the age of eight.

At the age of sixteen, he published his first substantial poetry under the pseudonym *Bhanushingho* ("Sun Lion") and wrote his first short stories and dramas in 1877. His home schooling, life in Shilaidaha, and travels made Tagore a nonconformist and pragmatist. Tagore strongly protested against the British Raj and gave his support to the Indian Independence Movement and Mahatma Gandhi. Tagore's life was tragic—he lost virtually his entire family and was devastated to witness Bengal's decline—but his life's work endured, in the form of his poetry and the institution he founded, Visva-Bharati University. Tagore wrote novels, short stories, songs, dance-dramas, and essays on political and personal topics.

Gitanjali (*Song Offerings*), *Gora* (*Fair-Faced*), and *Ghare-Baire* (*The Home and the World*) are among his best-known works. His verse, short stories, and novels, which often exhibited rhythmic lyricism, colloquial language, meditative naturalism, and philosophical contemplation, received worldwide acclaim. Tagore was also a cultural reformer and polymath who modernised Bengali art by rejecting strictures binding it to classical Indian forms. Two songs from his *rabindrasangeet* canon are now the national anthems of Bangladesh and India: the *Amar Shonar Bangla* and the *Jana Gana Mana*.

EARLY LIFE

Tagore (nicknamed "Rabi") was born the youngest of thirteen surviving children in the Jorasanko mansion in Calcutta (now Kolkata, India) of parents Debendranath Tagore and Sarada Devi. After undergoing his *upanayan* (the *sacred thread* ceremony, a coming-of-age rite) at age eleven, Tagore and his father left Calcutta on 14 February 1873 to tour India for several months, visiting his father's Santiniketan estate and Amritsar before reaching the Himalayan hill station of Dalhousie. There, Tagore read biographies, studied history, astronomy, modern science, and Sanskrit, and examined the classical poetry of Klidsa.

In 1877, he rose to notability when he composed several works, including a long poem set in the Maithili style pioneered by Vidyapati. As a joke, he maintained that these were the lost works of BhnusiCha, a newly discovered 17th-century VaicGava poet. He also wrote "Bhikharini" (1877; "The Beggar Woman"—the Bengali language's first short story) and *Sandhya Sangit* (1882)—including the famous poem "Nirjharer Swapnabhanga" ("The Rousing of the Waterfall"). Seeking to become a barrister, Tagore enrolled at a public school in Brighton, England in 1878. He studied law at University College London, but returned to Bengal in 1880 without a degree.

On 9 December 1883 he married Mrinalini Devi (born Bhabatarini, 1873–1902); they had five children, two of whom later died before reaching adulthood. In 1890, Tagore began managing his family's estates in Shilaidaha, a region now in Bangladesh; he was joined by his wife and children in 1898. Known as "Zamindar Babu", Tagore traveled across the vast estate while living out of the family's luxurious barge, the *Padma*, to collect (mostly token) rents and bless villagers; in return, appreciative villagers held feasts in his honour. These years, which composed Tagore's *Sadhana* period (1891–1895; named for one of Tagore's magazines), were among his most fecund. More than half the stories of the three-volume and eighty-four-story *Galpaguchchha* written. With irony and emotional weight, they depicted a wide range of Bengali lifestyles, particularly village life.

SANTINIKETAN

In 1901, Tagore left Shilaidaha and moved to Santiniketan (West Bengal) to found an ashram, which would grow to include a marble-floored prayer hall ("The Mandir"), an experimental school, groves of trees, gardens, and a library. There, Tagore's wife and two of his children died. His father died on 19 January 1905, and he began receiving monthly payments as part of his inheritance. He received additional income from the Maharaja of Tripura, sales of his family's jewellery, his seaside bungalow in Puri, and mediocre royalties (Rs. 2,000) from his works. These works gained him a large following among Bengali and foreign readers alike, and he published such works as *Naivedya* (1901) and *Kheya* (1906) while translating his poems into free verse. On 14 November 1913, Tagore learned that he had won the 1913 Nobel Prize in Literature. According to the Swedish Academy, it was given due to the idealistic and—for Western readers—accessible nature of a small body of his translated material, including the 1912 *Gitanjali: Song Offerings*.

In 1915, Tagore also accepted knighthood from the British Crown. In 1921, Tagore and agricultural economist Leonard Elmhirst set up the Institute for Rural Reconstruction (which Tagore later renamed Shriniketan—"Abode of Peace") in Surul, a village near the ashram at Santiniketan. Through it, Tagore sought to provide an alternative to Gandhi's symbol- and protest-based *Swaraj* movement, which he denounced. He recruited scholars, donors, and officials from many countries to help the Institute use schooling to "free village[s] from the shackles of helplessness and ignorance" by "vitaliz[ing] knowledge". In the early 1930s, he also grew more concerned about India's "abnormal caste consciousness" and untouchability, lecturing on its evils, writing poems and dramas with untouchable protagonists, and appealing to authorities at the Guruvayoor Temple to admit Dalits.

TWILIGHT YEARS

In his last decade, Tagore remained in the public limelight, publicly upbraiding Gandhi for stating that a massive 15 January 1934 earthquake in Bihar constituted divine retribution for the subjugation of Dalits. He also mourned the incipient socioeconomic decline of Bengal and the endemic poverty of Calcutta; he detailed the latter in an unrhymed hundred-line poem whose technique of searing double-vision would foreshadow Satyajit Ray's film *Apur Sansar*. Tagore also compiled fifteen volumes of writings, including the prose-poems works *Punashcha* (1932), *Shes Saptak* (1935), and *Patraput* (1936). He continued his experimentations by developing prose-songs and dance-dramas, including *Chitrangada* (1914), *Shyama* (1939), and *Chandalika* (1938), and wrote the novels *Dui Bon* (1933), *Malancha* (1934), and *Char Adhyay* (1934). Tagore took an interest in science in his last years, writing *Visva-Parichay* (a collection of essays) in 1937. His exploration of biology, physics, and astronomy impacted his poetry, which often contained extensive naturalism that underscored his respect for scientific laws.

He also wove the process of science (including narratives of scientists) into many stories contained in such volumes as *Se* (1937), *Tin Sangi* (1940), and *Galpasalpa* (1941). Tagore's last four years were marked by chronic pain and two long periods of illness. These began when Tagore lost consciousness in late 1937; he remained comatose and near death for an extended period. This was followed three years later in late 1940 by a similar spell, from which he never recovered. The poetry Tagore wrote in these years is among his finest, and is distinctive for its preoccupation with death. After extended suffering, Tagore died on 7 August 1941 (22 Shravan 1348) in an upstairs room of the Jorasanko mansion in which he was raised; his death anniversary is still mourned in public functions held across the Bengali-speaking world.

TRAVELS

Owing to his notable wanderlust, between 1878 and 1932, Tagore visited more than thirty countries on five continents;

many of these trips were crucial in familiarising non-Indian audiences to his works and spreading his political ideas. In 1912, he took a sheaf of his translated works to England, where they impressed missionary and Gandhi protégé Charles F. Andrews, Anglo-Irish poet William Butler Yeats, Ezra Pound, Robert Bridges, Ernest Rhys, Thomas Sturge Moore, and others.

Indeed, Yeats wrote the preface to the English translation of Gitanjali, while Andrews joined Tagore at Santiniketan. On 10 November 1912, Tagore toured the United States and the United Kingdom, staying in Butterton, Staffordshire with Andrews' clergymen friends. From 3 May 1916 until April 1917, Tagore went on lecturing circuits in Japan and the United States, during which he denounced nationalism—particularly that of the Japanese and Americans. He also wrote the essay "Nationalism in India", attracting both derision and praise (the latter from pacifists, including Romain Rolland). Shortly after returning to India, the 63-year-old Tagore visited Peru at the invitation of the Peruvian government, and took the opportunity to visit Mexico as well. Both governments pledged donations of $100,000 to the school at Shantiniketan (Visva-Bharati) in commemoration of his visits. A week after his November 6, 1924 arrival in Buenos Aires, Argentina, an ill Tagore moved into the Villa Miralrío at the behest of Victoria Ocampo. He left for India in January 1925. On 30 May 1926, Tagore reached Naples, Italy; he met fascist dictator Benito Mussolini in Rome the next day. Their initially warm rapport lasted until Tagore spoke out against Mussolini on 20 July 1926.

On 14 July 1927, Tagore and two companions began a four-month tour of Southeast Asia, visiting Bali, Java, Kuala Lumpur, Malacca, Penang, Siam, and Singapore. Tagore's travelogues from the tour were collected into the work "Jatri". In early 1930 he left Bengal for a nearly year-long tour of Europe and the United States. Once he returned to the UK, while his paintings were being exhibited in Paris and London, he stayed at a Friends settlement in Birmingham. There, he wrote his Hibbert Lectures for the University of Oxford (which dealt with the "idea of the humanity of our God, or the divinity of Man the Eternal") and spoke at London's annual Quaker gathering. There (addressing relations between the British and Indians, a topic he would grapple with over the next two years), Tagore spoke of a "dark chasm of aloofness". He later visited Aga Khan III, stayed at Dartington Hall, then toured Denmark, Switzerland, and Germany from June to mid-September 1930, then the Soviet Union.

Lastly, in April 1932, Tagore—who was acquainted with the legends and works of the Persian mystic Hafez—was invited as a personal guest of Shah Reza Shah Pahlavi of Iran. Such extensive travels allowed Tagore to interact with many notable contemporaries, including Henri Bergson, Albert Einstein, Robert Frost, Thomas Mann, George Bernard Shaw, H.G. Wells and Romain Rolland. Tagore's last travels abroad, including visits to Persia and Iraq (in 1932) and Ceylon in 1933, only sharpened his opinions regarding human divisions and nationalism.

WORKS

Tagore's Bengali-language initials are worked into this "Ra-Tha" wooden seal, which bears close stylistic similarity to designs used in traditional Haida carvings. Tagore often embellished his manuscripts with such art. (Dyson 2001) Tagore's literary reputation is disproportionately influenced by regard for his poetry; however, he also wrote novels, essays, short stories, travelogues, dramas, and thousands of songs. Of Tagore's prose, his short stories are perhaps most highly regarded; indeed, he is credited with originating the Bengali-language version of the genre. His works are frequently noted for their rhythmic, optimistic, and lyrical nature. Such stories mostly borrow from deceptively simple subject matter: the lives of ordinary people.

NOVELS AND NON-FICTION

Tagore wrote eight novels and four novellas, including *Chaturanga*, *Shesher Kobita*, *Char Odhay*, and *Noukadubi*. *Ghare Baire* (*The Home and the World*)—through the lens of the idealistic *zamindar* protagonist Nikhil—excoriates rising Indian nationalism, terrorism, and religious zeal in the *Swadeshi* movement; a frank expression of Tagore's conflicted sentiments, it emerged out of a 1914 bout of depression. Indeed, the novel bleakly ends with Hindu-Muslim sectarian violence and Nikhil's being (probably mortally) wounded. In some sense, *Gora* shares the same theme, raising controversial questions regarding the Indian identity. As with *Ghore Baire*, matters of self-identity (*jti*), personal freedom, and religion are developed in the context of a family story and love triangle. Another powerful story is *Yogayog* (*Nexus*), where the heroine Kumudini—bound by the ideals of *Shiva-Sati*, exemplified by Dkshyani—is torn between her pity for the sinking fortunes of her progressive and compassionate elder brother and his foil: her exploitative, rakish, and patriarchical husband. In it, Tagore demonstrates his feminist leanings, using *pathos* to depict the plight and ultimate demise of Bengali women trapped by pregnancy, duty, and family honour; simultaneously, he treats the decline of Bengal's landed oligarchy.

Other novels were more uplifting: *Shesher Kobita* (translated twice—*Last Poem* and *Farewell Song*) is his most lyrical novel, with poems and rhythmic passages written by the main character (a poet). It also contains elements of satire and postmodernism; stock characters gleefully attack the reputation of an old, outmoded, oppressively renowned poet who, incidentally, goes by the name of Rabindranath Tagore. Though his novels remain among the least-appreciated of his works, they have been given renewed attention via film adaptations by such directors as Satyajit Ray; these include *Chokher Bali* and *Ghare Baire*; many have soundtracks featuring selections from Tagore's own *rabindrasangit*. Tagore wrote many non-fiction books, writing on topics ranging from Indian history to linguistics. Aside from autobiographical works, his travelogues, essays, and lectures were compiled into several volumes, including *Iurop Jatrir Patro* (*Letters from Europe*) and *Manusher Dhormo* (*The Religion of Man*).

MUSIC AND ARTWORK

Tagore was a prolific musician and painter, writing around 2,230 songs. They compose *rabindrasangit* now an integral part of Bengali culture. Tagore's music is inseparable from his literature, most of which—poems or parts of novels, stories, or plays alike—became lyrics for his songs. Primarily influenced by the *thumri* style of Hindustani classical music, they ran the entire gamut of human emotion, ranging from his early dirge-like Brahmo devotional hymns to quasi-erotic compositions. They emulated the tonal colour of classical *ragas* to varying extents. Though at times his songs mimicked a given raga's melody and rhythm faithfully, he also blended elements of different ragas to create innovative works.

For Bengalis, their appeal, stemming from the combination of emotive strength and beauty described as surpassing even Tagore's poetry, was such that the *Modern Review* observed that "[t]here is in Bengal no cultured home where Rabindranath's songs are not sung or at least attempted to be sung ... Even illiterate villagers sing his songs". Music critic Arthur Strangways of *The Observer* first introduced non-Bengalis to *rabindrasangeet* with his book *The Music of Hindostan*, which described it as a "vehicle of a personality ... [that] go behind this or that system of music to that beauty of sound which all systems put out their hands to seize." Among them are Bangladesh's national anthem *Amar Shonar Bangla* and India's national anthem *Jana Gana Mana*; Tagore thus became the only person ever to have written the national anthems of two nations. In turn, *rabindrasangeet* influenced the styles of such musicians as sitar maestro Vilayat Khan, and the *sarodiyas* Buddhadev Dasgupta and Amjad Ali Khan.

At age sixty, Tagore took up drawing and painting; successful exhibitions of his many works—which made a debut appearance in Paris upon encouragement by artists he met in the south of France—were held throughout Europe. Tagore—who likely exhibited protanopia ("colour blindness"), or partial lack of (red-green, in Tagore's case) colour discernment—painted in a style characterised by peculiarities in aesthetics and colouring schemes. Nevertheless, Tagore took to emulating numerous styles, including that of craftwork by the Malanggan people of northern New Ireland, Haida carvings from the west coast of Canada (British Columbia), and woodcuts by M

Pechstein. Tagore also had an artist's eye for his own handwriting, embellishing the scribbles, cross-outs, and word layouts in his manuscripts with simple artistic leitmotifs, including simple rhythmic designs.

THEATRICAL PIECES

Tagore's experience in theatre began at age sixteen, when he played the lead role in his brother Jyotirindranath's adaptation of Molière's *Le Bourgeois Gentilhomme*. At age twenty, he wrote his first drama-opera—*Valmiki Pratibha* (*The Genius of Valmiki*)—which describes how the bandit Valmiki reforms his ethos, is blessed by Saraswati, and composes the *Ramayana*. Through it, Tagore vigorously explores a wide range of dramatic styles and emotions, including usage of revamped *kirtans* and adaptation of traditional English and Irish folk melodies as drinking songs. Another notable play, *Dak Ghar* (*The Post Office*), describes how a child—striving to escape his stuffy confines—ultimately "fall[s] asleep" (which suggests his physical death). A story with worldwide appeal (it received rave reviews in Europe), *Dak Ghar* dealt with death as, in Tagore's words, "spiritual freedom" from "the world of hoarded wealth and certified creeds".

His other works—emphasizing fusion of lyrical flow and emotional rhythm tightly focused on a core idea—were unlike previous Bengali dramas. His works sought to articulate, in Tagore's words, "the play of feeling and not of action". In 1890 he wrote *Visarjan* (*Sacrifice*), regarded as his finest drama. The Bengali-language originals included intricate subplots and extended monologues. Later, his dramas probed more philosophical and allegorical themes; these included *Dak Ghar*. Another is Tagore's *Chandalika* (*Untouchable Girl*), which was modeled on an ancient Buddhist legend describing how Ananda—the Gautama Buddha's disciple—asks water of an *Adivasi* ("untouchable") girl. Lastly, among his most famous dramas is *Raktakaravi* (*Red Oleanders*), which tells of a kleptocratic king who enriches himself by forcing his subjects to mine. The heroine, Nandini, eventually rallies the common people to destroy these symbols of subjugation. Tagore's other plays include *Chitrangada*, *Raja*, and *Mayar Khela*. Dance dramas based on Tagore's plays are commonly referred to as *rabindra nritya natyas*.

SHORT STORIES

Tagore's "Sadhana" period, comprising the four years from 1891 to 1895, was named for one of Tagore's magazines. This period was among Tagore's most fecund, yielding more than half the stories contained in the three-volume *Galpaguchchha*, which itself is a collection of eighty-four stories. Such stories usually showcase Tagore's reflections upon his surroundings, on modern and fashionable ideas, and on interesting mind puzzles (which Tagore was fond of testing his intellect with). Tagore typically associated his earliest stories (such as those of the "*Sadhana*" period) with an exuberance of vitality and spontaneity; these characteristics were intimately connected with Tagore's life in the common villages of, among others, Patisar, Shajadpur, and Shilaida while managing the Tagore family's vast landholdings. There, he beheld the lives of India's poor and common people; Tagore thereby took to examining their lives with a penetrative depth and feeling that was singular in Indian literature up to that point.

In "The Fruitseller from Kabul", Tagore speaks in first person as town-dweller and novelist who chances upon the Afghani seller. He attempts to distil the sense of longing felt by those long trapped in the mundane and hardscrabble confines of Indian urban life, giving play to dreams of a different existence in the distant and wild mountains: "There were autumn mornings, the time of year when kings of old went forth to conquest; and I, never stirring from my little corner in Calcutta, would let my mind wander over the whole world. At the very name of another country, my heart would go out to it ... I would fall to weaving a network of dreams: the mountains, the glens, the forest .... ". Many of the other *Galpaguchchha* stories were written in Tagore's *Sabuj Patra* period (1914–1917; also named for one of Tagore's magazines).

Tagore's *Golpoguchchho* (*Bunch of Stories*) remains among Bengali literature's most popular fictional works, providing subject matter for many successful films and theatrical plays. Satyajit Ray's film *Charulata* was based upon Tagore's controversial novella, *Nastanirh* (*The Broken Nest*). In *Atithi* (also made into a film), the young Brahmin boy Tarapada shares a boat ride with a village zamindar.

The boy reveals that he has run away from home, only to wander around ever since. Taking pity, the zamindar adopts him and ultimately arranges his marriage to the zamindar's own daughter. However, the night before the wedding, Tarapada runs off—again. *Strir Patra* (*The Letter from the Wife*) is among Bengali literature's earliest depictions of the bold emancipation of women. The heroine Mrinal, the wife of a typical patriarchical Bengali middle class man, writes a letter while she is traveling (which constitutes the whole story). It details the pettiness of her life and struggles; she finally declares that she will not return to her husband's home with the statement *Amio bachbo. Ei bachlum* ("And I shall live. Here, I live").

In *Haimanti*, Tagore takes on the institution of Hindu marriage, describing the dismal lifelessness of married Bengali women, hypocrisies plaguing the Indian middle classes, and how Haimanti, a sensitive young woman, must—due to her sensitiveness and free spirit—sacrifice her life. In the last passage, Tagore directly attacks the Hindu custom of glorifying Sita's attempted self-immolation as a means of appeasing her husband Rama's doubts. Tagore also examines Hindu-Muslim tensions in *Musalmani Didi*, which in many ways embodies the essence of Tagore's humanism. On the other hand, *Darpaharan* exhibits Tagore's self-consciousness, describing a young man harboring literary ambitions.

Though he loves his wife, he wishes to stifle her own literary career, deeming it unfeminine. Tagore himself, in his youth, seems to have harboured similar ideas about women. *Darpaharan* depicts the final humbling of the man via his acceptance of his wife's talents. As many other Tagore stories, *Jibito o Mrito* provides the Bengalis with one of their more widely used epigrams: *Kadombini moriya proman korilo she more nai* ("Kadombini died, thereby proved that she hadn't").

POETRY

Tagore's poetry—which varied in style from classical formalism to the comic, visionary, and ecstatic—proceeds out a lineage established by 15th- and 16th-century VaicGava poets. Tagore was also influenced by the mysticism of the *rishi*-authors who—including Vyasa—wrote the Upanishads, the Bhakta-Sufi mystic Kabir, and Ramprasad. Yet Tagore's poetry became most innovative and mature after his exposure to rural Bengal's folk music, which included ballads sung by Bul folk singers—especially the bard Llan Zh.

These—which were rediscovered and popularised by Tagore—resemble 19th-century Kartbhaj hymns that emphasize inward divinity and rebellion against religious and social orthodoxy. During his Shilaidaha years, his poems took on a lyrical quality, speaking via the *maner manus* (the Bauls' "man within the heart") or meditating upon the *jivan devata* ("living God within"). This figure thus sought connection with divinity through appeal to nature and the emotional interplay of human drama. Tagore used such techniques in his BhnusiCha poems (which chronicle the romanticism between Radha and Krishna), which he repeatedly revised over the course of seventy years.

Later, Tagore responded to the (mostly) crude emergence of modernism and realism in Bengali literature by writing experimental works in the 1930s. Examples works include *Africa* and *Camalia*, which are among the better known of his latter poems. He also occasionally wrote poems using *Shadhu Bhasha* (a Sanskritised dialect of Bengali); later, he began using *Cholti Bhasha* (a more popular dialect).

Other notable works include *Manasi*, *Sonar Tori* (*Golden Boat*), *Balaka* (*Wild Geese*—the title being a metaphor for migrating souls), and *Purobi*. *Sonar Tori*'s most famous poem—dealing with the ephemeral nature of life and achievement—goes by the same name; it ends with the haunting phrase ("*Shunno nodir tire rohinu po°i / Jaha chhilo loe gêlo shonar tori*"—"all I had achieved was carried off on the golden boat—only I was left behind."). Internationally, *Gitanjali* is Tagore's best-known collection, winning him his Nobel Prize.

"My song has put off her adornments. She has no pride of dress and decoration. Ornaments would mar our union; they would come between thee and me; their jingling would drown thy whispers."

"My poet's vanity dies in shame before thy sight. O master poet, I have sat down at thy feet. Only let me make my life simple and straight, like a flute of reed for thee to fill with music."

"Klanti" the sixth poem in *Gitali*, reads:

Klanti amar khôma kôro, probhuPôthe jodi pichhie po°i kobhuEi je hia thôro thôro kãpe aji êmontôro,Ei bedona khôma kôro, khôma kôro probhu.Ei dinota khôma kôro, probhu,Pichhon-pane takai jodi kobhu.Diner tape roudrojalae shukae mala pujar thalae,Shei mlanota khôma kôro, khôma kôro, probhu.

Tagore's poetry has been set to music by various composers, among them classical composer Arthur Shepherd's triptych for soprano and string quartet.

POLITICAL VIEWS

Marked complexities characterise Tagore's political views. He criticised European imperialism and supported Indian nationalists and although he himself vehemently denied it at the time, the evidence produced during the Hindu-German Conspiracy trial, as well as some later accounts, he was aware of the conspiracy and even interviewed the then Japanese premier Count Terauchi and former premier Count Okuma on behalf of the conspirators to try and enlist Japanese support. However, he also lampooned the Swadeshi movement, denouncing it in "The Cult of the Charka", an acrid 1925 essay. Instead, he emphasized self-help and intellectual uplift of the masses, stating that British imperialism was not a primary evil, but instead a "political symptom of our social disease", urging Indians to accept that "there can be no question of blind revolution, but of steady and purposeful education". Such views inevitably enraged many, placing his life in danger: during his stay in a San Francisco hotel in late 1916, Tagore narrowly escaped assassination by Indian expatriates. The plot failed only because the would-be assassins fell into argument. Yet Tagore wrote songs lionizing the Indian independence movement and renounced his knighthood in protest against the 1919 Jallianwala Bagh Massacre. Two of Tagore's more politically charged compositions, "Chitto Jetha Bhayshunyo" ("Where the Mind is Without Fear") and "Ekla Chalo Re" ("If They Answer Not to Thy Call, Walk Alone"), gained mass appeal, with the latter favoured by Gandhi. Despite his tumultuous relations with Gandhi, Tagore was key in resolving a Gandhi-Ambedkar dispute involving separate electorates for untouchables, ending Gandhi's fast "unto death".

Tagore also criticised orthodox (rote-oriented) education, lampooning it in the short story "The Parrot's Training", where a bird—which ultimately dies—is caged by tutors and force-fed pages torn from books. These views led Tagore—while visiting Santa Barbara, California on 11 October 1917—to conceive of a new type of university, desiring to "make [his ashram at] Santiniketan the connecting thread between India and the world ... [and] a world center for the study of humanity ... somewhere beyond the limits of nation and geography." The school—which he named Visva-Bharati—had its foundation stone laid on 22 December 1918; it was later inaugurated on 22 December 1921. Here, Tagore implemented a *brahmacharya* pedagogical structure employing *gurus* to provide individualised guidance for pupils. Tagore worked hard to fundraise for and staff the school, even contributing all of his Nobel Prize monies. Tagore's duties as steward and mentor at Santiniketan kept him busy; he taught classes in mornings and wrote the students' textbooks in afternoons and evenings. Tagore also fundraised extensively for the school in Europe and the U.S. between 1919 and 1921.

IMPACT AND LEGACY

Tagore's post-death impact can be felt through the many festivals held worldwide in his honour—examples include the annual Bengali festival/celebration of *Kabipranam* (Tagore's birthday anniversary), the annual Tagore Festival held in

Urbana, Illinois in the United States, the *Rabindra Path Parikrama* walking pilgrimages leading from Calcutta to Shantiniketan, and ceremonial recitals of Tagore's poetry held on important anniversaries. This legacy is most palpable in Bengali culture, ranging from language and arts to history and politics; indeed, Nobel laureate Amartya Sen noted that even for modern Bengalis, Tagore was a "towering figure", being a "deeply relevant and many-sided contemporary thinker". Tagore's collected Bengali-language writings—the 1939 *Rab+ndra Racanval+*—is also canonized as one of Bengal's greatest cultural treasures, while Tagore himself has been proclaimed "the greatest poet India has produced".

Tagore was famed throughout much of Europe, North America, and East Asia. He was key in founding Dartington Hall School, a progressive coeducational institution; in Japan, he influenced such figures as Nobel laureate Yasunari Kawabata. Tagore's works were widely translated into English, Dutch, German, Spanish, and other European languages by Czech indologist Vincent Slesny, French Nobel laureate André Gide, Russian poet Anna Akhmatova, and others. In the United States, Tagore's popular lecturing circuits (especially those between 1916–1917) were widely attended and acclaimed. Nevertheless, several controversies involving Tagore resulted in a decline in his popularity in Japan and North America after the late 1920s, contributing to his "near total eclipse" outside of Bengal.

Tagore, through Spanish translations of his works, also influenced leading figures of Spanish literature, including Chileans Pablo Neruda and Gabriela Mistral, Mexican writer Octavio Paz, and Spaniards José Ortega y Gasset, Zenobia Camprubí, and Juan Ramón Jiménez. Between 1914 and 1922, the Jiménez-Camprubí spouses translated no less than twenty-two of Tagore's books from English into Spanish. Jiménez, as part of this work, also extensively revised and adapted such works as Tagore's *The Crescent Moon*. Indeed, during this time, Jiménez developed the now-heralded innovation of "naked poetry" (Spanish: *«poesia desnuda»*). Ortega y Gasset wrote that "Tagore's wide appeal [may stem from the fact that] he speaks of longings for perfection that we all have ... Tagore awakens a dormant sense of childish wonder, and he saturates the air with all kinds of enchanting promises for the reader, who ... pays little attention to the deeper import of Oriental mysticism". Tagore's works were published in free editions around 1920 alongside works by Dante Alighieri, Miguel de Cervantes, Johann Wolfgang von Goethe, Plato, and Leo Tolstoy.

Tagore's talents came to be regarded as overrated by several westerners. Graham Greene doubted that "anyone but Mr. Yeats can still take his poems very seriously." Modern remnants of a once widespread Latin American reverence of Tagore were discovered, for example, by an astonished Salman Rushdie during a trip to Nicaragua.

LIFE OF RABINDRANATH TAGORE (1861–1901)

The life of Rabindranath Tagore (1861–1941) covers the first four decades of his life; these were formative of both his artistic and much of his political thinking. Rabindranath Tagore was a Bengali poet, Brahmo philosopher, and scholar.

FAMILY BACKGROUND

Tagore was born at No. 6 Dwarkanath Tagore Lane, Jorasanko — the address of his family mansion. In turn, Jorasanko was located in the Bengali section of north Kolkata, located near Chitpur Road. The area immediately around the Jorasanko Tagore mansion was rife with poverty and prostitution. He was the son of Debendranath Tagore and Sarada Devi. Debendranath Tagore had formulated the Brahmo faith propagated by his friend, the reformer Raja Ram Mohan Roy. Debendranath became the central figure in Brahmo society after Ray's death, who was addressed out of respect by followers as *maharishi.* He continued to lead the *Adi Brahmo Shomaj* until he died. Women who married into Tagore's clan were generally from the villages of East Bengal (now Bangladesh).

CHILDHOOD (1861–1878)

Tagore was born the youngest of fourteen children. As a child, Tagore lived amidst an atmosphere where literary magazines were published, musical recitals were held, and theatre performed. The Jorasanko Tagores were indeed at the center of a large and art-loving social group. Tagore's oldest brother, Dwijendranath, was a respected philosopher and poet. Another brother, Satyendranath, was the first ethnically Indian member appointed to the elite and formerly all-white Indian Civil Service. Yet another brother, Jyotirindranath Tagore, was a talented musician, composer, and playwright.

Among his sisters, Swarnakumari Devi earned fame as a novelist in her own right. Jyotirindranath's wife, Kadambari — who was slightly older than Tagore — was a dear friend and a powerful influence on Tagore. Her abrupt suicide in 1884 left him distraught for years, and left a profound mark on the emotional timbre of Tagore's literary life.

Tagore — nicknamed "Rabi" — was born the youngest of fourteen children. As part of the Jorasanko branch of the Tagore family, Tagore grew up exposed to the publication of literary magazines, in-home musical recitals, and theatrical performances. Tagore was also influenced by older brothers Dwijendranath (a philosopher), Satyendranath (the first Indian appointed to the elite Indian Civil Service), and Jyotirindranath (a musician, composer, and playwright). His female relatives included sister Swarna Kumari Devi (a novelist) and Kadambari (Jyotirindranath's wife, whose 1884 suicide burdened Tagore for years).

For the first decade or so of his life, Tagore remained distant from his father, who was frequently away touring northern India, England, and other places. Meanwhile, Tagore was mostly confined to the family compound — he was forbidden to leave it for any purpose other than traveling to school. He thereby grew increasingly restless for the outside world, open spaces, and nature. On the other hand, Tagore was intimidated by the mansion's perceived ghostly and enigmatic aura.

Further, Tagore was ordered about the house by servants in a period he would later designate as a "servocracy". Incidents included servants dunking the heads of Tagore and his siblings into drinking water held by giant clay cisterns — used as a means to quiet the children. In addition, Tagore often refused food to satisfy servants, was confined to a chalk circle by the second-in-command servant named Shyam in parody of an analogous forest trial that Sita underwent in the *Ramayana*, and was told horrific stories telling the bloody exploits of outlaw dacoits.

Tagore was also was tutored at home by Hemendranath, his brother. While being physically conditioned — for example, swimming in the Ganges River, taking long treks through hilly areas, and practicing judo and wrestling — he was also given Bengali-language lessons in anatomy, drawing, English language (Tagore's least favorite subject), geography, gymnastics, history, literature, mathematics, and Sanskrit imparted before and after school. Meanwhile, Tagore was developed an aversion towards formal learning and schooling, stating later that the role of teaching was not to explain things, but rather to

> *"knock at the doors of the mind. If any boy is asked to give an account of what is awakened in him by such knocking, he will probably say something silly. For what happens within is much bigger than what comes out in words. Those who pin their faith on university examinations as the test of education take no account of this."*

Tagore started writing poems around age eight, and he was urged by an older brother to recite these to people in the mansion — including to an impressed Brahmo nationalist, newspaper editor, and Hindu Mela organizer. At age eleven, Tagore underwent the *upanayan* coming-of-age rite: he and two relatives were shaved bald and sent into retreat, where they were to chant and meditate. Tagore instead rollicked, beating drums and pulling his brothers' ears, after which he received a sacred thread of investiture. Afterward, on February 14, 1873, Tagore experienced the first close contact with his father when they set out together from Calcutta on a months-long tour of India. They first made for Shantiniketan ("Abode of Peace"), a family estate acquired in 1863 by Debendranath composed of two rooms set amidst a mango grove, trees, and plants. Tagore later recalled his stay among the rice paddies:

> *"What I could not see did not take me long to get over— what I did see was quite enough. There was no servant rule, and the only ring which encircled me was the blue of the horizon, drawn around these [rural] solitudes by their presiding goddess. Within this I was free to move about as I chose."*

After several weeks, they traveled to Amritsar, staying near the Harmandir Sahib and worshipping at a Sikh gurudwara. They also read English- and Sanskrit-language books, exposing Tagore to astronomy, biographies of such figures as Benjamin Franklin, and Edward Gibbon's *The History of the Decline and Fall of the Roman Empire.*

Later, in mid-April, Tagore and his father set off for the remote and frigid Himalayan hill station of Dalhousie, India, near what is now Himachal Pradesh's border with Kashmir. There, at an elevation of some 2,300 meters (7,500 feet), they lived in a house high atop Bakrota hill. Tagore was taken aback by the region's deep gorges, alpine forests, and mossy streams and waterfalls. Yet Tagore was also made to study lessons — including such things as Sanskrit declensions — starting in the icy pre-dawn twilight. Tagore took a break from his readings for a noontime meal; thereafter, Tagore was to continue his studies, although Tagore was often allowed to fall asleep. Some two months later, Tagore left his father in Dalhousie and journeyed back to Calcutta.

SCHOOLING IN ENGLAND

In early October 1878, Tagore traveled to England with the intent of becoming a barrister. He first stayed for some months at a house that the Tagore family owned near Brighton and Hove, in Medina Villas; there, he attended a Brighton school (not, as has been claimed, Brighton College — his name does not appear in its admissions register). In 1877, his nephew and niece — Suren and Indira, the children of Tagore's brother Satyendranath — were sent together with their mother (Tagore's sister-in-law) to live with him. Later, after spending Christmas of 1878 with his family, Tagore was escorted by his elder brother's friend to London; there, Tagore's relatives hoped that he would focus more on his studies. He enrolled at University College London.

However, he never did complete his degree, leaving England after just over a year's stay. This exposure to English culture and language would later percolate into his earlier acquaintance with Bengali musical tradition, allowing him to create new modes of music, poetry, and drama. Nevertheless, Tagore neither fully embraced English strictures nor his family's traditionally strict Hindu religious observances in either his life or in his art, choosing instead to pick the best from both realms of experience.

SHELAIDAHA

In 1890, Tagore began managing his family's estates in Shelaidaha, a region now in Bangladesh; he was joined by his wife and children in 1898.

Tagore, known then as "Zamindar Babu", often traveled dozens of miles across the vast estate while living out of the *Padma*, the family's converted flat-bottomed keel-less barge (known as a "budgerow" or a *Daccai bajras*). His dealings with his tenants included the annual collection of (mostly token) rents and the blessing of villagers; in exchange for his generosity, villagers regularly held feasts in Tagore's honour — these featured such fare as dried rice and sour milk.

In this decade, Tagore authored many works and founded a new genre of Bengali writing: the short story. Tagore wrote some fifty-nine of them in 1891–1901; many had ironic elements or had emotional appeal while they dealt with a wide range of Bengali lifestyles. Examples include *Sonar Tari* (1894), *Chitra* (1896), and *Katha O Kahini* (1900); his essays, poems, and plays of the time also touched on village life.

LIFE OF RABINDRANATH TAGORE (1901–1932)

The life of Rabindranath Tagore (1901–1924) concerns his life in Santiniketan and extensive travels throughout Asia, Europe, and Japan. Rabindranath Tagore was a Bengali poet, Brahmo philosopher, and scholar.

SANTINIKETAN

In 1901, Tagore left Shelaidaha and moved to Shantiniketan, about one hundred miles to Calcutta's northwest in what is now West Bengal. Shantiniketan, a spread of relatively arid and eroded red soil of seven acres bought in the 1860s by Debendranth, was made the home of Tagore's new ashram, a marble-floored prayer hall ("The Mandir"), experimental school, groves of trees, gardens, and a library. Unfortunately, his wife along with two of his children — Renuka (in 1903) and Samindranath (in 1907) — died in this period, leaving Tagore distraught. When Tagore's father — aged 87 — also died on January 19, 1905, Tagore began receiving 1,250–1,500 rupees (Rs.) monthly as an inheritance. This combined with income from the Maharaja of Tripura, sales of jewelry owned by him and his late wife, his bungalow at the seaside Puri, and mediocre royalties (Rs. 2,000) gleaned from the licensed publishing of thousands of copies of his works.

Thus, he gained a large following among Bengali readers. He published such works as *Naivedya* (1901) and *Kheya* (1906). Non-Bangla translations were also published, but these were frequently of mediocre quality. In response to requests by admirers (including painter William Rothenstein), Tagore began translating his poems into free verse. In 1912, he went to England while carrying a sheaf of his translated works. At readings there, these works impressed a number of Englishmen, including English missionary and Gandhi protégé Charles F. Andrews, Anglo-Irish poet William Butler Yeats, Ezra Pound, Robert Bridges, Ernest Rhys, and Thomas Sturge Moore. Indeed, Yeats later wrote the preface to the English translation of Gitanjali (published by the India Society), while Andrews joined Tagore in India to work with him.

On 10 November 1912, Tagore traveled to the United States, speaking at a Unitarian church in Urbana, Illinois. In that year, Tagore also toured the United Kingdom, meeting William Rothenstein and William Butler Yeats, who read his *Gitanjali*. Later, he stayed in Butterton, Staffordshire with C.F. Andrews' clergymen friends. On 14 November 1913, he received word that he had won the Nobel Prize in Literature;

the award stemmed from the idealistic and accessible (for Western readers) nature of a small body of translated material, including the 1912 *Gitanjali: Song Offerings*.

Together with Mukul Dey, Charles F. Andrews and W. W. Pearson, Tagore again set off by boat on 3 May 1916, embarking on a lecturing circuit of Japan and the United States that was to last until April 1917. During a four-month layover in Japan, Tagore authored "On the Way to Japan" and "In Japan", which were later compiled into the book *Japanyatri* ("A Sojourn to Japan"), which detailed his admiration for the Japanese aesthetic. Yet Tagore also denounced nationalism, particularly that of the Japanese and Americans.

He wrote the essay "Nationalism in India", attracting both derision and praise (the latter from pacifists and fellow internationalists like Romain Rolland). Yet these views also endangered him: during his stay in a San Francisco hotel, Tagore narrowly escaped being assassinated by a pair of Indian expatriates— the plot failed only because the would-be assassins fell into argument concerning whether they should carry through with the murder.

The following morning, Tagore left for Santa Barbara, near Los Angeles. There, Tagore meditated among orange groves and conceived of a new type of university, desiring to "make Shantiniketan the connecting thread between India and the world ... [and] a world center for the study of humanity ... somewhere beyond the limits of nation and geography."

The school — which he named Visva-Bharati — had its foundation stone ceremoniously laid on 22 December 1918; it was later inaugurated on 22 December 1921. Tagore's duties as steward and mentor at Santiniketan kept him busy; he taught classes in mornings and wrote textbooks for his students in afternoons and evenings. Of this routine, he wrote that "I long to discover some fairyland of holidays ... where all duties look delightfully undutiful, like clouds bearing rain appearing perfectly inconsequential". Tagore was also occupied with fundraising between 1919 and 1921, undertaking trips to Europe and the U.S.

LIFE OF RABINDRANATH TAGORE (1932–1941)

Last Works of 1932-1937

Tagore's international travels also sharpened his opinion that human divisions were shallow. During a May 1932 visit to a Bedouin encampment in the Iraqi desert, the tribal chief told him that "Our prophet has said that a true Muslim is he by whose words and deeds not the least of his brother-men may ever come to any harm ..." Tagore noted in his diary: "I was startled into recognizing in his words the voice of essential humanity." In his last decade, Tagore compiled fifteen volumes of writings, including works of prose-poems such as *Punashcha* (1932), *Shes Saptak* (1935), and *Patraput* (1936). He also continued his experimentations by developing prose-songs and dance-dramas, including *Chitrangada* (1936), *Shyama* (1939), and *Chandalika* (1938). He also wrote the novels *Dui Bon* (1933), *Malancha* (1934), and *Char Adhyay* (1934). Tagore also took an interest in science in his last years, writing *Visva-Parichay* (a collection of essays) in 1937. He wrote on topics ranging from biology to physics, and astronomy; meanwhile, his poetry — containing extensive naturalism — underscored his respect for scientific laws. He also wove the process of science (including narratives of scientists) into many stories contained in such volumes as *Se* (1937), *Tin Sangi* (1940), and *Galpasalpa* (1941).

Illness of 1937-1941

Tagore's last four years (1937–1941) were marked by chronic pain and two long periods of illness. These began when Tagore lost consciousness in late 1937; he remained comatose and near death for an extended period. This was followed three years later in late 1940 by a similar spell, from which he never recovered. The poetry Tagore wrote in these twilight years are distinctive for their preoccupation with death; these more profound and mystical experimentations allowed Tagore to be branded a "modern poet". After extended suffering, Tagore died on August 7, 1941 (22 Shravan 1348) in an upstairs room of the Jorasanko mansion in which he was raised. This date is still mourned in public functions held across the Bangla-speaking world. The last person to see Tagore alive was Amiya Kumar Sen (brother of Sukumar Sen, the first chief election commissioner); Tagore dictated his last poem to Sen, who wrote it down. Sen later donated the resulting draft to a museum in Kolkata.

Chokher Bali

Chokher Bali, literally *Sand of the Eye*, equivalent to *eye-sore*, is a Bengali novel written by Rabindranath Tagore in the early twentieth century, against the backdrop of the Indian Independence Movement.

Plot Summary

Binodini is a young widow left to her own devices when her sickly husband dies soon after they are married. She returns to her village and lives there for a couple of months until she accepts the invitation of Rajlakshmi to live with her and her son, Mahendra (who had rejected a former marriage proposal with Binodini). He is newly married to Ashalata, but eventually realises that he and Binodini are more compatible. The story details the relationships of these three and Mahendra's best friend Behari as they deal with issues like distrust, adultery, lies, and numerous fallings-out between them.

Critical Acclaim

Tagore elaborately records early 20th century Bengali society, through his central character, the rebellious widow, who wants to live a life of her own. In writing this novel he exposes the custom of perpetual mourning on the part of widows, who were not allowed to remarry and were condemned to a life of seclusion and loneliness. It is a melancholy, stirring tale of the deceit and sorrow that arise from dissatisfaction and sorrow. Tagore has said about the novel, "I have always regretted the ending".

ADAPTATIONS

Gitanjali

Gitanjali (Bangla *Gitanjoli*) is a collection of 103 English poems, largely translations, by the Bengali poet Rabindranath

Tagore. This volume became very famous in the West, and was widely translated.

Gitanjali is also the title of an earlier Bengali volume (1910) of mostly devotional songs. The word *gitanjoli* is a composed from "git", song, and "anjoli", offering, and thus means - "An offering of songs"; but the word for offering, *anjoli*, has a strong devotional connotation, so the title may also be interpreted as "prayer offering of song".

The English collection is not a translation of poems from the Bengali volume of the same name. While half the poems (52 out of 103) in the English text were selected from the Bengali volume, others were taken from these works (given with year and number of songs selected for the English text): *Gitimallo* (1914,17), *Noibeddo* (1901,15), *Khea* (1906,11) and a handful from other works. The translations were often radical, leaving out or altering large chunks of the poem and in one instance even fusing two separate poems (song 95, which unifies songs 89,90 of naivedya).

The translations were undertaken prior to a visit to England in 1912, where the poems were extremely well received. A slender volume was published in 1913, with an exhilarating preface by W. B. Yeats. In the same year, based on a corpus of three thin translations, Rabindranath became the first non-European to win the Nobel prize.

Poetry

The poems of Gitanjali express a largely metaphysical outlook, talking about a union with the "supreme"; but like much western poetry that explores similar themes, the language suggests the union of two earthly lovers. This type of anthropomorphic depiction of celestial love is quite common in the Vaishnava literature of India since the 12th c. (see Vidyapati or Jayadeva). Rabindranath encountered it also in his interactions with the Baul community in rural Bengal. For example, poem 7 in the English volume renders poem 125 from the Bengali gItanjali, *Amar e gan chhe°echhe tar shôkol ôlongkar* and talks of heavenly love in terms of the lover taking off her jewelry, which is getting in the way of the union. See also the poem 18, at the bottom of this page. Some poems involve themes related to nature, but here, too, the spiritual is subtly present, as in this poem (no. 57), given here along with the Bangla text in Roman script: Light, my light, the world-filling light, the eye-kissing light, heart-sweetening light!

Ah, the light dances, my darling, at the centre of my life; the light strikes, my darling, the chords of my love; the sky opens, the wind runs wild, laughter passes over the earth. The butterflies spread their sails on the sea of light. Lilies and jasmines surge up on the crest of the waves of light.

The light is shattered into gold on every cloud, my darling, and it scatters gems in profusion. Mirth spreads from leaf to leaf, my darling, and gladness without measure. The heaven's river has drowned its banks and the flood of joy is abroad. Alo amar, alo ogo, alo bhubôn bhôraalo nôeon dhôoa amar, alo hridôe hara.Nache alo nache, o bhai, amar praner kachhe — baje alo baje, o bhai, hridôe binar majhe —jage akash, chhoþe batash, hashe shôkol dhôra.Alor srote pal tulechhe hajar projapoti.Alor ðheue uþhlo mete mollika maloti.Meghe meghe shona, o bhai, jae na manik gona —patae patae hashi, o bhai, pulôk rashi rashi.Shuronodir kul bhorechhe shudha-nijhôr-jhôra. -Ôcholaeotôn

Legacy

In the English-speaking world, the writings of Tagore are no longer widely read. Nonetheless, for millions of Bangla speakers, the Bengali originals continue to resonate, as in this verse:

Alo amar, alo ogo, alo bhubon bhora alo noeon dhooa amar, alo hridoe hara.

Nache alo nache, o bhai, amar praner kachhe -- baje alo baje, o bhai, hridoe binar majhe —

jage akash, chhoþe batash, hashe shokol dhora.

Alor srote pal tulechhe hajar projapoti.

Alor ðheue uþhlo mete mollika maloti.

Meghe meghe shona, o bhai, jae na manik gona —patae patae hashi, o bhai, pulok rashi rashi.

Shuronodir kul bhorechhe shudha-nijhor-jhora. - *Ocholaeoton*

I stand mesmerized, wondering how you sing your notes hold the world spellbound - the light of your music lights up my universe.

(song 22 of Bengali Gitanjali, song 3 in the English.)

SATYAJIT RAY'S ADAPTATION OF TAGORE

As we think of the models of adaptation we are forced to work with formal definitions of literature or film. It is necessary to recognise the modes and limits of transaction, and that demands positing stable entities between which the transaction takes place. Nevertheless, we also know that it is not a medium but a practice that one has to think of as literary or film texts are produced, practice being itself always adaptive, always redefining the borders between what falls within the medium and what does not. To place adaptation in a historical context could mean considering practice itself as something that conditions the medium rather than the other way round. Besides social and historical contexts one has to also consider here the contexts of the media in question, their own levels of historical development. I would like to illustrate the point with the help of a modern classic from India, Satyajit Ray's *Charulata* (1964).

Soon after the release of *Charulata*, Ray became involved in an intense debate over the changes he made in the original text, 'Nastaneer' (The Broken Nest'), a 1901 story written by Rabindranath Tagore (Ray 1982). An eminent critic called into question the very necessity of presenting the film as an adaptation of Tagore, whatever the merits of the film were, after such changes as those that Ray brought into 'both the theme and the plot' of the film (Rudra 1996). The story has the structure of a novelette; it is divided into twenty short chapters posing a challenge to a filmmaker who is looking for a tightly integrated narrative. The critic pointed out how Ray has virtually done away with the material of the last seven chapters and added several new elements, to mark a definite break with Tagore. Can departure itself be a mode of adaptation? Ray's reply came up with the most extensive analysis he ever wrote of his own films. He defended the deviations from the original in terms of the treatment of time, causality and character delineation, and in the process explained the primary imperatives of storytelling in cinema.

The story is set in the late nineteenth century Bengal. Bhupati, a well-meaning member of the nationalist gentry, spends most of his time on the political magazine he brings out in English. His young wife Charulata, following the custom, is confined to the inner quarters of the house, spends lonely hours reading novels and doing embroidery. She finds a companion in Bhupati's cousin Amal, a university student of her age. They exchange knowledge of novels, share enthusiasm for literary periodicals, they help each other grow into creative writers. All this happens with encouragement from Bhupati. For Amal, the realisation will come too late that the relationship has grown into love; and he will be in a position to break away from the bond, he will leave the house. For Charu, this organic aspect of growing up, of articulating herself into the world, will not be as easy to disown. She creates a new secret interior within the interior she inhabits as she learns to live with the new reality. Bhupati will come to know about all this after Charu has built that secret chamber, after she returns to him as a wife, so to speak. This discovery of the truth of the home also comes for Bhupati after his public enterprise, the magazine, fails, when he comes back to the inner quarters seeking his wife's company for the first time.

In his essay, Ray explains the basic rules of screenwriting and direction in order to point out the specificity of his medium. The debate took place in the pages of one of the most prestigious literary periodicals of the time, *Parichay*, the readers and contributors of which might have been intellectually advanced in other ways but seemed to require a lesson in film language. The film society movement was still in its early phase, and it is Ray the film society activist speaking here, still engaged in some kind of awareness raising exercise, making audiences familiar with arguments about the autonomy of film. The struggle for autonomy is launched here against a 'literary' perception of cinema.

Ray was one of the founders of the Calcutta Film Society, the first of its kind in India, established in 1947. The critical discourse that he and his colleagues at the Film Society launched can be seen in many ways as a preamble to the realist break that Ray's debut film, *Pather Panchali*, brought about in 1955. But serious discussion of cinema began before this cineaste intervention, it goes back at least to the late 1920s. A spate of film magazines followed the arrival of sound in 1931. The new sound studios employed a large number of writers. Sound redefined Indian cinema in terms of regional practices, regions being linguistically divided in India.

A language - cinema- literature correspondence was established in critical discourse which also set into relief the categories of realism, authenticity and authorship. Writings on cinema from the 1930s and 40s, often by the writers and critics who had joined the industry, present a more or less consistent argument for a regionally grounded contemporary cinema that should mould itself into a novelistic discourse. The *Mythological* film, often thought to be characteristic of Indian popular cinema, became a minor genre in the sound cinema of the Studio Era (1931-55), giving way to the *Social* film as the dominant mode. The *Social* was the mainstream middle-class cinema negotiating the theme of social reform that has informed the novel in all Indian languages since the nineteenth century. The mutations set in motion in the *Social* in the 1940s will finally give rise to two formations, the realist art film launched with *Pather Panchali*, and the classic melodrama that came into being around the same time that *Pather Panchali* appeared. The question of autonomy figured prominently in the new criticism that arrived in the wake of the Calcutta Film Society. Informed by an exposure to world cinema this criticism came to posit the idea of a national modern cinema, a cinema that would fashion a rational, democratic language free of the pre-modern, non-secular compulsions of the popular film. The arguments for textual autonomy and for rational form were of necessity interrelated.

The heteronomous address of Indian popular cinema, where blocks of spectacle are often combined through a logic of interruption, was the target of this critical discourse; but initially, there was also an older practice of the Studio- *Social* that had to be confronted. This was a kind of 'cinema du papa'- dominated by literary practitioners, where screenplays and films were often judged on the basis of the literary value of dialogue and characters.

Major novelists such as Premendra Mitra and Sailajananda Mukhopadhyay were seen to have failed to break into a cinematic language because of their inability to conceive such language in its autonomy. Ray's defence of his adaptation is pitched against the lingering resistance to perceiving the film text in its own terms, the challenge being all the more serious here because of the Tagore factor.

Can we judge *Charulata* on the basis of its independence of literary procedures, of the generic protocols of the original story? As we watch the film adaptation itself becomes an object of scrutiny. We relish the transformation that Tagore's rich prose has undergone in the wordless passages of *Charulata*, enjoy the method that translates spaces between the words into volume and movement.

But there is a second level of contact between the two texts where the whole question of word and image transaction has to be re-considered. At this level, the film takes its distance in time from the original text as a material basis of adaptation; it begins to look at a past of which the literary text itself has become a constitutive element. Hence it was not only the camera penetrating the world captured in the story in order to transform it into another language, it was also a question of framing the story itself as part of a fabric of the past.

'Broken Nest' reads more like a compressed novel than a short story, it moves through extended passages and gaps in time, through episodes and broad developments in characters and situations. The long introductory sequence of *Charulata* is probably the best example of the masterly technique of compression and telescoping Ray uses to translate descriptive passages. Almost without any dialogue the sequence establishes a typical afternoon in Charu's life, her loneliness, her affinity to novels, the spatial limits of her movements. It brings to life an object-world that embodies time – the wallpaper, the furniture, the items of daily use, but also the street sounds and the street images.

These images are glimpsed by Charu through an opera glass: as she opens one blind after another on the wall to peek at the comically graphic characters moving in the street, her socially restricted movement momentarily turns into a playful choreography. And then Charu frames the figure of her husband Bhupati with the opera glass - passing down the corridor not noticing her, lost in his book. Ray conjures up this interior with a dexterity that reminds us of the image of Charu's embroidery in the title sequence, A texture of words is dissolved into a weave of images effortlessly before our eyes.

But the world that is conjured up is also a world of texts in *Charulata*. And at this level, the cinematic moves are negotiated through literature rather than in terms of separation from it. The alphabet that Charu embroiders on the handkerchief signals the insistence of the letter in the film. The written word will take on a particular luminosity as the film progresses, and the world of writing that is invoked in the opening sequence will form the very basis of the re-created time and place. Charu hums the name of her favourite novelist, Bankim, as she browses idly through the bookshelf. Bankimchandra Chatterjee was a pioneer of the novel form in India and a crucial ideologue of nationalism.

The film constantly refers to his novels; through a shared knowledge of these novels Charu and Amal come close to each other. Bhupati, and Charu's sister-in-law, Manda, fall outside this domain of exchange because of their lack of appreciation of Bankim. The name of Bankim will end up in a play of alliteration between Charu and Amal in their last extended conversation.

At a more discursive level, the whole film can be seen to be engaged in a dialogue with one of Bankim's essays, 'Women, Old and New', a major statement on what is known as the 'Women's Question' in the nineteenth century. All this is added to Tagore's original text which finds itself embedded in a tapestry of literary signs. Writers people the world - Taraknath Gangopadhyay, Rammohun Roy, Shakespeare, Byron, Addison, Steele, Emerson. The image of writing, the written word, forms a major visual motif – we closely watch Amal writing, Charu writing, Bhupati getting intoxicated with the printed word. The alphabet shining on the embroidery over the titles signals a process which will lead us to the very last image of the film: the hands of Charu and Bhupati freeze before they could meet, the title of Tagore's story appears on the screen in calligraphic design.

This would appear as merely explanatory and redundant (to say 'Broken Nest' here is to be literal) unless we follow the logic of appearance of the written word in the film. It is a final gesture of receding from the original story, of turning the work itself into an object of the film's gaze.

The scene in which Bhupati comes to know about Charu's feelings for his cousin the camera makes a gesture very unusual for Ray: it climbs up the leg of a marble table slowly to reveal a letter lying on it while Charu and Bhupati are heard talking off-screen. The letter is from Amal and it will bring about an emotional outburst in Charu giving her feelings away. The very tendentious movement of the camera, drawing attention to the letter as the dramatic agent, would look odd in a work of concealed narration unless one remembers the role of the letter as such in the film.

Bankim's 'Women Old and New' was published in 1879 (Ray gives an exact time for the events, 1879, as we know from the dateline on the copy of the magazine that Bhupati shows Amal) where he argues for a new woman who would be modern in the traditional way. She would embody the resolution of the conflict between tradition and modernity by finding her place in a re-invented patriarchy. She would learn to be the new old woman. As the film launches a dialogue with this essay it maps Tagore's story onto a historical grid, the political drama is brought out into the open. The story tells us of the formation of the colonial subject, male and female, and of the inevitable irony and pain that attend the process.

Tagore begins his story by an ironic description of the domains his characters occupy. The idealistic, English educated Bhupati is worried about the expansion of British territories beyond the Afghan borders, but hasn't had the time to notice how his child bride has bloomed into womanhood; Charu's idleness is of a different kind, reminding one of a fruitless tree. As she develops an expressive selfhood, through her love and through her writing, the challenge of the demarcation of domains comes to face her, it demands a heavy price.

Tagore, writing more or less from within the social reality that he portrays, was not in a position to uncover the historical dynamics of this matrix. Ray casts a historical gaze at the story at this level too; he creates a design with characters and spaces and distributes the story along discursive lines of divide. The dichotomy of literature and politics suggested in the story is developed into a strong motif in the film. The first is associated with the woman, the second belongs to the man. Bhupati entrusts Amal with Charu's literary education admitting that he has no taste for such things, busy as he is with the 'real world' of politics. Ray also makes him say to Amal that this politics, critical though it is of the colonial government's policies, is not meant to be disloyal to the masters. And from Bhupati we also learn that how worried he and friends are about the outcome of the parliamentary elections in Britain; one of his friends has vowed to sacrifice a goat at the Kali temple if the liberals win.

Bhupati writes politics in English, Amal and Charu write literature in Bengali. And then we come to a further division: Amal writes for public circulation, in an ornate register, Charu would like to write for a strictly private exchange, in an unadorned style through which she can evoke personal experiences. Towards the end, after Amal has left the house and Bhupati's magazine has failed, Charu and Bhupati go on a visit to the seaside and plan a poignantly illusory reconciliation between the poles of opposition – between the public and the private, home and the world, politics and culture. Why not bring out another magazine, they propose, which will have politics in English and literature in Bengali.

One can see Charu never believing in this. She is coming to a harder knowledge, she has had to grow up paying a dreadful price. The film brings out this irony of growing up in its most acute historical-political dimensions. It does away with a whole lot of events present in the original story not so much to bring out its essence but the political essence of the predicament that it deals with. Growing into modernity, into citizenship, into subjectivity of a nameable kind - all this, marked indelibly with the reality of living through colonialism, would not have been so strongly captured without the grand design of polarities that the film is grounded in. In devising his language Ray moves in and out of the field of literature, it would be difficult to recognise this aspect of his craft if we conceived of literature or film in their pure autonomy.

2

TAGORE AND HIS SONGS

The *Rabindrasangeet*, which deal with varied themes are immensely popular and form a foundation for the Bengali ethos that is comparable to, perhaps even greater than, that which Shakespeare has on the English-speaking world. It is said that his songs are the outcome of 500 years of literary & cultural churning that the Bengali community has gone through.In his book *Caste and Outcaste*, Dhan Gopal Mukerji has said that these songs transcend the mundane to the aesthetic and express all ranges and categories of human emotion.

The poet had given a voice to all—big or small, rich or poor. The poorest boatman on the Ganges as well as the rich landlord find expression for their emotional trials and tribulations in Tagore's songs. *Rabindrasangeet* has evolved into a distinctive school of music. Practitioners of this genre are known to be fiercely protective of tradionalist practice.

Novel interpretations and variations have drawn severe censure in both West Bengal and Bangladesh. And like Beethoven's symphonies or Vilayat Khan's sitar, Rabindrasangeet demands an educated, intelligent & cultured audience to appreciate the lyrical beauty of his compositions.

He was among the first to recognize that cinema should have its own language. In 1929 he wrote, "The beauty and grandeur of this form in motion has to be developed in such a way that it becomes self-sufficient without the use of words." The inherent beauty & depth of tagore's songs have persuaded a number of filmmakers to use Tagore's songs in their films including Satyajit Ray, Ritwik Ghatak, Mrinal Sen, Nitin Bose,

Tapan Sinha and Kumar Shahani.His songs were also used in British, European & Australian movies just to capture the mood of a cinematic situation & to reveal a delicate interplay of relationships. Ritwik Ghatak said of Tagore, "That man has culled all my feelings from long before my birth...I read him and find that...I have nothing new to say." In his *Meghe Dhaka Tara* (The Cloud-capped Star) and *Subarnarekha*, Ghatak uses *Rabindrasangeet* to express the poignancy of post-Partition Bengal. Two of the songs written by Tagore are the national anthems of India and Bangladesh. These are:

- Bangladesh: "*Amar Shonar Bangla*"
- India: "*Jana Gana Mana*"

SINGERS OF RABINDRASANGEET

Some of the well-known singers of *Rabindrasangeet* are:

- Pankaj Mullick also known as the *First Man* of Rabindrasangeet.
- Hemanta Kumar Mukhopadhyay
- Debabrata Biswas also known as the *Second Man* of Rabindrasangeet & unarguably the most popular among male voices.
- Subinoy Roy.
- Kanika Bandyopadhyay her original name was "Anima" but Tagore had renamed her "Kanika" and Abanindranath Tagore used to call her *Mohar* by which name she is known to many of her dedicated listeners.
- Suchitra Mitra
- Rajeshwari Dutta was originally from Punjab. She was married to a well-known Bengali poet, Sudhindranath Dutta. She made her mark in the classical-based *tappa* and other compositions
- Argha Sen
- Ashoketaru Bandyopadhyay
- Beethin Bandopadhyay
- Banani Ghosh

- Dwijen Mukhopadhay
- Chinmay Chattopadhyay
- Gita Ghatak
- Iffatara Khan
- Mita Huq
- Nilima Sen
- Promita Mollik
- Purba Dam
- Rajasree
- Rajeswari Dutta
- Rezwana Chowdhury Banya
- Ritu Guha
- Roma Mondal
- Rono Gohathakurota
- Ruma Guha Thakurta
- Sadi Mohammad
- Sagar Sen
- Sumitra Sen
- Sanghamitramitra Gupta
- Susil Mullick
- Swagatalakshmi Dasgupta
- Swapan Gupta
- Ashok Das
- Monica Ghose
- Sasha A.K. Ghoshal

TEACHERS OF *RABINDRASANGEET*

Some of the well-known teachers of Rabindrasangeet (barring Tagore himself) are:

- Dinendra Nath Tagore
- Shantideb Ghosh
- Ashoketaru Bandyopadhyay

- Dwijen Mukhopadhay
- Shailaja Ranjan Majumdar
- Maya Sen
- Suchitra Mitra
- Rajasree
- Kanika Bandyopadhyay
- Rezwana Chowdhury Banya
- Subinoy Roy
- Swagatalakshmi Dasgupta

In Bangladesh, prominent Rabindrasangeet trainers who have contributed immensely in developing new artistes include :

- Sanjida Khatun
- Wahidul Haq deceased
- Ajit Ray
- Anisur Rahman
- Papia Sarwar
- Lily Islam
- Rezwana Chowdhury Banya
- Selina Malek
- Mita Haq
- Sadi Mohammad
- Fazle Nizami deceased
- Hamida Haq
- Atiqul Islamdeceased
- Chanchal Khan (In Australia now)
- Kaderi Kibria (In USA)
- Sirajus Salekin (In Australia)
- Rakhi Chakravarti (Overseas)
- Salma Akhbar
- Tapan Mahmud
- Bulbul Islam
- Mahadev Shaha

- Shahjahan Kamal Taught at Jhankar Academy, Bongio Sankskritic Chakra (Dhaka), Presently teaching at Alampia School of Music (Toronto).

Ekla Chalo Re

Jodi Tor Dak Shune Keu Na Ashe is a song written by Rabindranath Tagore, part of the Rabindra Sangeet canon. It exhorts the listener to continue his or her journey, despite abandonment or lack of support from others.

The song is often quoted in the context of political or social change movements; Mahatma Gandhi cited it as one his favorite songs.

In Bengali Romanization

Jodi tor ðak shune keu na ashe tôbe êkla chôlo re, Ekla chôlo, êkla chôlo, êkla chôlo, êkla chôlo re.

Jodi keu kôtha na kôe, ore ore o ôbhaga, Jodi shôbai thake mukh firaee shôbai kôre bhôe—

Tôbe pôran khule

O tui mukh fuþe tor moner kôtha êkla bôlo re.

Jodi shôbai fire jae, ore ore o ôbhaga, Jodi gôhon pôthe jabar kale keu fire na chae—

Tôbe pôther kãþa

O tui rôktomakha chôrontôle êkla dôlo re.

Jodi alo na dhôre, ore ore o ôbhaga, Jodi jhô°-badole ãdhar rate duar dêe ghôre—

Tôbe bojranôle

Apon buker pãjor jalie nie êkla jôlo re.

Tagore's English Translation

If they answer not to thy call walk alone, If they are afraid and cower mutely facing the wall, O thou of evil luck, open thy mind and speak out alone.

If they turn away, and desert you when crossing the wilderness, O thou of evil luck, trample the thorns under thy tread, and along the blood-lined track travel alone.

If they do not hold up the light when the night is troubled with storm, O thou of evil luck, with the thunder flame of pain ignite thy own heart and let it burn alone.

In Popular Culture

- The song was used in the 2005 film Netaji Subhas Chandra Bose: The Forgotten Hero
- "Ekla Chalo Re" is the title of a book by the Jain Acharya Mahaprajna
- The song was famously sung by Vinoba Bhave during the beginnings of his Bhoodan movement, with "blessed" substituted for "unfortunate".

Tagore Songs unique treasure of Rabindranath's creative life. Opinions differ on when he first started composing songs. According to some authorities, his first song was composed when he was 12; some others say he began composing songs in 1875 at the age of 14. He then composed 'Jval jval chita dvigun dvigun' for the play *Sarojini* written by his elder brother JYOTIRINDRANATH TAGORE.

The same year two songs by him appeared in print as offerings for HINDU MELA. One of them, 'Tomari tare ma sanpinu e deha' (O mother, this body of mine is dedicated to you), was undisputedly composed by Tagore; but the other, 'Ek sutre bandhiyachhi sahasrati man' (I have tied a thousand minds with one string), is regarded by some as having been composed or set to music by Jyotirindranath Tagore. If 'Tomari tare ma …' was composed at the age of 12, it was certainly Tagore's first song. For his last birthday he composed 'He nutan, dekha dik ar-bar janmer pratham shubhaksan' (Hail the new, let the auspicious moment of birth appear again) on 7 May 1941. This means he composed songs for 68 years. All his 2,232 songs have been compiled in his *Gitabitan*.

The tradition of pre-Rabindranath Bangla songs took a new turn in the Tagore family. Rabindranath's father Debendranath Tagore , brothers SATYENDRANATH TAGORE and Jyotirindranath Tagore and others composed a genre of devotional songs for Brahma Samaj prayers. In this respect they were following RAMMOHUN ROY. Rabindranath enriched the genre by following his brothers in composing Brahma Sangit in the classical style.

Tagore songs are deeply influenced by classical influence. Although he himself did not learn CLASSICAL MUSIC formally, the family atmosphere of cultivating this form of music enables him to compose many of his songs in the Hindustani classical style. On the occasion of Brahmo Samaj's *Magh* festival, he composed many devotional songs in the Hindustani classical style. The Tagore songs composed in this tradition are treasures of our music. Many of his songs abound in the classical forms of *sthayi*, *antara*, *sanchari* and *abhog*. The influence of the classical style is also manifested in the tunes. words and articulation of the songs. During his childhood, several music teachers from the Vishnupur gharana used to come to the Tagore house. Of them, Vishnuchandra Chakravarty and Radhikaprasad Goswami left a deep impression on Tagore's mind. The RAGAS and *raginis* heard in his childhood managed to cast long shadows on his songs.

Rabindranath established his uniqueness by applying multiple ragas and raginis in a single song. For instance, he applied four ragas - *lalit*, *vibhas*, *jogiya* and *ashavari* - in his song 'Achhe duhkha achhe mrtyu, biraha dahana lage'. To him, theme was more important than ragas. Even in folk tunes he experimented with a mixture of ragas to create a genre of his own TAPPA is yet another form that has enriched Tagore songs. The use of tappa in giving expression to Bengali emotions has been noteworthy. Rabindranath composed some songs following the tappa tradition of 'Shori Miar Punjabi'. His own tappas utilize no discernible combination of TALS. The use of folk tunes is also obvious in Tagore tappas.

Rabindranath composed tunes for some Vedic and Bauddha hymns to create devotional songs. He also composed a number of songs with the help of South Indian tunes. The folksongs of Bengal have significantly influenced Tagore songs too. He used extensively tunes and styles from BAUL, KIRTAN, shyamasangit, *sari* and even *kathakata* to give his songs a distinctive flavour and beauty.

Rabindranath's familiarity with the folk tunes, and kirtan, syamasangit and ramprasadi is seen in the songs he composed between 1884 and 1886. The use of baul tunes became noticeable since 1905. While agitating against the PARTITION OF BENGAL, Rabindranath realized that the best way to touch the hearts of the people was to utilize the tunes drawn from the soil. Twenty songs composed by him at the time were published in a book entitled *Baul*. Among them were Gandhiji's favourite song 'Yadi tor dak shune keu na ase tabe ekla chalo re' (If no one comes to respond to your call, go forth all alone) and 'Amar sonar Bangla, ami tomay bhalobasi' (My Bengal of gold, I love you), later adopted as the NATIONAL ANTHEM of Bangladesh. Rabindranath also used folk tunes from different Indian states like Mumbai, Gujarat, Madras, Mysore and Punjab (Sikh bhajan).

The Tagore family was familiar with many western musical tunes. In his AUTOBIOGRAPHY, Rabindranath speaks of a book called *Irish Melodies* that he read early in life. His grandfather DWARAKANATH TAGORE was known to have taken lessons in western music. The family of Rabindranath's elder brother Satyendranath Tagore used to cultivate western music. His knowledge about western music was enhanced when at the age of 17 he went to England to study bar-at-law and had an opportunity to live with different English families. He applied many western tunes in the songs of his musical plays *Valmiki Pratibha* (1881) and *Kalmrgaya* (1882). Thanks to his unique abilities, he could maintain his own distinctive note even after using varied elements from other musical sources. Because of this quality, his tunes can be easily identified even when he has based them on other musical forms.

Rabindranath has used many tals in composing songs. These included *chautal*, *ada chautal*, *dhamar*, *adatheka*, *surfankta*, *yat*, *jhanptal*, *trital*, *ektal*, *teoda*, *dadra*, *kaharba* and *adkhemta*. He has utilized some tals which are new to North Indian music; these include *sasthi*, *jhampak*, *rupkada*, *navatal*, *ekadashi* and *navapanchatal*. In poetic measures too, Rabindranath showed some distinctiveness, especially in using multiple times. He has occasionally used multiple tempos in a single song and has skillfully mixed times and tempos to create a very unusual musical form. Usually songs have a preponderance of tunes and measures but Tagore songs are essentially poetic and therefore their poetic themes are as important as their tunes. The thematic variety of his songs reflects the rich emotional life of Bengalis. *Gitabitan*, his main and final compilation of songs, has a large number of sections. His devotional songs have been listed under 'Puja', love songs under 'Prem', songs on seasons under 'Prakrti', patriotic songs under 'Swadesh', occasional songs under 'Anusthanik', and miscellaneous songs under 'Vichitra'. Some of his songs for his stage plays are satirical. The divisions of his songs relating to worship, love and nature are no doubt arbitrary as the themes are often intermixed so overwhelmingly that drawing clear lines between them becomes difficult.

His occasional songs treat an amazing variety of themes. He wrote songs on weddings, births and deaths, house warming, tree planting, plowing land, sinking a tubewell, tying rakhi, convocations, inauguration ceremonies, harvesting and even teaching of martial art to women. This has made Tagore songs an essential part of life of the Bengalis who sing them in happiness, in distress, and at work.

Rabindranath once said that a song begins where a poem ends and that the message of music travels further than that of words. He used to ride on the wings of music in utter delight to spread his ideals, something he also did through his poems. Visva-Bharati has so far published 63 volumes of *Gitabitan*, arranging the Tagore songs in alphabetical order with notations. A few more volumes remain to be published.

Rabindra-Sangeet as a Resource for Indian Classical Bandishes

Rabindranath's titanic intellect found manifestation in almost every facet of fine art. One of the most outstanding amongst them is Rabindra-sangeet, which embodies a breathtaking fusion of his musicianship and poetic genius. Such was the impact of this creation, that it not only withstood the test of time for more than a century, but also secured a unique place for itself in the subcontinent's musical culture. The objective of this article is not to deliberate on the beauty and depth of Rabindra-sangeet. There are countless works in this regard by people far more knowledgeable on Rabindranath and Rabindra-sangeet, and the influence of Classical music on Rabindra Sangeet has been amply analyzed and now stands as an accepted fact. What this article aims to focus on, is how and to what extent has Rabindra-sangeet, in its turn, influenced the more traditional forms of music and its exponents. In particular, there has been a pronounced influence of Rabindra-sangeet on some of the noted classical instrumentalists of North India. There are indeed scopes of debate over the rationale and the extent of potential of this influence, but the fact remains that it cannot be denied. There are far too many precedents in its favor.

In the succeeding sections of this article, it has been attempted to investigate, what elements in Rabindra-sangeet triggered this kind of influence on Indian Classical instrumentalists and what consequences it led to.

Traditional elements in Rabindra-sangeet

It is an accepted fact that elements of Indian classical music have been used in an extremely intelligent and effective fashion in Rabindra-sangeet. It is indeed one of its most significant features. The application of this ingredient was however dictated principally by the perceived requirements of the mood evoked in the song, which was after all the core entity of his creation. An overt application of elements derived from classical music would have conflicted with this requirement. Therefore the application of classical elements, more often than not, had been subtle, and only to the extent necessary to express the emotive content of the song. Many of his songs therefore have only a partial conformity to ragas. Of course, in cases where he found the tonal colour of the raga in almost total conformity to the sentiment of the song, he adopted the raga in its entirety. On certain instances, we even see authentic classical compositions adopted faithfully in respect of both melody and rhythm, set to outstanding Bengali lyric. The urge to evoke a particular mood to his own satisfaction, often led him to blend ragas in unexpectedly beautiful and interesting ways, or to look for uncharted and unexplored nuances within the known frameworks of ragas. It was on these occasions that some of his most beautiful and intellectually challenging creations came forth. The influence of Rabindra-sangeet on Indian classical Instrumental music is perhaps due to the fact that much of what is played on Indian classical instruments today is derived from vocal music, principally of classical as also to some extent, of non classical origin (like lighter variety of compositions derived from folk music such as *Kirtan* or *Bhatiyali*). Classical instrumentalists have always looked for newer ideas and inspirations to feed their imagination not merely from these sources. Rabindra-sangeet with its sheer beauty and lyricism combined with the exquisite embodiment of the classical genre, naturally turns out to be a very potential resource to prospect.

INFLUENCE OF RABINDRA SANGEET ON CLASSICAL INSTRUMENTS AND INSTRUMENTALISTS

The Beginning

The pioneering example in this regard was set by none other than the great Ustad Vilayat Khan Sahib. He had adopted the famous song, *Bhenge Mor Gharer Chabi,* into a beautiful, lilting light-classical composition. This was an interesting instance of a distinguished classical musician being motivated to imbibe the beauty and lyricism in Rabindra-sangeet . The next example in this regard was set by Sri Buddhadev Dasgupta, the renowned sarodiya. Being a person with cultural roots in Bengal, he might have had a greater exposure to Rabindra-sangeet in general. His approach towards adoption of Rabindra-sangeet to classical music, naturally, was a more involved one. Out of the numerous classical compositions he has derived so far from Rabindra Sangeet, there are examples of transformations inspired by a variety of different aspects such as melodic appeal, interesting and unexpected application of raga movements, interesting ways of blending of ragas and even re-discovery of old classical compositions. His work in this area is based on years of exhaustive study and research in collaboration with Rabindra-sangeet experts like Shubhash Chowdhury.

The introduction of these kind of compositions in the arena of authentic Indian Classical Music took place over the decades of sixties and seventies. The initiation had been cautious and measured, considering the conventional mind-set of most of the contemporary musicians and listeners. For example, Sri Dasgupta played his first sarod composition, derived from the Rabindrasageet *Shedin dujone*, in his AIR National Program in 1978, dubbing it as a "light classical composition set to Pilu" and not as "a sarod gat based on Rabindra Sangeet".

The Endeavour and its Acceptance

It took quite some time for this novel approach to be accepted by the musicians, critics and listeners in its correct perspective. At the initial stage, presentation of such compositions were limited to more intimate gatherings rather than important and full fledged classical concerts. The response of the musical community, though not of outright rejection was somewhat confused. On one hand they were moved by the aesthetic appeal of the compositions, but on the other, were not quite sure of the categorization of such compositions. These compositions were definitely not like light classical compositions (commonly termed as "*dhun*").

Their appeal was definitely more dignified, and were set to purer forms of Ragas for the *Dhuns* are mostly set to lighter and blended Ragas with an ambience akin to that of folk music. They could also not be classified as authentic classical compositions or *bandishes* propagated over musical generations, as their origin was quite different.

Sometimes they were sweepingly described as "Rabindra-sangeet played on sarod". This was a totally inappropriate description as well, as the compositions, more often than not, were quite different in their overall melodic construction, rythmic orientation and tempo than the original Rabindra-sangeet it had been derived from. In most cases the similarity was at a much more abstract level of melodic ideas and movements.

Therefore it was left to the proponents of this approach to educate and appraise the audience over the true characteristic of these compositions. This led to the formulation of certain experimental presentations featuring exponents of Rabindra-sangeet and classical musicians on a common stage, where some selected songs were presented along with their transformed versions of instrumental composition (or "*gat*" in the parlance of Hindusthani music), with adequate explanations in between. One of the earliest presentations of this kind was featured by Doordarshan Kendra, Calcutta with Budhhadev Dasgupta, V.Balsara (the famous pianist and film music personality) and Sri Ramanuj Dasgupta, (one of the contemporary upcoming Rabindra Sangeet singers). The reception to this program was very positive. Noted personalities from the sphere of Rabindra-sangeet as well as classical music acclaimed the effort. Further, as an interesting spin off, a large section of lay music-lovers and Tagore enthusiasts found an interesting cue towards the so-called "abstract" appeal of classical music.

A number of similar experimental programs were staged over the following years, with other eminent personalities from spheres of classical music and Rabindra-sangeet, volunteering to take part in such ventures. There have been quite a few presentations of these nature featuring Suchitra Mitra and Budhhadev Dasgupta, Subinoy Roy, Ravi Kichlu and Jaya Biswas and many others. Programs on this theme were accepted and presented by the AIR and Doordarshan on a number of occasions as well. Following suit, the Sangeet Natak Academy also funded a complete project on this theme. From this point onwards, it can be said, that the endeavour received its formal acceptance from the connoisseurs and listeners of classical music as also from the mass media. The idea was thereafter emulated by some of the most well known classical instrumentalists like Ustad Amjad Ali Khan. The trend continues to this day with dedicated stage programs focusing on classical compositions derived from Rabindra-sangeet. The interesting thing to note here is that just as the stage is shared by Rabindra-sangeet singers and classical instrumentalists, the galleries as well are shared by listeners of Rabindra-sangeet and classical music.

The Aspects of Transformation

Having delineated the course of evolution of this interesting work, it would be worthwhile to take a closer look at the aspects of transformation that it involves. Since this has to be examined on the basis of concrete examples, the author has chosen a few, from the works of Sri Budhhadev Dasgupta, whose contribution in this regard has not only been a pioneering one, but perhaps also the most profound and exhaustive. The compositions derived by him had been based on a number of different perspectives of musical thinking.

It should be borne in mind that when we talk of transformation, we are obviously not talking about simply playing Rabindra-sangeet on sarod. Certain ideas are taken from the original Rabindra-sangeet and used to formulate a composition suitable for the context of a classical instrument. The original song therefore, undergoes a change or a sort of reconstruction in that certain salient ideas taken from the song are represented using the elements of sarod vocabulary. The resulting composition can consequently differ to a considerable extent from the orginal song that inspired its creation. The difference mostly is on counts of rhythmic construction or tempo but sometimes also in details of melodic construction. The similarity on the other hand is rather abstract and more often than not at the level of an overall melodic outline. There are a few examples of course, where the nature of the original song itself is so akin to that of a classical presentation that it finds its way almost unaltered into a classical composition.

Revisiting Lost Domains in Ragas or Ragas Themselves

As mentioned before, in many of his creations Rabindranath had focussed on ragas from rather striking and unexpected perspectives. Some of the movements he had used, though unusual, could not be challenged on counts of beauty and conformity to the raga. Some of these movements were taken from very old and traditional conventions in classical music. One such example is the use of R, G, M, P, D.., M G in the opening lines of *Shanti karo borishono*, based on Rag Tilak Kamod. From this took birth a beautiful, medium tempo

(Madhya Laya) sarod composition (gat). An almost forgotten but exceedingly lyrical and romantic usage of Komal Gandhar in the latter part of the opening stanza (sthayee) of the song *Oi Janalar dhare* (Click here for an excerpt of the song or the *bandish* (Singer: Aniruddha Sinha; Ensemble: Sitar - Sugata Nag, Rahul Chatterjee, Sarod - Anirban Dasgupta, Pratyush Banerjee) is another outstanding example of such an application. In *Emono dine tare bola jai* we find a beautiful yet unconventional portrayal of Desh Malhar.

Both of these songs have inspired excellent sarod gats set to teental. In some of the songs there has been an excellent delineation of uncommon Ragas. *Aji jato tara tabo akashe* (Excerpts: of the song or sarod-solo *bandish* . Artists: Sriradha Banerjee, sarod solo: Buddhadev Dasgupta) beautifully pictures Manjh Khambaj, a Raga which existed in the days of yore, but was somewhat rarely heard in the arena of pure classical music.

This song was almost completely imbibed into an excellent slow teental (Vilambit) composition by Buddhadev, and has been rendered by him in many of his important concerts. (Excerpt: Anirban Dasgupta, Buddhadev Dasgupta and Zakir Hussain playing Manjh Khamaj at Vassar College, Poughkeepsie, 1985.) Incidentally, the same raga which Tagore so adeptly applied in his song, was later revived and popularised in the world of classical music by Acharya Alauddin Khan and his son, Ustad Ali Akbar Khan, the legendary sarodiya.

Beauty of Approach, Movement and Melody

As mentioned before, many of the songs, have such a poignant and emotionally moving representation of commonly known ragas, that it would become rather difficult for a sensitive classical musician to overlook their intrinsic musicality. This poignancy or musicality in more objective terms can be interpreted as interesting application of note sequences. Many of the derived sarod compositions have been inspired by this factor.

For example, in the song *Shedin dujone* one finds such an entrancing portrayal of the raga Pilu; here the notes of this rather common raga have been played with creative mastery. This was, in fact, Budhadev's first inspiration to derive a sarod composition from Rabindra sangeet. In "*Chokhe-r aaloey*" one finds a simple yet serenely beautiful depiction of Yaman Kalyan. This was converted into a medium tempo composition set to Teen tal.

A scintillating fast Tintal composition of Khambaj was created from *Amar kantha hote gaan ke nilo*. The rhythm of the original song (Dadra) had to be entirely changed in order to adapt it to the ambience of an instrumental presentation. This was necessary as the idea was to present not just the song but a full-fledged classical composition derived out of it. The basis of this transformation was the beauty of the melodic outline of the song. In contrast, *Jodi e amaro* is a striking example where not only is the melodic construction but also the rhythmic framework has been followed in to-to in the derived instrumental composition based on raga Kafi. Here as well, Tagore entrances us with the rare, beautiful yet unmistakable approach to Kafi starting from the note *Dhaibat*.

Out of Tagore's many songs based on Bhairabi, *Tabo daya* is one of the most outstanding considering the exquisite application of notes the heightens the expression of beauty and devotion. This prompted the creation of a medium tempo gat, largely maintaining the note sequences but changing the rhythmic framework to the somewhat-more-brisk Teen tal. There are more examples of this nature, such as *Shey kon boner horin* (Hemant) vocal [by Agnibha Banerjee] or instrumental *bandish* [by the "Ensemble"}, or *Shopney amar mone holo* (Hameer). vocal [by Aniruddha Sinha] or instrumental *bandish* [composed by the "Ensemble"].

Rediscovering Old Classical Compositions

Most of the songs composed by Rabindranath are characterised by their outstanding individuality, both from the point of views of lyric and melody. But on a certain instances we also find him faithfully adapting the melodic content of old classical compositions. In certain cases where he found the melodic as well as rhythmic orientation of existing or old classical compositions in keeping with the clime of the song being composed he never hesitated to follow them with complete faith.

It was perhaps his tribute to a rich tradition of classical music. Hence in some of the songs like *Shukho hin nishi din,* (vocal [by Haimanti Shukla], sarod *bandish* [by Buddhadev Dasgupta] or *Shunyo hate phiri he* we find priceless classical *bandishes,* faithfully captured and set to outstanding poetry. Even playing these songs verbatim on an instrument would make them sound like authentic classical instrumental compositions. An interesting commentary on this is provided in the audio-cassette series named "Rupantori", featuring stalwarts like Subinoy Roy and Prasun Banerjee.

Highlighting Tagore's Outstanding Ideations on Blending Ragas

Sometimes, his flights of imagination had led Tagore to such emotional moods, that the tonal colors available from the basic ragas were not adequate to express them. Under such circumstances he used his artistic liberty to blend ragas. This resulted in masterful combination of some of the known ragas producing unforeseen melodic shades of the highest artistic order. One sees such a marriage between the ragas Todi and Bhairvi in the song *Rajani-r shesh tara.* Another unparalleled confluence of Bahar and Basant is noted in the song *Ami tomari shonge* (vocal [by Sriradha Banerjee] or *bandish* [by Buddhadev Dasgupta]). There may be many more examples. However, in the context of this discussion, it can be mentioned that both of these songs have provided potent ideas not only towards framing beautiful *bandishes* but also creating new kinds of blended ragas.

What it Means for a Classical Instrumentalist

Evolution of new ideas in the realm of classical instrumental music inspired by Rabindra-sangeet is of more than incidental significance to some classical instrumentalists. An instrumentalist who has experienced, understood the classical appeal in Rabindra Sangeet and has succeeded in deriving useful ideas from it will obviously find his musical horizon widening much more than ever before. He will develop the insight to discover interesting and unknown corners of known ragas, which will not only apply to the derived compositions but also to the more conventional aspects of his playing like Alap and Vistar. At a more abstract level it might also have significant effects and possibly improvements on his perspective of thinking on ragas. The derived compositions, which as metioned before, have a very distinctive aesthetic ambience would considerably expand his repertoire. He will find himself in possession the magic key to an inexhaustible repository of ideas.

CONCLUSION

It is a known fact that classical musicians over all ages and centuries have derived musical ideas from classical as well as non-classical sources. In a sense, therefore, this example of Rabindra-sangeet inspiring creation of classical compositions may be interpreted as a repetition of history. However, a closer look suggests a difference. This lies in the artistic maturity of the source material in this case, so that a strong temptation to plagiarize must be resisted and the essence gleaned, and this can be an extremely challenging task.

Also, this endeavour has encouraged an interesting cross-influence. Some of the classical musicians have come down from their ivory towers and given Rabindra-sangeet its much overdue recognition. The exponents of Rabindra-sangeet by and large have welcomed this dialogue between these two islands of India's musical culture which were so far largely isolated from each other. For classical instrumentalists it opened up an extremely potent resource to excavate for newer ideas which are applicable to their own realm. Finally, the subtle yet long-term consequence could be to motivate future generations of musicians to enrich the realm of Classical Music from similar sources beyond the boundary their own domain.

3

STORIES BY RABINDRANATH TAGORE

BIMALA'S STORY

Mother, today there comes back to mind the vermilion mark at the parting of your hair, the *sari* which you used to wear, with its wide red border, and those wonderful eyes of yours, full of depth and peace. They came at the start of my life's journey, like the first streak of dawn, giving me golden provision to carry me on my way. The sky which gives light is blue, and my mother's face was dark, but she had the radiance of holiness, and her beauty would put to shame all the vanity of the beautiful.

Everyone says that I resemble my mother. In my childhood I used to resent this. It made me angry with my mirror. I thought that it was God's unfairness which was wrapped round my limbs—that my dark features were not my due, but had come to me by some misunderstanding. All that remained for me to ask of my God in reparation was, that I might grow up to be a model of what woman should be, as one reads it in some epic poem.

When the proposal came for my marriage, an astrologer was sent, who consulted my palm and said, "This girl has good signs. She will become an ideal wife." And all the women who heard it said: "No wonder, for she resembles her mother."

I was married into a Rajah's house. When I was a child, I was quite familiar with the description of the Prince of the fairy story. But my husband's face was not of a kind that one's imagination would place in fairyland. It was dark, even as mine was. The feeling of shrinking, which I had about my own lack of physical beauty, was lifted a little; at the same time a touch of regret was left lingering in my heart.

But when the physical appearance evades the scrutiny of our senses and enters the sanctuary of our hearts, then it can forget itself. I know, from my childhood's experience, how devotion is beauty itself, in its inner aspect. When my mother arranged the different fruits, carefully peeled by her own loving hands, on the white stone plate, and gently waved her fan to drive away the flies while my father sat down to his meals, her service would lose itself in a beauty which passed beyond outward forms. Even in my infancy I could feel its power. It transcended all debates, or doubts, or calculations: it was pure music. I distinctly remember after my marriage, when, early in the morning, I would cautiously and silently get up and take the dust of my husband's feet without waking him, how at such moments I could feel the vermilion mark upon my forehead shining out like the morning star. One day, he happened to awake, and smiled as he asked me: "What is that, Bimala? What *are* you doing?"

I can never forget the shame of being detected by him. He might possibly have thought that I was trying to earn merit secretly. But no, no! That had nothing to do with merit. It was my woman's heart, which must worship in order to love.

My father-in-law's house was old in dignity from the days of the *Badshahs*. Some of its manners were of the Moguls and Pathans, some of its customs of Manu and Parashar. But my husband was absolutely modern. He was the first of the house to go through a college course and take his M.A. degree. His elder brother had died young, of drink, and had left no children. My husband did not drink and was not given to dissipation. So foreign to the family was this abstinence, that to many it hardly seemed decent! Purity, they imagined, was only becoming in those on whom fortune had not smiled. It is the moon which has room for stains, not the stars.

My husband's parents had died long ago, and his old grandmother was mistress of the house. My husband was the apple of her eye, the jewel on her bosom. And so he never met with much difficulty in overstepping any of the ancient usages. When he brought in Miss Gilby, to teach me and be my companion, he stuck to his resolve in spite of the poison secreted by all the wagging tongues at home and outside.

My husband had then just got through his B.A. examination and was reading for his M.A. degree; so he had to stay in Calcutta to attend college. He used to write to me almost every day, a few lines only, and simple words, but his bold, round handwriting would look up into my face, oh, so tenderly! I kept his letters in a sandalwood box and covered them every day with the flowers I gathered in the garden.

At that time the Prince of the fairy tale had faded, like the moon in the morning light. I had the Prince of my real world enthroned in my heart. I was his queen. I had my seat by his side. But my real joy was, that my true place was at his feet. Since then, I have been educated, and introduced to the modern age in its own language, and therefore these words that I write seem to blush with shame in their prose setting. Except for my acquaintance with this modern standard of life, I should know, quite naturally, that just as my being born a woman was not in my own hands, so the element of devotion in woman's love is not like a hackneyed passage quoted from a romantic poem to be piously written down in round hand in a school-girl's copy-book.

But my husband would not give me any opportunity for worship. That was his greatness. They are cowards who claim absolute devotion from their wives as their right; that is a humiliation for both. His love for me seemed to overflow my limits by its flood of wealth and service. But my necessity was more for giving than for receiving; for love is a vagabond, who can make his flowers bloom in the wayside dust, better than in the crystal jars kept in the drawing-room.

My husband could not break completely with the old-time traditions which prevailed in our family. It was difficult, therefore, for us to meet at any hour of the day we pleased.

I knew exactly the time that he could come to me, and therefore our meeting had all the care of loving preparation. It was like the rhyming of a poem; it had to come through the path of the metre. After finishing the day's work and taking my afternoon bath, I would do up my hair and renew my vermilion mark and put on my *sari*, carefully crinkled; and then, bringing back my body and mind from all distractions of household duties, I would dedicate it at this special hour, with special ceremonies, to one individual. That time, each day, with him was short; but it was infinite.

My husband used to say, that man and wife are equal in love because of their equal claim on each other. I never argued the point with him, but my heart said that devotion never stands in the way of true equality; it only raises the level of the ground of meeting. Therefore the joy of the higher equality remains permanent; it never slides down to the vulgar level of triviality.

My beloved, it was worthy of you that you never expected worship from me. But if you had accepted it, you would have done me a real service. You showed your love by decorating me, by educating me, by giving me what I asked for, and what I did not. I have seen what depth of love there was in your eyes when you gazed at me. I have known the secret sigh of pain you suppressed in your love for me. You loved my body as if it were a flower of paradise. You loved my whole nature as if it had been given you by some rare providence. Such lavish devotion made me proud to think that the wealth was all my own which drove you to my gate. But vanity such as this only checks the flow of free surrender in a woman's love. When I sit on the queen's throne and claim homage, then the claim only goes on magnifying itself; it is never satisfied. Can there be any real happiness for a woman in merely feeling that she has power over a man? To surrender one's pride in devotion is woman's only salvation.

It comes back to me today how, in the days of our happiness, the fires of envy sprung up all around us. That was only natural, for had I not stepped into my good fortune by a mere chance, and without deserving it? But providence does not allow a run of luck to last for ever, unless its debt of honour be fully paid, day by day, through many a long day, and thus made secure. God may grant us gifts, but the merit of being able to take and hold them must be our own. Alas for the boons that slip through unworthy hands!

My husband's grandmother and mother were both renowned for their beauty. And my widowed sister-in-law was also of a beauty rarely to be seen. When, in turn, fate left them desolate, the grandmother vowed she would not insist on having beauty for her remaining grandson when he married. Only the auspicious marks with which I was endowed gained me an entry into this family—otherwise, I had no claim to be here.

In this house of luxury, but few of its ladies had received their meed of respect. They had, however, got used to the ways of the family, and managed to keep their heads above water, buoyed up by their dignity as *Ranis* of an ancient house, in spite of their daily tears being drowned in the foam of wine, and by the tinkle of the dancing girls" anklets. Was the credit due to me that my husband did not touch liquor, nor squander his manhood in the markets of woman's flesh? What charm did I know to soothe the wild and wandering mind of men? It was my good luck, nothing else. For fate proved utterly callous to my sister-in-law. Her festivity died out, while yet the evening was early, leaving the light of her beauty shining in vain over empty halls—burning and burning, with no accompanying music! His sister-in-law affected a contempt for my husband's modern notions. How absurd to keep the family ship, laden with all the weight of its time-honoured glory, sailing under the colours of his slip of a girl-wife alone! Often have I felt the lash of scorn. "A thief who had stolen a husband's love!" "A sham hidden in the shamelessness of her new-fangled finery!" The many-coloured garments of modern fashion with which my husband loved to adorn me roused jealous wrath. "Is not she ashamed to make a show-window of herself—and with her looks, too!" My husband was aware of all this, but his gentleness knew no bounds. He used to implore me to forgive her.

I remember I once told him: "Women's minds are so petty. so crooked!" "Like the feet of Chinese women," he replied. "Has not the pressure of society cramped them into pettiness and crookedness? They are but pawns of the fate which gambles with them. What responsibility have they of their own?" My sister-in-law never failed to get from my husband whatever she wanted. He did not stop to consider whether her requests were right or reasonable. But what exasperated me most was that she was not grateful for this. I had promised my husband that I would not talk back at her, but this set me raging all the more, inwardly. I used to feel that goodness has a limit, which, if passed, somehow seems to make men cowardly. Shall I tell the whole truth? I have often wished that my husband had the manliness to be a little less good.

My sister-in-law, the Bara Rani, was still young and had no pretensions to saintliness. Rather, her talk and jest and laugh inclined to be forward. The young maids with whom she surrounded herself were also impudent to a degree. But there was none to gainsay her—for was not this the custom of the house? It seemed to me that my good fortune in having a stainless husband was a special eyesore to her. He, however, felt more the sorrow of her lot than the defects of her character.

My husband was very eager to take me out of purdah.

One day I said to him: "What do I want with the outside world?"

"The outside world may want you," he replied.

"If the outside world has got on so long without me, it may go on for some time longer. It need not pine to death for want of me."

"Let it perish, for all I care! That is not troubling me. I am thinking about myself."

"Oh, indeed. Tell me what about yourself?"

My husband was silent, with a smile.

I knew his way, and protested at once: "No, no, you are not going to run away from me like that! I want to have this out with you."

"Can one ever finish a subject with words?"

"Do stop speaking in riddles. Tell me. . ."

"What I want is, that I should have you, and you should have me, more fully in the outside world. That is where we are still in debt to each other."

"Is anything wanting, then, in the love we have here at home?"

"Here you are wrapped up in me. You know neither what you have, nor what you want."

"I cannot bear to hear you talk like this."

"I would have you come into the heart of the outer world and meet reality. Merely going on with your household duties, living all your life in the world of household conventions and the drudgery of household tasks—you were not made for that! If we meet, and recognize each other, in the real world, then only will our love be true."

"If there be any drawback here to our full recognition of each other, then I have nothing to say. But as for myself, I feel no want."

"Well, even if the drawback is only on my side, why shouldn't you help to remove it?"

Such discussions repeatedly occurred. One day he said: "The greedy man who is fond of his fish stew has no compunction in cutting up the fish according to his need. But the man who loves the fish wants to enjoy it in the water; and if that is impossible he waits on the bank; and even if he comes back home without a sight of it he has the consolation of knowing that the fish is all right. Perfect gain is the best of all; but if that is impossible, then the next best gain is perfect losing.

I never liked the way my husband had of talking on this subject, but that is not the reason why I refused to leave the zenana. His grandmother was still alive. My husband had filled more than a hundred and twenty per cent of the house with the twentieth century, against her taste; but she had borne it uncomplaining. She would have borne it, likewise, if the daughter-in-law of the Rajah's house had left its seclusion. She was even prepared for this happening. But I did not consider it important enough to give her the pain of it. I have read in books that we are called "caged birds". I cannot speak for others, but I had so much in this cage of mine that there was not room for it in the universe—at least that is what I then felt. The grandmother, in her old age, was very fond of me. At the bottom of her fondness was the thought that, with the conspiracy of favourable stars which attended me, I had been able to attract my husband's love. Were not men naturally inclined to plunge downwards? None of the others, for all their beauty, had been able to prevent their husbands going headlong into the burning depths which consumed and destroyed them. She believed that I had been the means of extinguishing this fire, so deadly to the men of the family. So she kept me in the shelter of her bosom, and trembled if I was in the least bit unwell.

His grandmother did not like the dresses and ornaments my husband brought from European shops to deck me with. But she reflected: "Men will have some absurd hobby or other, which is sure to be expensive. It is no use trying to check their extravagance; one is glad enough if they stop short of ruin. If my Nikhil had not been busy dressing up his wife there is no knowing whom else he might have spent his money on!" So whenever any new dress of mine arrived she used to send for my husband and make merry over it. Thus it came about that it was her taste which changed. The influence of the modern age fell so strongly upon her, that her evenings refused to pass if I did not tell her stories out of English books.

After his grandmother's death, my husband wanted me to go and live with him in Calcutta. But I could not bring myself to do that. Was not this our House, which she had kept under her sheltering care through all her trials and troubles? Would not a curse come upon me if I deserted it and went off to town? This was the thought that kept me back, as her empty seat reproachfully looked up at me. That noble lady had come into this house at the age of eight, and had died in her seventy-ninth year. She had not spent a happy life. Fate had hurled shaft after shaft at her breast, only to draw out more and more the imperishable spirit within. This great house was hallowed with her tears. What should I do in the dust of Calcutta, away from it? My husband's idea was that this would be a good opportunity for leaving to my sister-in-law the consolation of ruling over the household, giving our life, at the same time, more room to branch out in Calcutta. That is just where my difficulty came in. She had worried my life out, she ill brooked my husband's happiness, and for this she was to be rewarded! And what of the day when we should have to come back here? Should I then get back my seat at the head?

"What do you want with that seat?" my husband would say. "Are there not more precious things in life?"

Men never understand these things. They have their nests in the outside world; they little know the whole of what the household stands for. In these matters they ought to follow womanly guidance. Such were my thoughts at that time.

I felt the real point was, that one ought to stand up for one's rights. To go away, and leave everything in the hands of the enemy, would be nothing short of owning defeat. But why did not my husband compel me to go with him to Calcutta? I know the reason. He did not use his power, just because he had it. If one had to fill in, little by little, the gap between day and night, it would take an eternity to do it. But the sun rises and the darkness is dispelled—a moment is sufficient to overcome an infinite distance. One day there came the new era of *Swadeshi* in Bengal; but as to how it happened, we had no distinct vision. There was no gradual slope connecting the past with the present. For that reason, I imagine, the new epoch came in like a flood, breaking down the dykes and sweeping all our prudence and fear before it. We had no time even to think about, or understand, what had happened, or what was about to happen.

My sight and my mind, my hopes and my desires, became red with the passion of this new age. Though, up to this time, the walls of the home—which was the ultimate world to my mind—remained unbroken, yet I stood looking over into the distance, and I heard a voice from the far horizon, whose meaning was not perfectly clear to me, but whose call went straight to my heart. From the time my husband had been a college student he had been trying to get the things required by our people produced in our own country. There are plenty of date trees in our district. He tried to invent an apparatus for extracting the juice and boiling it into sugar and treacle. I heard that it was a great success, only it extracted more money than juice. After a while he came to the conclusion that our attempts at reviving our industries were not succeeding for want of a bank of our own. He was, at the time, trying to teach me political economy. This alone would not have done much harm, but he also took it into his head to teach his countrymen ideas of thrift, so as to pave the way for a bank; and then he actually started a small bank. Its high rate of interest, which made the villagers flock so enthusiastically to put in their money, ended by swamping the bank altogether.

The old officers of the estate felt troubled and frightened. There was jubilation in the enemy's camp. Of all the family, only my husband's grandmother remained unmoved. She would scold me, saying: "Why are you all plaguing him so? Is it the fate of the estate that is worrying you? How many times have I seen this estate in the hands of the court receiver! Are men like women? Men are born spendthrifts and only know how to waste. Look here, child, count yourself fortunate that your husband is not wasting himself as well!"

My husband's list of charities was a long one. He would assist to the bitter end of utter failure anyone who wanted to invent a new loom or rice-husking machine. But what annoyed me most was the way that Sandip Babu used to fleece him on the pretext of *Swadeshi* work. Whenever he wanted to start a newspaper, or travel about preaching the Cause, or take a change of air by the advice of his doctor, my husband would unquestioningly supply him with the money. This was over and above the regular living allowance which Sandip Babu also received from him. The strangest part of it was that my husband and Sandip Babu did not agree in their opinions.

As soon as the *Swadeshi* storm reached my blood, I said to my husband:

"I must burn all my foreign clothes."

"Why burn them?" said he. "You need not wear them as long as you please."

"As long as I please! Not in this life . . ."

"Very well, do not wear them for the rest of your life, then. But why this bonfire business?"

"Would you thwart me in my resolve?"

"What I want to say is this: Why not try to build up something? You should not waste even a tenth part of your energies in this destructive excitement."

"Such excitement will give us the energy to build."

"That is as much as to say, that you cannot light the house unless you set fire to it."

Then there came another trouble. When Miss Gilby first came to our house there was a great flutter, which afterwards calmed down when they got used to her. Now the whole thing was stirred up afresh. I had never bothered myself before as to whether Miss Gilby was European or Indian, but I began to do so now. I said to my husband: "We must get rid of Miss Gilby."

He kept silent.

I talked to him wildly, and he went away sad at heart.

After a fit of weeping, I felt in a more reasonable mood when we met at night. "I cannot," my husband said, "look upon Miss Gilby through a mist of abstraction, just because she is English. Cannot you get over the barrier of her name after such a long acquaintance? Cannot you realize that she loves you?"

I felt a little ashamed and replied with some sharpness: "Let her remain. I am not over anxious to send her away." And Miss Gilby remained.

But one day I was told that she had been insulted by a young fellow on her way to church. This was a boy whom we were supporting. My husband turned him out of the house. There was not a single soul, that day, who could forgive my husband for that act—not even I. This time Miss Gilby left of her own accord. She shed tears when she came to say good-bye, but my mood would not melt. To slander the poor boy so—and such a fine boy, too, who would forget his daily bath and food in his enthusiasm for *Swadeshi*.

My husband escorted Miss Gilby to the railway station in his own carriage. I was sure he was going too far. When exaggerated accounts of the incident gave rise to a public scandal, which found its way to the newspapers, I felt he had been rightly served. I had often become anxious at my husband's doings, but had never before been ashamed; yet now I had to blush for him! I did not know exactly, nor did I care, what wrong poor Noren might, or might not, have done to Miss Gilby, but the idea of sitting in judgement on such a matter at such a time! I should have refused to damp the spirit which prompted young Noren to defy the Englishwoman. I could not but look upon it as a sign of cowardice in my husband, that he should fail to understand this simple thing. And so I blushed for him.

And yet it was not that my husband refused to support *Swadeshi*, or was in any way against the Cause. Only he had not been able whole-heartedly to accept the spirit of *Bande Mataram*. "I am willing," he said, "to serve my country; but my worship I reserve for Right which is far greater than my country. To worship my country as a god is to bring a curse upon it."

This was the time when Sandip Babu with his followers came to our neighbourhood to preach *Swadeshi*.

There is to be a big meeting in our temple pavilion. We women are sitting there, on one side, behind a screen. Triumphant shouts of *Bande Mataram* come nearer: and to them I am thrilling through and through. Suddenly a stream of barefooted youths in turbans, clad in ascetic ochre, rushes into the quadrangle, like a silt-reddened freshet into a dry river-bed at the first burst of the rains. The whole place is filled with an immense crowd, through which Sandip Babu is borne, seated in a big chair hoisted on the shoulders of ten or twelve of the youths.

Bande Mataram! *Bande Mataram*! *Bande Mataram*! It seems as though the skies would be rent and scattered into a thousand fragments.

I had seen Sandip Babu's photograph before. There was something in his features which I did not quite like. Not that he was bad-looking—far from it: he had a splendidly handsome face. Yet, I know not why, it seemed to me, in spite of all its brilliance, that too much of base alloy had gone into its making. The light in his eyes somehow did not shine true. That was why I did not like it when my husband unquestioningly gave in to all his demands. I could bear the waste of money; but it vexed me to think that he was imposing on my husband, taking advantage of friendship. His bearing was not that of an ascetic, nor even of a person of moderate means, but foppish all over. Love of comfort seemed to . . . any number of such reflections come back to me today, but let them be. When, however, Sandip Babu began to speak that afternoon, and the hearts of the crowd swayed and surged to his words, as though they would break all bounds, I saw him wonderfully transformed. Especially when his features were suddenly lit up by a shaft of light from the slowly setting sun, as it sunk below the roof-line of the pavilion, he seemed to me to be marked out by the gods as their messenger to mortal men and women.

From beginning to end of his speech, each one of his utterances was a stormy outburst. There was no limit to the confidence of his assurance. I do not know how it happened, but I found I had impatiently pushed away the screen from before me and had fixed my gaze upon him. Yet there was none in that crowd who paid any heed to my doings. Only once, I noticed, his eyes, like stars in fateful Orion, flashed full on my face. I was utterly unconscious of myself. I was no longer the lady of the Rajah's house, but the sole representative of Bengal's womanhood. And he was the champion of Bengal. As the sky had shed its light over him, so he must receive the consecration of a woman's benediction . . .

It seemed clear to me that, since he had caught sight of me, the fire in his words had flamed up more fiercely. Indra's steed refused to be reined in, and there came the roar of thunder and the flash of lightning. I said within myself that his language had caught fire from my eyes; for we women are not only the deities of the household fire, but the flame of the soul itself.

I returned home that evening radiant with a new pride and joy. The storm within me had shifted my whole being from one centre to another. Like the Greek maidens of old, I fain would cut off my long, resplendent tresses to make a bowstring for my hero. Had my outward ornaments been connected with my inner feelings, then my necklet, my armlets, my bracelets, would all have burst their bonds and flung themselves over that assembly like a shower of meteors. Only some personal sacrifice, I felt, could help me to bear the tumult of my exaltation.

When my husband came home later, I was trembling lest he should utter a sound out of tune with the triumphant paean which was still ringing in my ears, lest his fanaticism for truth should lead him to express disapproval of anything that had been said that afternoon. For then I should have openly defied and humiliated him. But he did not say a word . . . which I did not like either.

He should have said: "Sandip has brought me to my senses. I now realize how mistaken I have been all this time." I somehow felt that he was spitefully silent, that he obstinately refused to be enthusiastic. I asked how long Sandip Babu was going to be with us.

"He is off to Rangpur early tomorrow morning," said my husband.

"Must it be tomorrow?"

"Yes, he is already engaged to speak there."

I was silent for a while and then asked again: "Could he not possibly stay a day longer?"

"That may hardly be possible, but why?"

"I want to invite him to dinner and attend on him myself."

My husband was surprised. He had often entreated me to be present when he had particular friends to dinner, but I had never let myself be persuaded. He gazed at me curiously, in silence, with a look I did not quite understand.

I was suddenly overcome with a sense of shame. "No, no," I exclaimed, "that would never do!"

"Why not!" said he. "I will ask him myself, and if it is at all possible he will surely stay on for tomorrow."

It turned out to be quite possible. I will tell the exact truth. That day I reproached my Creator because he had not made me surpassingly beautiful—not to steal any heart away, but because beauty is glory. In this great day the men of the country should realize its goddess in its womanhood. But, alas, the eyes of men fail to discern the goddess, if outward beauty be lacking. Would Sandip Babu find the *Shakti* of the Motherland manifest in me? Or would he simply take me to be an ordinary, domestic woman? That morning I scented my flowing hair and tied it in a loose knot, bound by a cunningly intertwined red silk ribbon. Dinner, you see, was to be served at midday, and there was no time to dry my hair after my bath and do it up plaited in the ordinary way. I put on a gold-bordered white *sari*, and my short-sleeve muslin jacket was also gold-bordered.

I felt that there was a certain restraint about my costume and that nothing could well have been simpler. But my sister-in-law, who happened to be passing by, stopped dead before me, surveyed me from head to foot and with compressed lips smiled a meaning smile. When I asked her the reason, "I am admiring your get-up!" she said. "What is there so entertaining about it?" I enquired, considerably annoyed.

"It's superb," she said. "I was only thinking that one of those low-necked English bodices would have made it perfect." Not only her mouth and eyes, but her whole body seemed to ripple with suppressed laughter as she left the room.

I was very, very angry, and wanted to change everything and put on my everyday clothes. But I cannot tell exactly why I could not carry out my impulse. Women are the ornaments of society—thus I reasoned with myself—and my husband would never like it, if I appeared before Sandip Babu unworthily clad. My idea had been to make my appearance after they had sat down to dinner. In the bustle of looking after the serving the first awkwardness would have passed off. But dinner was not ready in time, and it was getting late. Meanwhile my husband had sent for me to introduce the guest.

I was feeling horribly shy about looking Sandip Babu in the face. However, I managed to recover myself enough to say: "I am so sorry dinner is getting late." He boldly came and sat right beside me as he replied: "I get a dinner of some kind every day, but the Goddess of Plenty keeps behind the scenes. Now that the goddess herself has appeared, it matters little if the dinner lags behind."

He was just as emphatic in his manners as he was in his public speaking. He had no hesitation and seemed to be accustomed to occupy, unchallenged, his chosen seat. He claimed the right to intimacy so confidently, that the blame would seem to belong to those who should dispute it.

I was in terror lest Sandip Babu should take me for a shrinking, old-fashioned bundle of inanity. But, for the life of me, I could not sparkle in repartees such as might charm or dazzle him. What could have possessed me, I angrily wondered, to appear before him in such an absurd way? I was about to retire when dinner was over, but Sandip Babu, as bold as ever, placed himself in my way.

"You must not," he said, "think me greedy. It was not the dinner that kept me staying on, it was your invitation. If you were to run away now, that would not be playing fair with your guest." If he had not said these words with a careless ease, they would have been out of tune. But, after all, he was such a great friend of my husband that I was like his sister.

While I was struggling to climb up this high wave of intimacy, my husband came to the rescue, saying: "Why not come back to us after you have taken your dinner?" "But you must give your word," said Sandip Babu, "before we let you off."

"I will come," said I, with a slight smile.

"Let me tell you," continued Sandip Babu, "why I cannot trust you. Nikhil has been married these nine years, and all this while you have eluded me. If you do this again for another nine years, we shall never meet again."

I took up the spirit of his remark as I dropped my voice to reply: "Why even then should we not meet?"

"My horoscope tells me I am to die early. None of my forefathers have survived their thirtieth year. I am now twenty-seven."

He knew this would go home. This time there must have been a shade of concern in my low voice as I said: "The blessings of the whole country are sure to avert the evil influence of the stars."

"Then the blessings of the country must be voiced by its goddess. This is the reason for my anxiety that you should return, so that my talisman may begin to work from today."

Sandip Babu had such a way of taking things by storm that I got no opportunity of resenting what I never should have permitted in another.

"So," he concluded with a laugh, "I am going to hold this husband of yours as a hostage till you come back."

As I was coming away, he exclaimed: "May I trouble you for a trifle?"

I started and turned round.

"Don't be alarmed," he said. "It's merely a glass of water. You might have noticed that I did not drink any water with my dinner. I take it a little later."

Upon this I had to make a show of interest and ask him the reason. He began to give the history of his dyspepsia. I was told how he had been a martyr to it for seven months, and how, after the usual course of nuisances, which included different allopathic and homoeopathic misadventures, he had obtained the most wonderful results by indigenous methods.

"Do you know," he added, with a smile, "God has built even my infirmities in such a manner that they yield only under the bombardment of *Swadeshi* pills."

My husband, at this, broke his silence. "You must confess," said he, "that you have as immense an attraction for foreign medicine as the earth has for meteors. You have three shelves in your sitting-room full of. . ."

Sandip Babu broke in: "Do you know what they are? They are the punitive police. They come, not because they are wanted, but because they are imposed on us by the rule of this modern age, exacting fines and-inflicting injuries."

My husband could not bear exaggerations, and I could see he disliked this. But all ornaments are exaggerations. They are not made by God, but by man. Once I remember in defence of some untruth of mine I said to my husband: "Only the trees and beasts and birds tell unmitigated truths, because these poor things have not the power to invent. In this men show their superiority to the lower creatures, and women beat even men. Neither is a profusion of ornament unbecoming for a woman, nor a profusion of untruth."

As I came out into the passage leading to the zenana I found my sister-in-law, standing near a window overlooking the reception rooms, peeping through the venetian shutter.

"You here?" I asked in surprise.

"Eavesdropping!" she replied.

When I returned, Sandip Babu was tenderly apologetic. "I am afraid we have spoilt your appetite," he said.

I felt greatly ashamed. Indeed, I had been too indecently quick over my dinner. With a little calculation, it would become quite evident that my non-eating had surpassed the eating. But I had no idea that anyone could have been deliberately calculating.

I suppose Sandip Babu detected my feeling of shame, which only augmented it. "I was sure," he said, "that you had the impulse of the wild deer to run away, but it is a great boon that you took the trouble to keep your promise with me."

I could not think of any suitable reply and so I sat down, blushing and uncomfortable, at one end of the sofa. The vision that I had of myself, as the *Shakti* of Womanhood, incarnate, crowning Sandip Babu simply with my presence, majestic and unashamed, failed me altogether. Sandip Babu deliberately started a discussion with my husband. He knew that his keen wit flashed to the best effect in an argument. I have often since observed, that he never lost an opportunity for a passage at arms whenever I happened to be present.

He was familiar with my husband's views on the cult of *Bande Mataram*, and began in a provoking way: "So you do not allow that there is room for an appeal to the imagination in patriotic work?"

"It has its place, Sandip, I admit, but I do not believe in giving it the whole place. I would know my country in its frank reality, and for this I am both afraid and ashamed to make use of hypnotic texts of patriotism."

"What you call hypnotic texts I call truth. I truly believe my country to be my God. I worship Humanity. God manifests Himself both in man and in his country."

"If that is what you really believe, there should be no difference for you between man and man, and so between country and country."

"Quite true. But my powers are limited, so my worship of Humanity is continued in the worship of my country."

"I have nothing against your worship as such, but how is it you propose to conduct your worship of God by hating other countries in which He is equally manifest?"

"Hate is also an adjunct of worship. Arjuna won Mahadeva's favour by wrestling with him. God will be with us in the end, if we are prepared to give Him battle."

"If that be so, then those who are serving and those who are harming the country are both His devotees. Why, then, trouble to preach patriotism?"

"In the case of one's own country, it is different. There the heart clearly demands worship."

"If you push the same argument further you can say that since God is manifested in us, our *self* has to be worshipped before all else; because our natural instinct claims it."

"Look here, Nikhil, this is all merely dry logic. Can't you recognize that there is such a thing as feeling?"

"I tell you the truth, Sandip," my husband replied. "It is my feelings that are outraged, whenever you try to pass off injustice as a duty, and unrighteousness as a moral ideal. The fact, that I am incapable of stealing, is not due to my possessing logical faculties, but to my having some feeling of respect for myself and love for ideals."

I was raging inwardly. At last I could keep silent no longer. "Is not the history of every country," I cried, "whether England, France, Germany, or Russia, the history of stealing for the sake of one's own country?"

"They have to answer for these thefts; they are doing so even now; their history is not yet ended."

"At any rate," interposed Sandip Babu, "why should we not follow suit? Let us first fill our country's coffers with stolen goods and then take centuries, like these other countries, to answer for them, if we must. But, I ask you, where do you find this 'answering' in history?"

"When Rome was answering for her sin no one knew it. All that time, there was apparently no limit to her prosperity. But do you not see one thing: how these political bags of theirs are bursting with lies and treacheries, breaking their backs under their weight?"

Never before had I had any opportunity of being present at a discussion between my husband and his men friends. Whenever he argued with me I could feel his reluctance to push me into a corner. This arose out of the very love he bore me. Today for the first time I saw his fencer's skill in debate.

Nevertheless, my heart refused to accept my husband's position. I was struggling to find some answer, but it would not come. When the word "righteousness" comes into an argument, it sounds ugly to say that a thing can be too good to be useful.

All of a sudden Sandip Babu turned to me with the question: "What do *you* say to this?"

"I do not care about fine distinctions," I broke out. "I will tell you broadly what I feel. I am only human. I am covetous. I would have good things for my country. If I am obliged, I would snatch them and filch them. I have anger. I would be angry for my country's sake. If necessary, I would smite and slay to avenge her insults. I have my desire to be fascinated, and fascination must be supplied to me in bodily shape by my country. She must have some visible symbol casting its spell upon my mind. I would make my country a Person, and call her Mother, Goddess, Durga—for whom I would redden the earth with sacrificial offerings. I am human, not divine." Sandip Babu leapt to his feet with uplifted arms and shouted "Hurrah!"—The next moment he corrected himself and cried: "*Bande Mataram.*"

A shadow of pain passed over the face of my husband. He said to me in a very gentle voice: "Neither am I divine: I am human. And therefore I dare not permit the evil which is in me to be exaggerated into an image of my country—never, never!"

Sandip Babu cried out: "See, Nikhil, how in the heart of a woman Truth takes flesh and blood. Woman knows how to be cruel: her virulence is like a blind storm. It is beautifully fearful. In man it is ugly, because it harbours in its centre the gnawing worms of reason and thought. I tell you, Nikhil, it is our women who will save the country. This is not the time for nice scruples. We must be unswervingly, unreasoningly brutal. We must sin. We must give our women red sandal paste with which to anoint and enthrone our sin. Don't you remember what the poet says:

Come, Sin, O beautiful Sin,

Let thy stinging red kisses pour down fiery red wine into our blood.

Sound the trumpet of imperious evil

And cross our forehead with the wreath of exulting lawlessness,

O Deity of Desecration,

Smear our breasts with the blackest mud of disrepute, unashamed.

Down with that righteousness, which cannot smilingly bring rack and ruin."

When Sandip Babu, standing with his head high, insulted at a moment's impulse all that men have cherished as their highest, in all countries and in all times, a shiver went right through my body.

But, with a stamp of his foot, he continued his declamation: "I can see that you are that beautiful spirit of fire, which burns the home to ashes and lights up the larger world with its flame. Give to us the indomitable courage to go to the bottom of Ruin itself. Impart grace to all that is baneful."

It was not clear to whom Sandip Babu addressed his last appeal. It might have been She whom he worshipped with his *Bande Mataram*. It might have been the Womanhood of his country. Or it might have been its representative, the woman before him. He would have gone further in the same strain, but my husband suddenly rose from his seat and touched him lightly on the shoulder saying: "Sandip, Chandranath Babu is here."

I started and turned round, to find an aged gentleman at the door, calm and dignified, in doubt as to whether he should come in or retire. His face was touched with a gentle light like that of the setting sun.

My husband came up to me and whispered: "This is my master, of whom I have so often told you. Make your obeisance to him."

I bent reverently and took the dust of his feet. He gave me his blessing saying: "May God protect you always, my little mother." I was sorely in need of such a blessing at that moment.

NIKHIL'S STORY

One day I had the faith to believe that I should be able to bear whatever came from my God. I never had the trial. Now I think it has come. I used to test my strength of mind by imagining all kinds of evil which might happen to me—poverty, imprisonment, dishonour, death—even Bimala's. And when I said to myself that I should be able to receive these with firmness, I am sure I did not exaggerate. Only I could never even imagine one thing, and today it is that of which I am thinking, and wondering whether I can really bear it. There is a thorn somewhere pricking in my heart, constantly giving me pain while I am about my daily work. It seems to persist even when I am asleep. The very moment I wake up in the morning, I find that the bloom has gone from the face of the sky. What is it? What has happened?

My mind has become so sensitive, that even my past life, which came to me in the disguise of happiness, seems to wring my very heart with its falsehood; and the shame and sorrow which are coming close to me are losing their cover of privacy, all the more because they try to veil their faces. My heart has become all eyes. The things that should not be seen, the things I do not want to see—these I must see. The day has come at last when my ill-starred life has to reveal its destitution in a long-drawn series of exposures. This penury, all unexpected, has taken its seat in the heart where plenitude seemed to reign. The fees which I paid to delusion for just nine years of my youth have now to be returned with interest to Truth till the end of my days.

What is the use of straining to keep up my pride? What harm if I confess that I have something lacking in me? Possibly it is that unreasoning forcefulness which women love to find in men. But is strength mere display of muscularity? Must strength have no scruples in treading the weak underfoot? But why all these arguments? Worthiness cannot be earned merely by disputing about it. And I am unworthy, unworthy, unworthy.

What if I am unworthy? The true value of love is this, that it can ever bless the unworthy with its own prodigality. For the worthy there are many rewards on God's earth, but God has specially reserved love for the unworthy.

Up till now Bimala was my home-made Bimala, the product of the confined space and the daily routine of small duties. Did the love which I received from her, I asked myself, come from the deep spring of her heart, or was it merely like the daily provision of pipe water pumped up by the municipal steam-engine of society? I longed to find Bimala blossoming fully in all her truth and power. But the thing I forgot to calculate was, that one must give up all claims based on conventional rights, if one would find a person freely revealed in truth.

Why did I fail to think of this? Was it because of the husband's pride of possession over his wife? No. It was because I placed the fullest trust upon love. I was vain enough to think that I had the power in me to bear the sight of truth in its awful nakedness. It was tempting Providence, but still I clung to my proud determination to come out victorious in the trial. Bimala had failed to understand me in one thing. She could not fully realize that I held as weakness all imposition of force. Only the weak dare not be just. They shirk their responsibility of fairness and try quickly to get at results through the short-cuts of injustice. Bimala has no patience with patience. She loves to find in men the turbulent, the angry, the unjust. Her respect must have its element of fear.

I had hoped that when Bimala found herself free in the outer world she would be rescued from her infatuation for tyranny. But now I feel sure that this infatuation is deep down in her nature. Her love is for the boisterous. From the tip of her tongue to the pit of her stomach she must tingle with red pepper in order to enjoy the simple fare of life. But my determination was, never to do my duty with frantic impetuosity, helped on by the fiery liquor of excitement. I know Bimala finds it difficult to respect me for this, taking my scruples for feebleness—and she is quite angry with me because I am not running amuck crying *Bande Mataram*.

For the matter of that, I have become unpopular with all my countrymen because I have not joined them in their carousals. They are certain that either I have a longing for some title, or else that I am afraid of the police. The police on their side suspect me of harbouring some hidden design and protesting too much in my mildness.

What I really feel is this, that those who cannot find food for their enthusiasm in a knowledge of their country as it actually is, or those who cannot love men just because they are men—who needs must shout and deify their country in order to keep up their excitement—these love excitement more than their country.

To try to give our infatuation a higher place than Truth is a sign of inherent slavishness. Where our minds are free we find ourselves lost. Our moribund vitality must have for its rider either some fantasy, or someone in authority, or a sanction from the pundits, in order to make it move. So long as we are impervious to truth and have to be moved by some hypnotic stimulus, we must know that we lack the capacity for self-government. Whatever may be our condition, we shall either need some imaginary ghost or some actual medicine-man to terrorize over us.

The other day when Sandip accused me of lack of imagination, saying that this prevented me from realizing my country in a visible image, Bimala agreed with him. I did not say anything in my defence, because to win in argument does not lead to happiness. Her difference of opinion is not due to any inequality of intelligence, but rather to dissimilarity of nature.

They accuse me of being unimaginative—that is, according to them, I may have oil in my lamp, but no flame. Now this is exactly the accusation which I bring against them. I would say to them: "You are dark, even as the flints are. You must come to violent conflicts and make a noise in order to produce your sparks. But their disconnected flashes merely assist your pride, and not your clear vision."

I have been noticing for some time that there is a gross cupidity about Sandip. His fleshly feelings make him harbour delusions about his religion and impel him into a tyrannical attitude in his patriotism. His intellect is keen, but his nature is coarse, and so he glorifies his selfish lusts under high-sounding names. The cheap consolations of hatred are as urgently necessary for him as the satisfaction of his appetites. Bimala has often warned me, in the old days, of his hankering after money. I understood this, but I could not bring myself to haggle with Sandip. I felt ashamed even to own to myself that he was trying to take advantage of me. It will, however, be difficult to explain to Bimala today that Sandip's love of country is but a different phase of his covetous self-love. Bimala's hero-worship of Sandip makes me hesitate all the more to talk to her about him, lest some touch of jealousy may lead me unwittingly into exaggeration. It may be that the pain at my heart is already making me see a distorted picture of Sandip. And yet it is better perhaps to speak out than to keep my feelings gnawing within me.

I have known my master these thirty years. Neither calumny, nor disaster, nor death itself has any terrors for him.

Nothing could have saved me, born as I was into the traditions of this family of ours, but that he has established his own life in the centre of mine, with its peace and truth and spiritual vision, thus making it possible for me to realize goodness in its truth.

My master came to me that day and said: "Is it necessary to detain Sandip here any longer?"

His nature was so sensitive to all omens of evil that he had at once understood. He was not easily moved, but that day he felt the dark shadow of trouble ahead. Do I not know how well he loves me?

At tea-time I said to Sandip: "I have just had a letter from Rangpur. They are complaining that I am selfishly detaining you. When will you be going there?"

Bimala was pouring out the tea. Her face fell at once. She threw just one enquiring glance at Sandip.

"I have been thinking," said Sandip, "that this wandering up and down means a tremendous waste of energy. I feel that if I could work from a centre I could achieve more permanent results."

With this he looked up at Bimala and asked: "Do you not think so too?"

Bimala hesitated for a reply and then said: "Both ways seem good—to do the work from a centre, as well as by travelling about. That in which you find greater satisfaction is the way for you."

"Then let me speak out my mind," said Sandip. "I have never yet found any one source of inspiration suffice me for good. That is why I have been constantly moving about, rousing enthusiasm in the people, from which in turn I draw my own store of energy. Today you have given me the message of my country. Such fire I have never beheld in any man. I shall be able to spread the fire of enthusiasm in my country by borrowing it from you. No, do not be ashamed. You are far above all modesty and diffidence. You are the Queen Bee of our hive, and we the workers shall rally around you. You shall be our centre, our inspiration." Bimala flushed all over with bashful pride and her hand shook as she went on pouring out the tea.

Another day my master came to me and said: "Why don't you two go up to Darjeeling for a change? You are not looking well. Have you been getting enough sleep?" I asked Bimala in the evening whether she would care to have a trip to the Hills. I knew she had a great longing to see the Himalayas. But she refused . . . The country's Cause, I suppose!

I must not lose my faith: I shall wait. The passage from the narrow to the larger world is stormy. When she is familiar with this freedom, then I shall know where my place is. If I discover that I do not fit in with the arrangement of the outer world, then I shall not quarrel with my fate, but silently take my leave . . . Use force? But for what? Can force prevail against Truth?

SANDIP'S STORY

The impotent man says: "That which has come to my share is mine." And the weak man assents. But the lesson of the whole world is: "That is really mine which I can snatch away." My country does not become mine simply because it is the country of my birth. It becomes mine on the day when I am able to win it by force. Every man has a natural right to possess, and therefore greed is natural. It is not in the wisdom of nature that we should be content to be deprived. What my mind covets, my surroundings must supply. This is the only true understanding between our inner and outer nature in this world. Let moral ideals remain merely for those poor anaemic creatures of starved desire whose grasp is weak. Those who can desire with all their soul and enjoy with all their heart, those who have no hesitation or scruple, it is they who are the anointed of Providence. Nature spreads out her riches and loveliest treasures for their benefit. They swim across streams, leap over walls, kick open doors, to help themselves to whatever is worth taking. In such a getting one can rejoice; such wresting as this gives value to the thing taken.

Nature surrenders herself, but only to the robber. For she delights in this forceful desire, this forceful abduction. And so she does not put the garland of her acceptance round the lean, scraggy neck of the ascetic. The music of the wedding march is struck. The time of the wedding I must not let pass. My heart therefore is eager. For, who is the bridegroom? It is I. The bridegroom's place belongs to him who, torch in hand, can come in time. The bridegroom in Nature's wedding hall comes unexpected and uninvited.

Ashamed? No, I am never ashamed! I ask for whatever I want, and I do not always wait to ask before I take it. Those who are deprived by their own diffidence dignify their privation by the name of modesty. The world into which we are born is the world of reality. When a man goes away from the market of real things with empty hands and empty stomach, merely filling his bag with big sounding words, I wonder why he ever came into this hard world at all. Did these men get their appointment from the epicures of the religious world, to play set tunes on sweet, pious texts in that pleasure garden where blossom airy nothings? I neither affect those tunes nor do I find any sustenance in those blossoms.

What I desire, I desire positively, superlatively. I want to knead it with both my hands and both my feet; I want to smear it all over my body; I want to gorge myself with it to the full. The scrannel pipes of those who have worn themselves out by their moral fastings, till they have become flat and pale like starved vermin infesting a long-deserted bed, will never reach my ear. I would conceal nothing, because that would be cowardly. But if I cannot bring myself to conceal when concealment is needful, that also is cowardly. Because you have your greed, you build your walls. Because I have my greed, I break through them. You use your power: I use my craft. These are the realities of life. On these depend kingdoms and empires and all the great enterprises of men.

As for those *avatars* who come down from their paradise to talk to us in some holy jargon—their words are not real. Therefore, in spite of all the applause they get, these sayings of theirs only find a place in the hiding corners of the weak. They are despised by those who are strong, the rulers of the world. Those who have had the courage to see this have won success, while those poor wretches who are dragged one way by nature and the other way by these ava tars, they set one foot in the boat of the real and the other in the boat of the unreal, and thus are in a pitiable plight, able neither to advance nor to keep their place. There are many men who seem to have been born only with an obsession to die. Possibly there is a beauty, like that of a sunset, in this lingering death in life which seems to fascinate them. Nikhil lives this kind of life, if life it may be called. Years ago, I had a great argument with him on this point.

"It is true," he said, "that you cannot get anything except by force. But then what is this force? And then also, what is this getting? The strength I believe in is the strength of renouncing." "So you," I exclaimed, "are infatuated with the glory of bankruptcy."

"Just as desperately as the chick is infatuated about the bankruptcy of its shell," he replied. "The shell is real enough, yet it is given up in exchange for intangible light and air. A sorry exchange, I suppose you would call it?"

When once Nikhil gets on to metaphor, there is no hope of making him see that he is merely dealing with words, not with realities. Well, well, let him be happy with his metaphors. We are the flesh-eaters of the world; we have teeth and nails; we pursue and grab and tear. We are not satisfied with chewing in the evening the cud of the grass we have eaten in the morning. Anyhow, we cannot allow your metaphor-mongers to bar the door to our sustenance.

In that case we shall simply steal or rob, for we must live. People will say that I am starting some novel theory just because those who are moving in this world are in the habit of talking differently though they are really acting up to it all the time. Therefore they fail to understand, as I do, that this is the only working moral principle. In point of fact, I know that my idea is not an empty theory at all, for it has been proved in practical life. I have found that my way always wins over the hearts of women, who are creatures of this world of reality and do not roam about in cloud-land, as men do, in idea-filled balloons.

Women find in my features, my manner, my gait, my speech, a masterful passion—not a passion dried thin with the heat of asceticism, not a passion with its face turned back at every step in doubt and debate, but a full-blooded passion. It roars and rolls on, like a flood, with the cry: "I want, I want, I want." Women feel, in their own heart of hearts, that this indomitable passion is the lifeblood of the world, acknowledging no law but itself, and therefore victorious. For this reason they have so often abandoned themselves to be swept away on the flood-tide of my passion, recking naught as to whether it takes them to life or to death. This power which wins these women is the power of mighty men, the power which wins the world of reality.

Those who imagine the greater desirability of another world merely shift their desires from the earth to the skies. It remains to be seen how high their gushing fountain will play, and for how long. But this much is certain: women were not created for these pale creatures—these lotus-eaters of idealism. "Affinity!" When it suited my need, I have often said that God has created special pairs of men and women, and that the union of such is the only legitimate union, higher than all unions made by law. The reason of it is, that though man wants to follow nature, he can find no pleasure in it unless he screens himself with some phrase—and that is why this world is so overflowing with lies. "Affinity!" Why should there be only one? There may be affinity with thousands. It was never in my agreement with nature that I should overlook all my innumerable affinities for the sake of only one. I have discovered many in my own life up to now, yet that has not closed the door to one more—and that one is clearly visible to my eyes. She has also discovered her own affinity to me.

And then?

Then, if I do not win I am a coward.

I wonder what could have happened to my feeling of shame. The fact is, I had no time to think about myself. My days and nights were passing in a whirl, like an eddy with myself in the centre. No gap was left for hesitation or delicacy to enter.

One day my sister-in-law remarked to my husband: "Up to now the women of this house have been kept weeping. Here comes the men's turn.

"We must see that they do not miss it," she continued, turning to me. "I see you are out for the fray, Chota Rani! Hurl your shafts straight at their hearts." Her keen eyes looked me up and down. Not one of the colours into which my toilet, my dress, my manners, my speech, had blossomed out had escaped her. I am ashamed to speak of it today, but I felt no shame then. Something within me was at work of which I was not even conscious. I used to overdress, it is true, but more like an automaton, with no particular design. No doubt I knew which effort of mine would prove specially pleasing to Sandip Babu, but that required no intuition, for he would discuss it openly before all of them.

One day he said to my husband: "Do you know, Nikhil, when I first saw our Queen Bee, she was sitting there so demurely in her gold-bordered *sari*. Her eyes were gazing inquiringly into space, like stars which had lost their way, just as if she had been for ages standing on the edge of some darkness, looking out for something unknown. But when I saw her, I felt a quiver run through me. It seemed to me that the gold border of her *sari* was her own inner fire flaming out and twining round her. That is the flame we want, visible fire! Look here, Queen Bee, you really must do us the favour of dressing once more as a living flame." So long I had been like a small river at the border of a village. My rhythm and my language were different from what they are now. But the tide came up from the sea, and my breast heaved; my banks gave way and the great drumbeats of the sea waves echoed in my mad current. I could not understand the meaning of that sound in my blood. Where was that former self of mine? Whence came foaming into me this surging flood of glory? Sandip's hungry eyes burnt like the lamps of worship before my shrine. All his gaze proclaimed that I was a wonder in beauty and power; and the loudness of his praise, spoken and unspoken, drowned all other voices in my world. Had the Creator created me afresh, I wondered? Did he wish to make up now for neglecting me so long? I who before was plain had become suddenly beautiful. I who before had been of no account now felt in myself all the splendour of Bengal itself.

For Sandip Babu was not a mere individual. In him was the confluence of millions of minds of the country. When he called me the Queen Bee of the hive, I was acclaimed with a chorus of praise by all our patriot workers. After that, the loud jests of my sister-in-law could not touch me any longer. My relations with all the world underwent a change. Sandip Babu made it clear how all the country was in need of me. I had no difficulty in believing this at the time, for I felt that I had the power to do everything. Divine strength had come to me. It was something which I had never felt before, which was beyond myself. I had no time to question it to find out what was its nature. It seemed to belong to me, and yet to transcend me. It comprehended the whole of Bengal. Sandip Babu would consult me about every little thing touching the Cause. At first I felt very awkward and would hang back, but that soon wore off. Whatever I suggested seemed to astonish him. He would go into raptures and say: "Men can only think. You women have a way of understanding without thinking. Woman was created out of God's own fancy. Man, He had to hammer into shape."

Letters used to come to Sandip Babu from all parts of the country which were submitted to me for my opinion. Occasionally he disagreed with me. But I would not argue with him. Then after a day or two—as if a new light had suddenly dawned upon him—he would send for me and say: "It was my mistake. Your suggestion was the correct one." He would often confess to me that wherever he had taken steps contrary to my advice he had gone wrong. Thus I gradually came to be convinced that behind whatever was taking place was Sandip Babu, and behind Sandip Babu was the plain common sense of a woman. The glory of a great responsibility filled my being.

My husband had no place in our counsels. Sandip Babu treated him as a younger brother, of whom personally one may be very fond and yet have no use for his business advice. He would tenderly and smilingly talk about my husband's childlike innocence, saying that his curious doctrine and perversities of mind had a flavour of humour which made them all the more lovable. It was seemingly this very affection for Nikhil which led Sandip Babu to forbear from troubling him with the burden of the country.

Nature has many anodynes in her pharmacy, which she secretly administers when vital relations are being insidiously severed, so that none may know of the operation, till at last one awakes to know what a great rent has been made. When the knife was busy with my life's most intimate tie, my mind was so clouded with fumes of intoxicating gas that I was not in the least aware of what a cruel thing was happening. Possibly this is woman's nature. When her passion is roused she loses her sensibility for all that is outside it. When, like the river, we women keep to our banks, we give nourishment with all that we have: when we overflow them we destroy with all that we are.

SANDIP'S STORY

I can see that something has gone wrong. I got an inkling of it the other day.

Ever since my arrival, Nikhil's sitting-room had become a thing amphibious—half women's apartment, half men's: Bimala had access to it from the zenana, it was not barred to me from the outer side. If we had only gone slow, and made use of our privileges with some restraint, we might not have fallen foul of other people. But we went ahead so vehemently that we could not think of the consequences. Whenever Bee comes into Nikhil's room, I somehow get to know of it from mine. There are the tinkle of bangles and other little sounds; the door is perhaps shut with a shade of unnecessary vehemence; the bookcase is a trifle stiff and creaks if jerked open. When I enter I find Bee, with her back to the door, ever so busy selecting a book from the shelves. And as I offer to assist her in this difficult task she starts and protests; and then we naturally get on to other topics. The other day, on an inauspicious Thursday afternoon, I sallied forth from my room at the call of these same sounds. There was a man on guard in the passage. I walked on without so much as glancing at him, but as I approached the door he put himself in my way saying: "Not that way, sir."

"Not that way! Why?"

"The Rani Mother is there."

"Oh, very well. Tell your Rani Mother that Sandip Babu wants to see her."

"That cannot be, sir. It is against orders."

I felt highly indignant. "I order you!" I said in a raised voice.

"Go and announce me."

The fellow was somewhat taken aback at my attitude. In the meantime I had neared the door. I was on the point of reaching it, when he followed after me and took me by the arm saying: "No, sir, you must not."

What! To be touched by a flunkey! I snatched away my arm and gave the man a sounding blow. At this moment Bee came out of the room to find the man about to insult me. I shall never forget the picture of her wrath! That Bee is beautiful is a discovery of my own. Most of our people would see nothing in her. Her tall, slim figure these boors would call "lanky". But it is just this lithesomeness of hers that I admire—like an up-leaping fountain of life, coming direct out of the depths of the Creator's heart. Her complexion is dark, but it is the lustrous darkness of a sword-blade, keen and scintillating.

"Nanku!" she commanded, as she stood in the doorway, pointing with her finger, "leave us."

"Do not be angry with him," said I. "If it is against orders, it is I who should retire."

Bee's voice was still trembling as she replied: "You must not go. Come in."

It was not a request, but again a command! I followed her in, and taking a chair fanned myself with a fan which was on the table. Bee scribbled something with a pencil on a sheet of paper and, summoning a servant, handed it to him saying: "Take this to the Maharaja."

"Forgive me," I resumed. "I was unable to control myself, and hit that man of yours.

"You served him right," said Bee.

"But it was not the poor fellow's fault, after all. He was only obeying his orders."

Here Nikhil came in, and as he did so I left my seat with a rapid movement and went and stood near the window with my back to the room.

"Nanku, the guard, has insulted Sandip Babu," said Bee to Nikhil. Nikhil seemed to be so genuinely surprised that I had to turn round and stare at him. Even an outrageously good man fails in keeping up his pride of truthfulness before his wife—if she be the proper kind of woman.

"He insolently stood in the way when Sandip Babu was coming in here," continued Bee. "He said he had orders . . ."

"Whose orders?" asked Nikhil.

"How am I to know?" exclaimed Bee impatiently, her eyes brimming over with mortification.

Nikhil sent for the man and questioned him. "It was not my fault," Nanku repeated sullenly. "I had my orders."

"Who gave you the order?"

"The Bara Rani Mother."

We were all silent for a while. After the man had left, Bee said: "Nanku must go!"

Nikhil remained silent. I could see that his sense of justice would not allow this. There was no end to his qualms. But this time he was up against a tough problem. Bee was not the woman to take things lying down. She would have to get even with her sister-in-law by punishing this fellow. And as Nikhil remained silent, her eyes flashed fire. She knew not how to pour her scorn upon her husband's feebleness of spirit. Nikhil left the room after a while without another word.

The next day Nanku was not to be seen. On inquiry, I learnt that he had been sent off to some other part of the estates, and that his wages had not suffered by such transfer.

I could catch glimpses of the ravages of the storm raging over this, behind the scenes. All I can say is, that Nikhil is a curious creature, quite out of the common.

The upshot was, that after this Bee began to send for me to the sitting-room, for a chat, without any contrivance, or pretence of its being an accident. Thus from bare suggestion we came to broad hint: the implied came to be expressed. The daughter-in-law of a princely house lives in a starry region so remote from the ordinary outsider that there is not even a regular road for his approach. What a triumphal progress of Truth was this which, gradually but persistently, thrust aside veil after veil of obscuring custom, till at length Nature herself was laid bare.

Truth? Of course it was the truth! The attraction of man and woman for each other is fundamental. The whole world of matter, from the speck of dust upwards, is ranged on its side. And yet men would keep it hidden away out of sight, behind a tissue of words; and with home-made sanctions and prohibitions make of it a domestic utensil. Why, it's as absurd as melting down the solar system to make a watch-chain for one's son-in-law!

When, in spite of all, reality awakes at the call of what is but naked truth, what a gnashing of teeth and beating of breasts is there! But can one carry on a quarrel with a storm? It never takes the trouble to reply, it only gives a shaking. I am enjoying the sight of this truth, as it gradually reveals itself. These tremblings of steps, these turnings of the face, are sweet to me: and sweet are the deceptions which deceive not only others, but also Bee herself. When Reality has to meet the unreal, deception is its principal weapon; for its enemies always try to shame Reality by calling it gross, and so it needs must hide itself, or else put on some disguise. The circumstances are such that it dare not frankly avow: "Yes, I am gross, because I am true. I am flesh. I am passion. I am hunger, unashamed and cruel."

All is now clear to me. The curtain flaps, and through it I can see the preparations for the catastrophe. The little red ribbon, which peeps through the luxuriant masses of her hair, with its flush of secret longing, it is the lolling tongue of the red storm cloud. I feel the warmth of each turn of her *sari*, each suggestion of her raiment, of which even the wearer may not be fully conscious.

Bee was not conscious, because she was ashamed of the reality; to which men have given a bad name, calling it Satan; and so it has to steal into the garden of paradise in the guise of a snake, and whisper secrets into the ears of man's chosen consort and make her rebellious; then farewell to all ease; and after that comes death! My poor little Queen Bee is living in a dream. She knows not which way she is treading. It would not be safe to awaken her before the time. It is best for me to pretend to be equally unconscious.

The other day, at dinner, she was gazing at me in a curious sort of way, little realizing what such glances mean! As my eyes met hers, she turned away with a flush. "You are surprised at my appetite," I remarked. "I can hide everything, except that I am greedy! Anyhow, why trouble to blush for me, since I am shameless?"

This only made her colour more furiously, as she stammered: "No, no, I was only. . ."

"I know," I interrupted. "Women have a weakness for greedy men; for it is this greed of ours which gives them the upper hand. The indulgence which I have always received at their hands has made me all the more shameless. I do not mind your watching the good things disappear, not one bit. I mean to enjoy every one of them."

The other day I was reading an English book in which sex-problems were treated in an audaciously realistic manner. I had left it lying in the sitting-room. As I went there the next afternoon, for something or other, I found Bee seated with this book in her hand. When she heard my footsteps she hurriedly put it down and placed another book over it—a volume of Mrs Hemans's poems. "I have never been able to make out," I began, "why women are so shy about being caught reading poetry. We men—lawyers, mechanics, or what not—may well feel ashamed. If we must read poetry, it should be at dead of night, within closed doors. But you women are so akin to poesy. The Creator Himself is a lyric poet, and Jayadeva must have practised the divine art seated at His feet."

Bee made no reply, but only blushed uncomfortably. She made as if she would leave the room. Whereupon I protested: "No, no, pray read on. I will just take a book I left here, and run away." With which I took up my book from the table. "Lucky you did not think of glancing over its pages," I continued, "or you would have wanted to chastise me."

"Indeed! Why?" asked Bee.

"Because it is not poetry," said I. "Only blunt things, bluntly put, without any finicking niceness. I wish Nikhil would read it." Bee frowned a little as she murmured: "What makes you wish that?"

"He is a man, you see, one of us. My only quarrel with him is that he delights in a misty vision of this world. Have you not observed how this trait of his makes him look on *Swadeshi* as if it was some poem of which the metre must be kept correct at every step? We, with the clubs of our prose, are the iconoclasts of metre."

"What has your book to do with *Swadeshi*?"

"You would know if you only read it. Nikhil wants to go by made-up maxims, in *Swadeshi* as in everything else; so he knocks up against human nature at every turn, and then falls to abusing it. He never will realize that human nature was created long before phrases were, and will survive them too." Bee was silent for a while and then gravely said: "Is it not a part of human nature to try and rise superior to itself?"

I smiled inwardly. "These are not your words", I thought to myself. "You have learnt them from Nikhil. You are a healthy human being. Your flesh and blood have responded to the call of reality. You are burning in every vein with life-fire—do I not know it? How long should they keep you cool with the wet towel of moral precepts?"

"The weak are in the majority," I said aloud. "They are continually poisoning the ears of men by repeating these shibboleths. Nature has denied them strength—it is thus that they try to enfeeble others."

"We women are weak," replied Bimala. "So I suppose we must join in the conspiracy of the weak."

"Women weak!" I exclaimed with a laugh. "Men belaud you as delicate and fragile, so as to delude you into thinking yourselves weak. But it is you women who are strong. Men make a great outward show of their so-called freedom, but those who know their inner minds are aware of their bondage. They have manufactured scriptures with their own hands to bind themselves; with their very idealism they have made golden fetters of women to wind round their body and mind. If men had not that extraordinary faculty of entangling themselves in meshes of their own contriving, nothing could have kept them bound. But as for you women, you have desired to conceive reality with body and soul. You have given birth to reality. You have suckled reality at your breasts." Bee was well read for a woman, and would not easily give in to my arguments. "If that were true," she objected, "men would not have found women attractive."

"Women realize the danger," I replied. "They know that men love delusions, so they give them full measure by borrowing their own phrases. They know that man, the drunkard, values intoxication more than food, and so they try to pass themselves off as an intoxicant. As a matter of fact, but for the sake of man, woman has no need for any make-believe."

"Why, then, are you troubling to destroy the illusion?"

"For freedom. I want the country to be free. I want human relations to be free."

I was aware that it is unsafe suddenly to awake a sleep-walker. But I am so impetuous by nature, a halting gait does not suit me. I knew I was overbold that day. I knew that the first shock of such ideas is apt to be almost intolerable. But with women it is always audacity that wins. Just as we were getting on nicely, who should walk in but Nikhil's old tutor Chandranath Babu. The world would have been not half a bad place to live in but for these schoolmasters, who make one want to quit in disgust. The Nikhil type wants to keep the world always a school. This incarnation of a school turned up that afternoon at the psychological moment.

We all remain schoolboys in some corner of our hearts, and I, even I, felt somewhat pulled up. As for poor Bee, she at once took her place solemnly, like the topmost girl of the class on the front bench. All of a sudden she seemed to remember that she had to face her examination.

Some people are so like eternal pointsmen lying in wait by the line, to shunt one's train of thought from one rail to another. Chandranath Babu had no sooner come in than he cast about for some excuse to retire, mumbling: "I beg your pardon, I. . ."

Before he could finish, Bee went up to him and made a profound obeisance, saying: "Pray do not leave us, sir. Will you not take a seat?" She looked like a drowning person clutching at him for support—the little coward!

But possibly I was mistaken. It is quite likely that there was a touch of womanly wile in it. She wanted, perhaps, to raise her value in my eyes. She might have been pointedly saying to me: "Please don't imagine for a moment that I am entirely overcome by you. My respect for Chandranath Babu is even greater." Well, indulge in your respect by all means! Schoolmasters thrive on it. But not being one of them, I have no use for that empty compliment.

Chandranath Babu began to talk about *Swadeshi*. I thought I would let him go on with his monologues. There is nothing like letting an old man talk himself out. It makes him feel that he is winding up the world, forgetting all the while how far away the real world is from his wagging tongue.

But even my worst enemy would not accuse me of patience. And when Chandranath Babu went on to say: "If we expect to gather fruit where we have sown no seed, then we . . ." I had to interrupt him.

"Who wants fruit?" I cried. "We go by the Author of the Gita who says that we are concerned only with the doing, not with the fruit of our deeds."

"What is it then that you do want?" asked Chandranath Babu.

"Thorns!" I exclaimed, "which cost nothing to plant."

"Thorns do not obstruct others only," he replied. "They have a way of hurting one's own feet."

"That is all right for a copy-book," I retorted. "But the real thing is that we have this burning at heart. Now we have only to cultivate thorns for others" soles; afterwards when they hurt us we shall find leisure to repent. But why be frightened even of that? When at last we have to die it will be time enough to get cold. While we are on fire let us seethe and boil."

Chandranath Babu smiled. "Seethe by all means," he said, "but do not mistake it for work, or heroism. Nations which have got on in the world have done so by action, not by ebullition. Those who have always lain in dread of work, when with a start they awake to their sorry plight, they look to short-cuts and scamping for their deliverance."

I was girding up my loins to deliver a crushing reply, when Nikhil came back. Chandranath Babu rose, and looking towards Bee, said: "Let me go now, my little mother, I have some work to attend to." As he left, I showed Nikhil the book in my hand. "I was telling Queen Bee about this book," I said.

Ninety-nine per cent of people have to be deluded with lies, but it. is easier to delude this perpetual pupil of the schoolmaster with the truth. He is best cheated openly. So, in playing with him, the simplest course was to lay my cards on the table.

Nikhil read the title on the cover, but said nothing. "These writers," I continued, "are busy with their brooms, sweeping away the dust of epithets with which men have covered up this world of ours. So, as I was saying, I wish you would read it."

"I have read it," said Nikhil.

"Well, what do you say?"

"It is all very well for those who really care to think, but poison for those who shirk thought."

"What do you mean?"

"Those who preach 'Equal Rights of Property' should not be thieves. For, if they are, they would be preaching lies. When passion is in the ascendant, this kind of book is not rightly understood." "Passion," I replied, "is the street lamp which guides us. To call it untrue is as hopeless as to expect to see better by plucking out our natural eyes."

Nikhil was visibly growing excited. "I accept the truth of passion," he said, "only when I recognize the truth of restraint. By pressing what we want to see right into our eyes we only injure them: we do not see. So does the violence of passion, which would leave no space between the mind and its object, defeat its purpose."

"It is simply your intellectual foppery," I replied, "which makes you indulge in moral delicacy, ignoring the savage side of truth. This merely helps you to mystify things, and so you fail to do your work with any degree of strength."

"The intrusion of strength," said Nikhil impatiently, "where strength is out of place, does not help you in your work . . . But why are we arguing about these things? Vain arguments only brush off the fresh bloom of truth." I wanted Bee to join in the discussion, but she had not said a word up to now. Could I have given her too rude a shock, leaving her assailed with doubts and wanting to learn her lesson afresh from the schoolmaster? Still, a thorough shaking-up is essential. One must begin by realizing that things supposed to be unshakeable can be shaken.

"I am glad I had this talk with you," I said to Nikhil, "for I was on the point of lending this book to Queen Bee to read."

"What harm?" said Nikhil. "If I could read the book, why not Bimala too? All I want to say is, that in Europe people look at everything from the viewpoint of science. But man is neither mere physiology, nor biology, nor psychology, nor even sociology. For God's sake don't forget that. Man is infinitely more than the natural science of himself. You laugh at me, calling me the schoolmaster's pupil, but that is what you are, not I. You want to find the truth of man from your science teachers, and not from your own inner being."

"But why all this excitement?" I mocked.

"Because I see you are bent on insulting man and making him petty."

"Where on earth do you see all that?"

"In the air, in my outraged feelings. You would go on wounding the great, the unselfish, the beautiful in man."

"What mad idea is this of yours?"

Nikhil suddenly stood up. "I tell you plainly, Sandip," he said, "man may be wounded unto death, but he will not die. This is the reason why I am ready to suffer all, knowing all, with eyes open."

With these words he hurriedly left the room.

I was staring blankly at his retreating figure, when the sound of a book, falling from the table, made me turn to find Bee following him with quick, nervous steps, making a detour to avoid passing too near me.

A curious creature, that Nikhil! He feels the danger threatening his home, and yet why does he not turn me out? I know, he is waiting for Bimal to give him the cue. If Bimal tells him that their mating has been a misfit, he will bow his head and admit that it may have been a blunder! He has not the strength of mind to understand that to acknowledge a mistake is the greatest of all mistakes. He is a typical example of how ideas make for weakness. I have not seen another like him—so whimsical a product of nature! He would hardly do as a character in a novel or drama, to say nothing of real life.

And Bee? I am afraid her dream-life is over from today. She has at length understood the nature of the current which is bearing her along. Now she must either advance or retreat, open-eyed. The chances are she will now advance a step, and then retreat a step. But that does not disturb me. When one is on fire, this rushing to and fro makes the blaze all the fiercer. The fright she has got will only fan her passion.

Perhaps I had better not say much to her, but simply select some modern books for her to read. Let her gradually come to the conviction that to acknowledge and respect passion as the supreme reality, is to be modern—not to be ashamed of it, not to glorify restraint. If she finds shelter in some such word as "modern", she will find strength.

Be that as it may, I must see this out to the end of the Fifth Act. I cannot, unfortunately, boast of being merely a spectator, seated in the royal box, applauding now and again. There is a wrench at my heart, a pang in every nerve. When I have put out the light and am in my bed, little touches, little glances, little words flit about and fill the darkness. When I get up in the morning, I thrill with lively anticipations, my blood seems to course through me to the strains of music . . . There was a double photo-frame on the table with Bee's photograph by the side of Nikhil's. I had taken out hers. Yesterday I showed Bee the empty side and said: "Theft becomes necessary only because of miserliness, so its sin must be divided between the miser and the thief. Do you not think so?"

"It was not a good one," observed Bee simply, with a little smile.

"What is to be done?" said I. "A portrait cannot be better than a portrait. I must be content with it, such as it is."

Bee took up a book and began to turn over the pages. "If you are annoyed," I went on, "I must make a shift to fill up the vacancy."

Today I have filled it up. This photograph of mine was taken in my early youth. My face was then fresher, and so was my mind. Then I still cherished some illusions about this world and the next. Faith deceives men, but it has one great merit: it imparts a radiance to the features.

My portrait now reposes next to Nikhil's, for are not the two of us old friends?

I was never self-conscious. But nowadays I often try to take an outside view—to see myself as Bimal sees me. What a dismally solemn picture it makes, my habit of taking things too seriously!

Better, surely, to laugh away the world than flood it with tears. That is, in fact, how the world gets on. We relish our food and rest, only because we can dismiss, as so many empty shadows, the sorrows scattered everywhere, both in the home and in the outer world. If we took them as true, even for a moment, where would be our appetite, our sleep? But I cannot dismiss myself as one of these shadows, and so the load of my sorrow lies eternally heavy on the heart of my world.

Why not stand out aloof in the highway of the universe, and feel yourself to be part of the all? In the midst of the immense, age-long concourse of humanity, what is Bimal to you? Your wife? What is a wife? A bubble of a name blown big with your own breath, so carefully guarded night and day, yet ready to burst at any pin-prick from outside.

My wife—and so, forsooth, my very own! If she says: "No, I am myself"—am I to reply: "How can that be? Are you not mine?"

"My wife"—Does that amount to an argument, much less the truth? Can one imprison a whole personality within that name?

My wife!—Have I not cherished in this little world all that is purest and sweetest in my life, never for a moment letting it down from my bosom to the dust? What incense of worship, what music of passion, what flowers of my spring and of my autumn, have I not offered up at its shrine? If, like a toy paper-boat, she be swept along into the muddy waters of the gutter—would I not also. . . ?

There it is again, my incorrigible solemnity! Why "muddy"? What "gutter,? Names, called in a fit of jealousy, do not change the facts of the world. If Bimal is not mine, she is not; and no fuming, or fretting, or arguing will serve to prove that she is. If my heart is breaking—let it break! That will not make the world bankrupt—nor even me; for man is so much greater than the things he loses in this life. The very ocean of tears has its other shore, else none would have ever wept. But then there is Society to be considered . . . which let Society consider! If I weep it is for myself, not for Society. If Bimal should say she is not mine, what care I where my Society wife may be?

Suffering there must be; but I must save myself, by any means in my power, from one form of self-torture: I must never think that my life loses its value because of any neglect it may suffer. The full value of my life does not all go to buy my narrow domestic world; its great commerce does not stand or fall with some petty success or failure in the bartering of my personal joys and sorrows. The time has come when I must divest Bimala of all the ideal decorations with which I decked her. It was owing to my own weakness that I indulged in such idolatry. I was too greedy. I created an angel of Bimala, in order to exaggerate my own enjoyment. But Bimala is what she is. It is preposterous to expect that she should assume the rôle of an angel for my pleasure. The Creator is under no obligation to supply me with angels, just because I have an avidity for imaginary perfection.

I must acknowledge that I have merely been an accident in Bimala's life. Her nature, perhaps, can only find true union with one like Sandip. At the same time, I must not, in false modesty, accept my rejection as my desert. Sandip certainly has attractive qualities, which had their sway also upon myself; but yet, I feel sure, he is not a greater man than I. If the wreath of victory falls to his lot today, and I am overlooked, then the dispenser of the wreath will be called to judgement.

I say this in no spirit of boasting. Sheer necessity has driven me to the pass, that to secure myself from utter desolation I must recognize all the value that I truly possess. Therefore, through the, terrible experience of suffering let there come upon me the joy of deliverance—deliverance from self-distrust. I have come to distinguish what is really in me from what I foolishly imagined to be there. The profit and loss account has been settled, and that which remains is myself—not a crippled self, dressed in rags and tatters, not a sick self to be nursed on invalid diet, but a spirit which has gone through the worst, and has survived.

My master passed through my room a moment ago and said with his hand on my shoulder. "Get away to bed, Nikhil, the night is far advanced."

The fact is, it has become so difficult for me to go to bed till late—till Bimal is fast asleep. In the day-time we meet, and even converse, but what am I to say when we are alone together, in the silence of the night?—so ashamed do I feel in mind and body. "How is it, sir, you have not yet retired?" I asked in my turn. My master smiled a little, as he left me, saying: "My sleeping days are over. I have now attained the waking age.

I had written thus far, and was about to rise to go off bedwards when, through the window before me, I saw the heavy pall of July cloud suddenly part a little, and a big star shine through. It seemed to say to me: "Dreamland ties are made, and dreamland ties are broken, but I am here for ever—the everlasting lamp of the bridal night."

All at once my heart was full with the thought that my Eternal Love was steadfastly waiting for me through the ages, behind the veil of material things. Through many a life, in many a mirror, have I seen her image—broken mirrors, crooked mirrors, dusty mirrors. Whenever I have sought to make the mirror my very own, and shut it up within my box, I have lost sight of the image. But what of that. What have I to do with the mirror, or even the image?

My beloved, your smile shall never fade, and every dawn there shall appear fresh for me the vermilion mark on your forehead!

"What childish cajolery of self-deception," mocks some devil from his dark corner—"silly prattle to make children quiet!"

That may be. But millions and millions of children, with their million cries, have to be kept quiet. Can it be that all this multitude is quieted with only a lie? No, my Eternal Love cannot deceive me, for she is true!

She is true; that is why I have seen her and shall see her so often, even in my mistakes, even through the thickest mist of tears. I have seen her and lost her in the crowd of life's market-place, and found her again; and I shall find her once more when I have escaped through the loophole of death. Ah, cruel one, play with me no longer! If I have failed to track you by the marks of your footsteps on the way, by the scent of your tresses lingering in the air, make me not weep for that for ever. The unveiled star tells me not to fear. That which is eternal must always be there.

Now let me go and see my Bimala. She must have spread her tired limbs on the bed, limp after her struggles, and be asleep. I will leave a kiss on her forehead without waking her—that shall be the flower-offering of my worship. I believe I could forget everything after death—all my mistakes, all my sufferings—but some vibration of the memory of that kiss would remain; for the wreath which is being woven out of the kisses of many a successive birth is to crown the Eternal Beloved. As the gong of the watch rang out, sounding the hour of two, my sister-in-law came into the room. "Whatever are you doing, brother dear?" she cried. "For pity's sake go to bed and stop worrying so. I cannot bear to look on that awful shadow of pain on your face." Tears welled up in her eyes and overflowed as she entreated me thus. I could not utter a word, but took the dust of her feet, as I went off to bed.

At first I suspected nothing, feared nothing; I simply felt dedicated to my country. What a stupendous joy there was in this unquestioning surrender. Verily had I realized how, in thoroughness of self-destruction, man can find supreme bliss. For aught I know, this frenzy of mine might have come to a gradual, natural end. But Sandip Babu would not have it so, he would insist on revealing himself. The tone of his voice became as intimate as a touch, every look flung itself on its knees in beggary. And, through it all, there burned a passion which in its violence made as though it would tear me up by the roots, and drag me along by the hair.

I will not shirk the truth. This cataclysmal desire drew me by day and by night. It seemed desperately alluring—this making havoc of myself. What a shame it seemed, how terrible, and yet how sweet! Then there was my overpowering curiosity, to which there seemed no limit. He of whom I knew but little, who never could assuredly be mine, whose youth flared so vigorously in a hundred points of flame—oh, the mystery of his seething passions, so immense, so tumultuous!

I began with a feeling of worship, but that soon passed away. I ceased even to respect Sandip; on the contrary, I began to look down upon him. Nevertheless this flesh-and-blood lute of mine, fashioned with my feeling and fancy, found in him a master-player. What though I shrank from his touch, and even came to loathe the lute itself; its music was conjured up all the same.

I must confess there was something in me which . . . what shall I say? . . . which makes me wish I could have died!

Chandranath Babu, when he finds leisure, comes to me. He has the power to lift my mind up to an eminence from where I can see in a moment the boundary of my life extended on all sides and so realize that the lines, which I took from my bounds, were merely imaginary.

But what is the use of it all? Do I really desire emancipation? Let suffering come to our house; let the best in me shrivel up and become black; but let this infatuation not leave me—such seems to be my prayer. When, before my marriage, I used to see a brother-in-law of mine, now dead, mad with drink—beating his wife in his frenzy, and then sobbing and howling in maudlin repentance, vowing never to touch liquor again, and yet, the very same evening, sitting down to drink and drink—it would fill me with disgust. But my intoxication today is still more fearful. The stuff has not to be procured or poured out: it springs within my veins, and I know not how to resist it.

Must this continue to the end of my days? Now and again I start and look upon myself, and think my life to be a nightmare which will vanish all of a sudden with all its untruth. It has become so frightfully incongruous. It has no connection with its past. What it is, how it could have come to this pass, I cannot understand.

One day my sister-in-law remarked with a cutting laugh: "What a wonderfully hospitable Chota Rani we have! Her guest absolutely will not budge. In our time there used to be guests, too; but they had not such lavish looking after—we were so absurdly taken up with our husbands. Poor brother Nikhil is paying the penalty of being born too modern. He should have come as a guest if he wanted to stay on. Now it looks as if it were time for him to quit . . . O you little demon, do your glances never fall, by chance, on his agonized face?" This sarcasm did not touch me; for I knew that these women had it not in them to understand the nature of the cause of my devotion. I was then wrapped in the protecting armour of the exaltation of sacrifice, through which such shafts were powerless to reach and shame me.

For some time all talk of the country's cause has been dropped. Our conversation nowadays has become full of modern sex-problems, and various other matters, with a sprinkling of poetry, both old Vaishnava and modern English, accompanied by a running undertone of melody, low down in the bass, such as I have never in my life heard before, which seems to me to sound the true manly note, the note of power. The day had come when all cover was gone. There was no longer even the pretence of a reason why Sandip Babu should linger on, or why I should have confidential talks with him every now and then. I felt thoroughly vexed with myself, with my sister-in-law, with the ways of the world, and I vowed I would never again go to the outer apartments, not if I were to die for it.

For two whole days I did not stir out. Then, for the first time, I discovered how far I had travelled. My life felt utterly tasteless. Whatever I touched I wanted to thrust away. I felt myself waiting—from the crown of my head to the tips of my toes—waiting for something, somebody; my blood kept tingling with some expectation.

I tried busying myself with extra work. The bedroom floor was clean enough but I insisted on its being scrubbed over again under my eyes. Things were arranged in the cabinets in one kind of order; I pulled them all out and rearranged them in a different way. I found no time that afternoon even to do up my hair; I hurriedly tied it into a loose knot, and went and worried everybody, fussing about the store-room. The stores seemed short, and pilfering must have been going on of late, but I could not muster up the courage to take any particular person to task—for might not the thought have crossed somebody's mind: "Where were your eyes all these days!"

In short, I behaved that day as one possessed. The next day I tried to do some reading. What I read I have no idea, but after a spell of absentmindedness I found I had wandered away, book in hand, along the passage leading towards the outer apartments, and was standing by a window looking out upon the verandah running along the row of rooms on the opposite side of the quadrangle. One of these rooms, I felt, had crossed over to another shore, and the ferry had ceased to ply. I felt like the ghost of myself of two days ago, doomed to remain where I was, and yet not really there, blankly looking out for ever.

As I stood there, I saw Sandip come out of his room into the verandah, a newspaper in his hand. I could see that he looked extraordinarily disturbed. The courtyard, the railings, in front, seemed to rouse his wrath. He flung away his newspaper with a gesture which seemed to want to rend the space before him. I felt I could no longer keep my vow. I was about to move on towards the sitting-room, when I found my sister-in-law behind me. "O Lord, this beats everything!" she ejaculated, as she glided away. I could not proceed to the outer apartments.

The next morning when my maid came calling, "Rani Mother, it is getting late for giving out the stores," I flung the keys to her, saying, "Tell Harimati to see to it," and went on with some embroidery of English pattern on which I was engaged, seated near the window.

Then came a servant with a letter. "From Sandip Babu," said he. What unbounded boldness! What must the messenger have thought? There was a tremor within my breast as I opened the envelope. There was no address on the letter, only the words: *An urgent matter—touching the Cause. Sandip.*

I flung aside the embroidery. I was up on my feet in a moment, giving a touch or two to my hair by the mirror. I kept the *sari* I had on, changing only my jacket—for one of my jackets had its associations.

I had to pass through one of the verandahs, where my sister-in-law used to sit in the morning slicing betel-nut. I refused to feel awkward. "Whither away, Chota Rani?" she cried.

"To the sitting-room outside."

"So early! A matinée, eh?"

And, as I passed on without further reply, she hummed after me a flippant song.

When I was about to enter the sitting-room, I saw Sandip immersed in an illustrated catalogue of British Academy pictures, with his back to the door. He has a great notion of himself as an expert in matters of Art.

One day my husband said to him: "If the artists ever want a teacher, they need never lack for one so long as you are there." It had not been my husband's habit to speak cuttingly, but latterly there has been a change and he never spares Sandip.

"What makes you suppose that artists need no teachers?" Sandip retorted.

"Art is a creation," my husband replied. "So we should humbly be content to receive our lessons about Art from the work of the artist."

Sandip laughed at this modesty, saying: "You think that meekness is a kind of capital which increases your wealth the more you use it. It is my conviction that those who lack pride only float about like water reeds which have no roots in the soil."

My mind used to be full of contradictions when they talked thus. On the one hand I was eager that my husband should win in argument and that Sandip's pride should be shamed. Yet, on the other, it was Sandip's unabashed pride which attracted me so. It shone like a precious diamond, which knows no diffidence, and sparkles in the face of the sun itself. I entered the room. I knew Sandip could hear my footsteps as I went forward, but he pretended not to, and kept his eyes on the book.

I dreaded his Art talks, for I could not overcome my delicacy about the pictures he talked of, and the things he said, and had much ado in putting on an air of overdone insensibility to hide my qualms. So, I was almost on the point of retracing my steps, when, with a deep sigh, Sandip raised his eyes, and affected to be startled at the sight of me. "Ah, you have come!" he said.

In his words, in his tone, in his eyes, there was a world of suppressed reproach, as if the claims he had acquired over me made my absence, even for these two or three days, a grievous wrong. I knew this attitude was an insult to me, but, alas, I had not the power to resent it. I made no reply, but though I was looking another way, I could not help feeling that Sandip's plaintive gaze had planted itself right on my face, and would take no denial. I did so wish he would say something, so that I could shelter myself behind his words. I cannot tell how long this went on, but at last I could stand it no longer. "What is this matter," I asked, "you are wanting to tell me about?"

Sandip again affected surprise as he said: "Must there always be some matter? Is friendship by itself a crime? Oh, Queen Bee, to think that you should make so light of the greatest thing on earth! Is the heart's worship to be shut out like a stray cur?"

There was again that tremor within me. I could feel the crisis coming, too importunate to be put off. Joy and fear struggled for the mastery. Would my shoulders, I wondered, be broad enough to stand its shock, or would it not leave me overthrown, with my face in the dust?

I was trembling all over. Steadying myself with an effort I repeated: "You summoned me for something touching the Cause, so I have left my household duties to attend to it."

"That is just what I was trying to explain," he said, with a dry laugh. "Do you not know that I come to worship? Have I not told you that, in you, I visualize the *Shakti* of our country? The Geography of a country is not the whole truth. No one can give up his life for a map! When I see you before me, then only do I realize how lovely my country is. When you have anointed me with your own hands, then shall I know I have the sanction of my country; and if, with that in my heart, I fall fighting, it shall not be on the dust of some map-made land, but on a lovingly spread skirt—do you know what kind of skirt?—like that of the earthen-red *sari* you wore the other day, with a broad blood-red border. Can I ever forget it? Such are the visions which give vigour to life, and joy to death!"

Sandip's eyes took fire as he went on, but whether it was the fire of worship, or of passion, I could not tell. I was reminded of the day on which I first heard him speak, when I could not be sure whether he was a person, or just a living flame. I had not the power to utter a word. You cannot take shelter behind the walls of decorum when in a moment the fire leaps up and, with the flash of its sword and the roar of its laughter, destroys all the miser's stores. I was in terror lest he should forget himself and take me by the hand. For he shook like a quivering tongue of fire; his eyes showered scorching sparks on me.

"Are you for ever determined," he cried after a pause, "to make gods of your petty household duties—you who have it in you to send us to life or to death? Is this power of yours to be kept veiled in a zenana? Cast away all false shame, I pray you; snap your fingers at the whispering around. Take your plunge today into the freedom of the outer world."

When, in Sandip's appeals, his worship of the country gets to be subtly interwoven with his worship of me, then does my blood dance, indeed, and the barriers of my hesitation totter. His talks about Art and Sex, his distinctions between Real and Unreal, had but clogged my attempts at response with some revolting nastiness.

This, however, now burst again into a glow before which my repugnance faded away. I felt that my resplendent womanhood made me indeed a goddess. Why should not its glory flash from my forehead with visible brilliance? Why does not my voice find a word, some audible cry, which would be like a sacred spell to my country for its fire initiation?

All of a sudden my maid Khema rushed into the room, dishevelled. "Give me my wages and let me go," she screamed. "Never in all my life have I been so . . ." The rest of her speech was drowned in sobs.

"What is the matter?"

Thako, the Bara Rani's maid, it appeared, had for no rhyme or reason reviled her in unmeasured terms. She was in such a state, it was no manner of use trying to pacify her by saying I would look into the matter afterwards.

The slime of domestic life that lay beneath the lotus bank of womanhood came to the surface. Rather than allow Sandip a prolonged vision of it, I had to hurry back within.

My sister-in-law was absorbed in her betel-nuts, the suspicion of a smile playing about her lips, as if nothing untoward had happened. She was still humming the same song.

"Why has your Thako been calling poor Khema names?" I burst out.

"Indeed? The wretch! I will have her broomed out of the house. What a shame to spoil your morning out like this! As for Khema, where are the hussy's manners to go and disturb you when you are engaged? Anyhow, Chota Rani, don't you worry yourself with these domestic squabbles. Leave them to me, and return to your friend."

How suddenly the wind in the sails of our mind veers round! This going to meet Sandip outside seemed, in the light of the zenana code, such an extraordinarily out-of-the-way thing to do that I went off to my own room, at a loss for a reply. I knew this was my sister-in-law's doing and that she had egged her maid on to contrive this scene. But I had brought myself to such an unstable poise that I dared not have my fling.

Why, it was only the other day that I found I could not keep up to the last the unbending hauteur with which I had demanded from my husband the dismissal of the man Nanku. I felt suddenly abashed when the Bara Rani came up and said: "It is really all my fault, brother dear. We are old-fashioned folk, and I did not quite like the ways of your Sandip Babu, so I only told the guard . . . but how was I to know that our Chota Rani would take this as an insult?—I thought it would be the other way about! Just my incorrigible silliness!"

The thing which seems so glorious when viewed from the heights of the country's cause, looks so muddy when seen from the bottom. One begins by getting angry, and then feels disgusted.

I shut myself into my room, sitting by the window, thinking how easy life would be if only one could keep in harmony with one's surroundings. How simply the senior Rani sits in her verandah with her betel-nuts and how inaccessible to me has become my natural seat beside my daily duties! Where will it all end, I asked myself? Shall I ever recover, as from a delirium, and forget it all; or am I to be dragged to depths from which there can be no escape in this life? How on earth did I manage to let my good fortune escape me, and spoil my life so? Every wall of this bedroom of mine, which I first entered nine years ago as a bride, stares at me in dismay.

When my husband came home, after his M.A. examination, he brought for me this orchid belonging to some far-away land beyond the seas. From beneath these few little leaves sprang such a cascade of blossoms, it looked as if they were pouring forth from some overturned urn of Beauty. We decided, together, to hang it here, over this window. It flowered only that once, but we have always been in hope of its doing so once more. Curiously enough I have kept on watering it these days, from force of habit, and it is still green.

It is now four years since I framed a photograph of my husband in ivory and put it in the niche over there. If I happen to look that way I have to lower my eyes. Up to last week I used regularly to put there the flowers of my worship, every morning after my bath. My husband has often chided me over this.

"It shames me to see you place me on a height to which I do not belong," he said one day.

"What nonsense!"

"I am not only ashamed, but also jealous!"

"Just hear him! Jealous of whom, pray?"

"Of that false me. It only shows that I am too petty for you, that you want some extraordinary man who can overpower you with his superiority, and so you needs must take refuge in making for yourself another 'me'."

"This kind of talk only makes me angry," said I.

"What is the use of being angry with me?" he replied. "Blame your fate which allowed you no choice, but made you take me blindfold. This keeps you trying to retrieve its blunder by making me out a paragon." I felt so hurt at the bare idea that tears started to my eyes that day. And whenever I think of that now, I cannot raise my eyes to the niche.

For now there is another photograph in my jewel case. The other day, when arranging the sitting-room, I brought away that double photo frame, the one in which Sandip's portrait was next to my husband's. To this portrait I have no flowers of worship to offer, but it remains hidden away under my gems. It has all the greater fascination because kept secret. I look at it now and then with doors closed. At night I turn up the lamp, and sit with it in my hand, gazing and gazing. And every night I think of burning it in the flame of the lamp, to be done with it for ever; but every night I heave a sigh and smother it again in my pearls and diamonds.

Ah, wretched woman! What a wealth of love was twined round each one of those jewels! Oh, why am I not dead? Sandip had impressed it on me that hesitation is not in the nature of woman. For her, neither right nor left has any existence—she only moves forward. When the women of our country wake up, he repeatedly insisted, their voice will be unmistakably confident in its utterance of the cry: "I want."

"I want!" Sandip went on one day—this was the primal word at the root of all creation. It had no maxim to guide it, but it became fire and wrought itself into suns and stars. Its partiality is terrible. Because it had a desire for man, it ruthlessly sacrificed millions of beasts for millions of years to achieve that desire. That terrible word "I want" has taken flesh in woman, and therefore men, who are cowards, try with all their might to keep back this primeval flood With their earthen dykes.

They are afraid lest, laughing and dancing as it goes, it should wash away all the hedges and props of their pumpkin field. Men, in every age, flatter themselves that they have secured this force within the bounds of their convenience, but it gathers and grows. Now it is calm and deep like a lake, but gradually its pressure will increase, the dykes will give way, and the force which has so long been dumb will rush forward with the roar: "I want!"

These words of Sandip echo in my heart-beats like a war-drum. They shame into silence all my conflicts with myself. What do I care what people may think of me? Of what value are that orchid and that niche in my bedroom? What power have they to belittle me, to put me to shame? The primal fire of creation burns in me.

I felt a strong desire to snatch down the orchid and fling it out of the window, to denude the niche of its picture, to lay bare and naked the unashamed spirit of destruction that raged within me. My arm was raised to do it, but a sudden pang passed through my breast, tears started to my eyes. I threw myself down and sobbed: "What is the end of all this, what is the end?" When I read these pages of the story of my life I seriously question myself: Is this Sandip? Am I made of words? Am I merely a book with a covering of flesh and blood?

The earth is not a dead thing like the moon. She breathes. Her rivers and oceans send up vapours in which she is clothed. She is covered with a mantle of her own dust which flies about the air. The onlooker, gazing upon the earth from the outside, can see only the light reflected from this vapour and this dust. The tracks of the mighty continents are not distinctly visible.

The man, who is alive as this earth is, is likewise always enveloped in the mist of the ideas which he is breathing out. His real land and water remain hidden, and he appears to be made of only lights and shadows.

It seems to me, in this story of my life, that, like a living plant, I am displaying the picture of an ideal world. But I am not merely what I want, what I think—I am also what I do not love, what I do not wish to be. My creation had begun before I was born. I had no choice in regard to my surroundings and so must make the best of such material as comes to my hand.

My theory of life makes me certain that the Great is cruel To be just is for ordinary men—it is reserved for the great to be unjust. The surface of the earth was even. The volcano butted it with its fiery horn and found its own eminence—its justice was not towards its obstacle, but towards itself. Successful injustice and genuine cruelty have been the only forces by which individual or nation has become millionaire or monarch. That is why I preach the great discipline of Injustice. I say to everyone: Deliverance is based upon injustice. Injustice is the fire which must keep on burning something in order to save itself from becoming ashes. Whenever an individual or nation becómes incapable of perpetrating injustice it is swept into the dust-bin of the world.

As yet this is only my idea—it is not completely myself. There are rifts in the armour through which sómething peeps out which is extremely soft and sensitive. Because, as I say, the best part of myself was created before I came to this stage of existence.

From time to time I try my followers in their lesson of cruelty. One day we went on a picnic. A goat was grazing by. I asked them: "Who is there among you that can cut off a leg of that goat, alive, with this knife, and bring it to me?" While they all hesitated, I went myself and did it. One of them fainted at the sight. But when they saw me unmoved they took the dust of my feet, saying that I was above all human weaknesses. That is to say, they saw that day the vaporous envelope which was my idea, but failed to perceive the inner me, which by a curious freak of fate has been created tender and merciful.

In the present chapter of my life, which is growing in interest every day round Bimala and Nikhil, there is also much that remains hidden underneath. This malady of ideas which afflicts me is shaping my life within: nevertheless a great part of my life remains outside its influence; and so there is set up a discrepancy between my outward life and its inner design which I try my best to keep concealed even from myself; otherwise it may wreck not only my plans, but my very life.

Life is indefinite—a bundle of contradictions. We men, with our ideas, strive to give it a particular shape by melting it into a particular mould—into the definiteness of success. All the world-conquerors, from Alexander down to the American millionaires, mould themselves into a sword or a mint, and thus find that distinct image of themselves which is the source of their success.

The chief controversy between Nikhil and myself arises from this: that though I say "know thyself", and Nikhil also says "know thyself", his interpretation makes this "knowing" tantamount to "not knowing".

"Winning your kind of success," Nikhil once objected, "is success gained at the cost of the soul: but the soul is greater than success."

I simply said in answer: "Your words are too vague."

"That I cannot help," Nikhil replied. "A machine is distinct enough, but not so life. If to gain distinctness you try to know life as a machine, then such mere distinctness cannot stand for truth. The soul is not as distinct as success, and so you only lose your soul if you seek it in your success."

"Where, then, is this wonderful soul?"

"Where it knows itself in the infinite and transcends its success."

"But how does all this apply to our work for the country?"

"It is the same thing. Where our country makes itself the final object, it gains success at the cost of the soul. Where it recognizes the Greatest as greater than all, there it may miss success, but gains its soul."

"Is there any example of this in history?"

"Man is so great that he can despise not only the success, but also the example. Possibly example is lacking, just as there is no example of the flower in the seed. But there is the urgence of the flower in the seed all the same."

It is not that I do not at all understand Nikhil's point of view; that is rather where my danger lies. I was born in India and the poison of its spirituality runs in my blood. However loudly I may proclaim the madness of walking in the path of self-abnegation, I cannot avoid it altogether.

This is exactly how such curious anomalies happen nowadays in our country. We must have our religion and also our nationalism; our Bhagavadgita and also our *Bande Mataram*. The result is that both of them suffer. It is like performing with an English military band, side by side with our Indian festive pipes. I must make it the purpose of my life to put an end to this hideous confusion.

I want the western military style to prevail, not the Indian. We shall then not be ashamed of the flag of our passion, which mother Nature has sent with us as our standard into the battlefield of life. Passion is beautiful and pure—pure as the lily that comes out of the slimy soil. It rises superior to its defilement and needs no Pears' soap to wash it clean.

A question has been worrying me the last few days. Why am I allowing my life to become entangled with Bimala's? Am I a drifting log to be caught up at any and every obstacle?

Not that I have any false shame at Bimala becoming an object of my desire. It is only too clear how she wants me, and so I look on her as quite legitimately mine. The fruit hangs on the branch by the stem, but that is no reason why the claim of the stem should be eternal. Ripe fruit cannot for ever swear by its slackening stem-hold. All its sweetness has been accumulated for me; to surrender itself to my hand is the reason of its existence, its very nature, its true morality. So I must pluck it, for it becomes me not to make it futile. But what is teasing me is that I am getting entangled. Am I not born to rule?—to bestride my proper steed, the crowd, and drive it as I will; the reins in my hand, the destination known only to me, and for it the thorns, the mire, on the road? This steed now awaits me at the door, pawing and champing its bit, its neighing filling the skies. But where am I, and what am I about, letting day after day of golden opportunity slip by?

I used to think I was like a storm—that the torn flowers with which I strewed my path would not impede my progress. But I am only wandering round and round a flower like a bee—not a storm. So, as I was saying, the colouring of ideas which man gives himself is only superficial. The inner man remains as ordinary as ever. If someone, who could see right into me, were to write my biography, he would make me out to be no different from that lout of a Panchu, or even from Nikhil!

Last night I was turning over the pages of my old diary . . . I had just graduated, and my brain was bursting with philosophy. Even so early I had vowed not to harbour any illusions, whether of my own or others" imagining, but to build my life on a solid basis of reality. But what has since been its actual story? Where is its solidity?

It has rather been a network, where, though the thread be continuous, more space is taken up by the holes. Fight as I may, these will not own defeat. Just as I was congratulating myself on steadily following the thread, here I am badly caught in a hole! For I have become susceptible to compunctions.

"I want it; it is here; let me take it"—This is a clear-cut, straightforward policy. Those who can pursue its course with vigour needs must win through in the end. But the gods would not have it that such journey should be easy, so they have deputed the siren Sympathy to distract the wayfarer, to dim his vision with her tearful mist.

I can see that poor Bimala is struggling like a snared deer. What a piteous alarm there is in her eyes! How she is torn with straining at her bonds! This sight, of course, should gladden the heart of a true hunter. And so do I rejoice; but, then, I am also touched; and therefore I dally, and standing on the brink I am hesitating to pull the noose fast.

There have been moments, I know, when I could have bounded up to her, clasped her hands and folded her to my breast, unresisting. Had I done so, she would not have said one word. She was aware that some crisis was impending, which in a moment would change the meaning of the whole world. Standing before that cavern of the incalculable but yet expected, her face went pale and her eyes glowed with a fearful ecstasy. Within that moment, when it arrives, an eternity will take shape, which our destiny awaits, holding its breath.

But I have let this moment slip by. I did not, with uncompromising strength, press the almost certain into the absolutely assured. I now see clearly that some hidden elements in my nature have openly ranged themselves as obstacles in my path.

That is exactly how Ravana, whom I look upon as the real hero of the Ramayana, met with his doom. He kept Sita in his

Asoka garden, awaiting her pleasure, instead of taking her straight into his harem. This weak spot in his otherwise grand character made the whole of the abduction episode futile. Another such touch of compunction made him disregard, and be lenient to, his traitorous brother Bibhisan, only to get himself killed for his pains.

Thus does the tragic in life come by its own. In the beginning it lies, a little thing, in some dark under-vault, and ends by overthrowing the whole superstructure. The real tragedy is, that man does not know himself for what he really is.

Then again there is Nikhil. Crank though he be, laugh at him as I may, I cannot get rid of the idea that he is my friend. At first I gave no thought to his point of view, but of late it has begun to shame and hurt me. Therefore I have been trying to talk and argue with him in the same enthusiastic way as of old, but it does not ring true. It is even leading me at times into such a length of unnaturalness as to pretend to agree with him. But such hypocrisy is not in my nature, nor in that of Nikhil either. This, at least, is something we have in common. That is why, nowadays, I would rather not come across him, and have taken to fighting shy of his presence.

All these are signs of weakness. No sooner is the possibility of a wrong admitted than it becomes actual, and clutches you by the throat, however you may then try to shake off all belief in it. What I should like to be able to tell Nikhil frankly is, that happenings such as these must be looked in the face—as great Realities—and that which is the Truth should not be allowed to stand between true friends. There is no denying that I have really weakened. It was not this weakness which won over Bimala; she burnt her wings in the blaze of the full strength of my unhesitating manliness. Whenever smoke obscures its lustre she also becomes confused, and draws back. Then comes a thorough revulsion of feeling, and she fain would take back the garland she has put round my neck, but cannot; and so she only closes her eyes, to shut it out of sight.

But all the same I must not swerve from the path I have chalked out. It would never do to abandon the cause of the country, especially at the present time. I shall simply make

Bimala one with my country. The turbulent west wind which has swept away the country's veil of conscience, will sweep away the veil of the wife from Bimala's face, and in that uncovering there will be no shame. The ship will rock as it bears the crowd across the ocean, flying the pennant of *Bande Mataram*, and it will serve as the cradle to my power, as well as to my love.

Bimala will see such a majestic vision of deliverance, that her bonds will slip from about her, without shame, without her even being aware of it. Fascinated by the beauty of this terrible wrecking power, she will not hesitate a moment to be cruel. I have seen in Bimala's nature the cruelty which is the inherent force of existence—the cruelty which with its unrelenting might keeps the world beautiful.

If only women could be set free from the artificial fetters put round them by men, we could see on earth the living image of Kali, the shameless, pitiless goddess. I am a worshipper of Kali, and one day I shall truly worship her, setting Bimala on her altar of Destruction. For this let me get ready.

The way of retreat is absolutely closed for both of us. We shall despoil each other: get to hate each other: but never more be free.

Everything is rippling and waving with the flood of August. The young shoots of rice have the sheen of an infant's limbs. The water has invaded the garden next to our house. The morning light, like the love of the blue sky, is lavished upon the earth . . . Why cannot I sing? The water of the distant river is shimmering with light; the leaves are glistening; the rice-fields, with their fitful shivers, break into gleams of gold; and in this symphony of Autumn, only I remain voiceless. The sunshine of the world strikes my heart, but is not reflected back.

When I realize the lack of expressiveness in myself, I know why I am deprived. Who could bear my company day and night without a break? Bimala is full of the energy of life, and so she has never become stale to me for a moment, in all these nine years of our wedded life.

My life has only its dumb depths; but no murmuring rush. I can only receive: not impart movement. And therefore my company is like fasting. I recognize clearly today that Bimala has been languishing because of a famine of companionship.

Then whom shall I blame? Like Vidyapati I can only lament:

It is August, the sky breaks into a passionate rain;

Alas, empty is my house.

My house, I now see, was built to remain empty, because its doors cannot open. But I never knew till now that its divinity had been sitting outside. I had fondly believed that she had accepted my sacrifice, and granted in return her boon. But, alas, my house has all along been empty.

Every year, about this time, it was our practice to go in a house-boat over the broads of Samalda. I used to tell Bimala that a song must come back to its refrain over and over again. The original refrain of every song is in Nature, where the rain-laden wind passes over the rippling stream, where the green earth, drawing its shadow-veil over its face, keeps its ear close to the speaking water. There, at the beginning of time, a man and a woman first met—not within walls. And therefore we two must come back to Nature, at least once a year, to tune our love anew to the first pure note of the meeting of hearts. The first two anniversaries of our married life I spent in Calcutta, where I went through my examinations. But from the next year onwards, for seven years without a break, we have celebrated our union among the blossoming water-lilies. Now begins the next octave of my life.

It was difficult for me to ignore the fact that the same month of August had come round again this year. Does Bimala remember it, I wonder?—she has given me no reminder. Everything is mute about me.

It is August, the sky breaks into a passionate rain;

And empty is my house.

The house which becomes empty through the parting of lovers, still has music left in the heart of its emptiness. But the house that is empty because hearts are asunder, is awful in its silence. Even the cry of pain is out of place there. This cry of pain must be silenced in me. So long as I continue to suffer, Bimala will never have true freedom. I must free her completely, otherwise I shall never gain my freedom from untruth . . . I think I have come to the verge of understanding one thing. Man has so fanned the flame of the loves of men and women, as to make it overpass its rightful domain, and now, even in the name of humanity itself, he cannot bring it back under control. Man's worship has idolized his passion. But there must be no more human sacrifices at its shrine . . .

I went into my bedroom this morning, to fetch a book. It is long since I have been there in the day-time. A pang passed through me as I looked round it today, in the morning light. On the clothes rack was hanging a *sari* of Bimala's, crinkled ready for wear. On the dressing-table were her perfumes, her comb, her hair-pins, and with them, still, her vermilion box! Underneath were her tiny gold-embroidered slippers.

Once, in the old days, when Bimala had not yet overcome her objections to shoes, I had got these out from Lucknow, to tempt her. The first time she was ready to drop for very shame, to go in them even from the room to the verandah. Since then she has worn out many shoes, but has treasured up this pair. When first showing her the slippers, I chaffed her over a curious practice of hers; "I have caught you taking the dust of my feet, thinking me asleep! These are the offerings of my worship to ward the dust off the feet of my wakeful divinity." "You must not say such things," she protested, "or I will never wear your shoes!"

This bedroom of mine—it has a subtle atmosphere which goes straight to my heart. I was never aware, as I am today, how my thirsting heart has been sending out its roots to cling round each and every familiar object. The severing of the main root, I see, is not enough to set life free. Even these little slippers serve to hold one back. My wandering eyes fall on the niche. My portrait there is looking the same as ever, in spite of the flowers scattered round it having been withered black! Of all the things in the room their greeting strikes me as sincere. They are still here simply because it was not felt worth while even to remove them. Never mind; let me welcome truth, albeit in such sere and sorry garb, and look forward to the time when I shall be able to do so unmoved, as does my photograph.

As I stood there, Bimal came in from behind. I hastily turned my eyes from the niche to the shelves as I muttered: "I came to get Amiel's Journal." What need had Ito volunteer an explanation? I felt like a wrong-doer, a trespasser, prying into a secret not meant for me. I could not look Bimal in the face, but hurried away.

I had just made the discovery that it was useless to keep up a pretence of reading in my room outside, and also that it was equally beyond me to busy myself attending to anything at all—so that all the days of my future bid fair to congeal into one solid mass and settle heavily on my breast for good—when Panchu, the tenant of a neighbouring *zamindar*, came up to me with a basketful of cocoa-nuts and greeted me with a profound obeisance.

"Well, Panchu," said I. "What is all this for?"

I had got to know Panchu through my master. He was extremely poor, nor was I in a position to do anything for him; so I supposed this present was intended to procure a tip to help the poor fellow to make both ends meet. I took some money from my purse and held it out towards him, but with folded hands he protested: "I cannot take that, sir!"

"Why, what is the matter?"

"Let me make a clean breast of it, sir. Once, when I was hard pressed, I stole some cocoa-nuts from the garden here. I am getting old, and may die any day, so I have come to pay them back." Amiel's Journal could not have done me any good that day. But these words of Panchu lightened my heart. There are more things in life than the union or separation of man and woman. The great world stretches far beyond, and one can truly measure one's joys and sorrows when standing in its midst.

Panchu was devoted to my master. I know well enough how he manages to eke out a livelihood. He is up before dawn every day, and with a basket of *pan* leaves, twists of tobacco, coloured cotton yarn, little combs, looking-glasses, and other trinkets beloved of the village women, he wades through the knee-deep water of the marsh and goes over to the Namasudra quarters. There he barters his goods for rice, which fetches him a little more than their price in money. If he can get back soon enough he goes out again, after a hurried meal, to the sweetmeat seller's, where he assists in beating sugar for wafers. As soon as he comes home he sits at his shell-bangle making, plodding on often till midnight. All this cruel toil does not earn, for himself and his family, a bare two meals a day during much more than half the year. His method of eating is to begin with a good filling draught of water, and his staple food is the cheapest kind of seedy banana. And yet the family has to go with only one meal a day for the rest of the year.

At one time I had an idea of making him a charity allowance, "But," said my master, "your gift may destroy the man, it cannot destroy the hardship of his lot. Mother Bengal has not only this one Panchu. If the milk in her breasts has run dry, that cannot be supplied from the outside." These are thoughts which give one pause, and I decided to devote myself to working it out. That very day I said to Bimal: "Let us dedicate our lives to removing the root of this sorrow in our country."

"You are my Prince Siddharta, I see," she replied with a smile. "But do not let the torrent of your feelings end by sweeping me away also!"

"Siddharta took his vows alone. I want ours to be a joint arrangement."

The idea passed away in talk. The fact is, Bimala is at heart what is called a "lady". Though her own people are not well off, she was born a Rani. She has no doubts in her mind that there is a lower unit of measure for the trials and troubles of the "lower classes". Want is, of course, a permanent feature of their lives, but does not necessarily mean "want" to them. Their very smallness protects them, as the banks protect the pool; by widening bounds only the slime is exposed.

The real fact is that Bimala has only come into my home, not into my life. I had magnified her so, leaving her such a large place, that when I lost her, my whole way of life became narrow and confined. I had thrust aside all other objects into a corner to make room for Bimala—taken up as I was with decorating her and dressing her and educating her and moving round her day and night; forgetting how great is humanity and how nobly precious is man's life. When the actualities of everyday things get the better of the man, then is Truth lost sight of and freedom missed. So painfully important did Bimala make the mere actualities, that the truth remained concealed from me. That is why I find no gap in my misery, and spread this minute point of my emptiness over all the world. And so, for hours on this Autumn morning, the refrain has been humming in my ears:

It is the month of August, and the sky breaks into a passionate rain;

Alas, my house is empty.

The change which had, in a moment, come over the mind of Bengal was tremendous. It was as if the Ganges had touched the ashes of the sixty thousand sons of Sagar which no fire could enkindle, no other water knead again into living clay. The ashes of lifeless Bengal suddenly spoke up: "Here am I."

I have read somewhere that in ancient Greece a sculptor had the good fortune to impart life to the image made by his own hand. Even in that miracle, however, there was the process of form preceding life. But where was the unity in this heap of barren ashes? Had they been hard like stone, we might have had hopes of some form emerging, even as Ahalya, though turned to stone, at last won back her humanity. But these scattered ashes must have dropped to the dust through gaps in the Creator's fingers, to be blown hither and thither by the wind. They had become heaped up, but were never before united. Yet in this day which had come to Bengal, even this collection of looseness had taken shape, and proclaimed in a thundering voice, at our very door: "Here I am."

How could we help thinking that it was all supernatural? This moment of our history seemed to have dropped into our hand like a jewel from the crown of some drunken god. It had no resemblance to our past; and so we were led to hope that all our wants and miseries would disappear by the spell of some magic charm, that for us there was no longer any boundary line between the possible and the impossible. Everything seemed to be saying to us: "It is coming; it has come!"

Thus we came to cherish the belief that our history needed no steed, but that like heaven's chariot it would move with its own inherent power—At least no wages would have to be paid to the charioteer; only his wine cup would have to be filled again and again. And then in some impossible paradise the goal of our hopes would be reached.

My husband was not altogether unmoved, but through all our excitement it was the strain of sadness in him which deepened and deepened. He seemed to have a vision of something beyond the surging present.

I remember one day, in the course of the arguments he continually had with Sandip, he said: "Good fortune comes to our gate and announces itself, only to prove that we have not the power to receive it—that we have not kept things ready to be able to invite it into our house."

"No," was Sandip's answer. "You talk like an atheist because you do not believe in our gods. To us it has been made quite visible that the Goddess has come with her boon, yet you distrust the obvious signs of her presence."

"It is because I strongly believe in my God," said my husband, "that I feel so certain that our preparations for his worship are lacking. God has power to give the boon, but we must have power to accept it."

This kind of talk from my husband would only annoy me. I could not keep from joining in: "You think this excitement is only a fire of drunkenness, but does not drunkenness, up to a point, give strength?" "Yes," my husband replied. "It may give strength, but not weapons."

"But strength is the gift of God," I went on. "Weapons can be supplied by mere mechanics."

My husband smiled. "The mechanics will claim their wages before they deliver their supplies," he said.

Sandip swelled his chest as he retorted: "Don't you trouble about that. Their wages shall be paid."

"I shall bespeak the festive music when the payment has been made, not before," my husband answered.

"You needn't imagine that we are depending on your bounty for the music," said Sandip scornfully. "Our festival is above all money payments."

And in his thick voice he began to sing:

"My lover of the unpriced love, spurning payments,
Plays upon the simple pipe, bought for nothing,
Drawing my heart away."

Then with a smile he turned to me and said: "If I sing, Queen Bee, it is only to prove that when music comes into one's life, the lack of a good voice is no matter. When we sing merely on the strength of our tunefulness, the song is belittled. Now that a full flood of music has swept over our country, let Nikhil practise his scales, while we rouse the land with our cracked voices:

"My house cries to me: Why go out to lose your all?
My life says: All that you have, fling to the winds!
If we must lose our all, let us lose it: what is it worth after all?
If I must court ruin, let me do it smilingly;
For my quest is the death-draught of immortality.

"The truth is, Nikhil, that we have all lost our hearts. None can hold us any longer within the bounds of the easily possible, in our forward rush to the hopelessly impossible.

"Those who would draw us back,
They know not the fearful joy of recklessness.
They know not that we have had our call
From the end of the crooked path.
All that is good and straight and trim—
Let it topple over in the dust."

I thought that my husband was going to continue the discussion, but he rose silently from his seat and left us.

The thing that was agitating me within was merely a variation of the stormy passion outside, which swept the country from one end to the other. The car of the wielder of my destiny was fast approaching, and the sound of its wheels reverberated in my being. I had a constant feeling that something extraordinary might happen any moment, for which, however, the responsibility would not be mine. Was I not removed from the plane in which right and wrong, and the feelings of others, have to be considered? Had I ever wanted this—had I ever been waiting or hoping for any such thing? Look at my whole life and tell me then, if I was in any way accountable.

Through all my past I had been consistent in my devotion—but when at length it came to receiving the boon, a different god appeared! And just as the awakened country, with its *Bande Mataram*, thrills in salutation to the unrealized future before it, so do all my veins and nerves send forth shocks of welcome to the unthought-of, the unknown, the importunate Stranger.

One night I left my bed and slipped out of my room on to the open terrace. Beyond our garden wall are fields of ripening rice. Through the gaps in the village groves to the North, glimpses of the river are seen. The whole scene slept in the darkness like the vague embryo of some future creation.

In that future I saw my country, a woman like myself, standing expectant. She has been drawn forth from her home corner by the sudden call of some Unknown. She has had no time to pause or ponder, or to light herself a torch, as she rushes forward into the darkness ahead. I know well how her very soul responds to the distant flute-strains which call her; how her breast rises and falls; how she feels she nears it, nay it is already hers, so that it matters not even if she run blindfold. She is no mother. There is no call to her of children in their hunger, no home to be lighted of an evening, no household work to be done. So; she hies to her tryst, for this is the land of the Vaishnava Poets. She has left home, forgotten domestic duties;

she has nothing but an unfathomable yearning which hurries her on—by what road, to what goal, she recks not.

I, also, am possessed of just such a yearning. I likewise have lost my home and also lost my way. Both the end and the means have become equally shadowy to me. There remain only the yearning and the hurrying on. Ah! wretched wanderer through the night, when the dawn reddens you will see no trace of a way to return. But why return? Death will serve as well. If the Dark which sounded the flute should lead to destruction, why trouble about the hereafter? When I am merged in its blackness, neither I, nor good and bad, nor laughter, nor tears, shall be any more!

In Bengal the machinery of time being thus suddenly run at full pressure, things which were difficult became easy, one following soon after another. Nothing could be held back any more, even in our corner of the country. In the beginning our district was backward, for my husband was unwilling to put any compulsion on the villagers. "Those who make sacrifices for their country's sake are indeed her servants," he would say, "but those who compel others to make them in her name are her enemies. They would cut freedom at the root, to gain it at the top."

But when Sandip came and settled here, and his followers began to move about the country, speaking in towns and market-places, waves of excitement came rolling up to us as well. A band of young fellows of the locality attached themselves to him, some even who had been known as a disgrace to the village. But the glow of their genuine enthusiasm lighted them up, within as well as without. It became quite clear that when the pure breezes of a great joy and hope sweep through the land, all dirt and decay are cleansed away. It is hard, indeed, for men to be frank and straight and healthy, when their country is in the throes of dejection.

Then were all eyes turned on my husband, from whose estates alone foreign sugar and salt and cloths had not been banished. Even the estate officers began to feel awkward and ashamed over it. And yet, some time ago, when my husband began to import country-made articles into our village, he had been secretly and openly twitted for his folly, by old and young alike. When *Swadeshi* had not yet become a boast, we had despised it with all our hearts.

My husband still sharpens his Indian-made pencils with his Indian-made knife, does his writing with reed pens, drinks his water out of a bell-metal vessel, and works at night in the light of an old-fashioned castor-oil lamp. But this dull, milk-and-water *Swadeshi* of his never appealed to us. Rather, we had always felt ashamed of the inelegant, unfashionable furniture of his reception-rooms, especially when he had the magistrate, or any other European, as his guest.

My husband used to make light of my protests. "Why allow such trifles to upset you?" he would say with a smile.

"They will think us barbarians, or at all events wanting in refinement."

"If they do, I will pay them back by thinking that their refinement does not go deeper than their white skins."

My husband had an ordinary brass pot on his writing-table which he used as a flower-vase. It has often happened that, when I had news of some European guest, I would steal into his room and put in its place a crystal vase of European make. "Look here, Bimala," he objected at length, "that brass pot is as unconscious of itself as those blossoms are; but this thing protests its purpose so loudly, it is only fit for artificial flowers."

The Bara Rani, alone, pandered to my husband's whims. Once she comes panting to say: "Oh, brother, have you heard? Such lovely Indian soaps have come out! My days of luxury are gone by; still, if they contain no animal fat, I should like to try some."

This sort of thing makes my husband beam all over, and the house is deluged with Indian scents and soaps. Soaps indeed! They are more like lumps of caustic soda. And do I not know that what my sister-in-law uses on herself are the European soaps of old, while these are made over to the maids for washing clothes?

Another time it is: "Oh, brother dear, do get me some of these new Indian pen-holders."

Her "brother" bubbles up as usual, and the Bara Rani's room becomes littered with all kinds of awful sticks that go by the name of *Swadeshi* pen-holders. Not that it makes any difference to her, for reading and writing are out of her line. Still, in her writing-case, lies the selfsame ivory pen-holder, the only one ever handled.

The fact is, all this was intended as a hit at me, because I would not keep my husband company in his vagaries. It was no good trying to show up my sister-in-law's insincerity; my husband's face would set so hard, if I barely touched on it. One only gets into trouble, trying to save such people from being imposed upon!

The Bara Rani loves sewing. One day I could not help blurting out: "What a humbug you are, sister! When your 'brother' is present, your mouth waters at the very mention of *Swadeshi* scissors, but it is the English-made article every time when you work."

"What harm?" she replied. "Do you not see what pleasure it gives him? We have grown up together in this house, since he was a boy. I simply cannot bear, as you can, the sight of the smile leaving his face. Poor dear, he has no amusement except this playing at shop-keeping. You are his only dissipation, and you will yet be his ruin!"

"Whatever you may say, it is not right to be double-faced," I retorted. My sister-in-law laughed out in my face. "Oh, our artless little Chota Rani!—straight as a schoolmaster's rod, eh? But a woman is not built that way. She is soft and supple, so that she may bend without being crooked."

I could not forget those words: "You are his dissipation, and will be his ruin!" Today I feel—if a man needs must have some intoxicant, let it not be a woman.

Suksar, within our estates, is one of the biggest trade centres in the district. On one side of a stretch of water there is held a daily bazar; on the other, a weekly market. During the rains when this piece of water gets connected with the river, and boats can come through, great quantities of cotton yarns, and woollen stuffs for the coming winter, are brought in for sale. At the height of our enthusiasm, Sandip laid it down that all foreign articles, together with the demon of foreign influence, must be driven out of our territory.

"Of course!" said I, girding myself up for a fight.

"I have had words with Nikhil about it," said Sandip. "He tells me, he does not mind speechifying, but he will not have coercion."

"I will see to that," I said, with a proud sense of power. I knew how deep was my husband's love for me. Had I been in my senses I should have allowed myself to be torn to pieces rather than assert my claim to that, at such a time. But Sandip had to be impressed with the full strength of my *Shakti*.

Sandip had brought home to me, in his irresistible way, how the cosmic Energy was revealed for each individual in the shape of some special affinity. Vaishnava Philosophy, he said, speaks of the *Shakti* of Delight that dwells in the heart of creation, ever attracting the heart of her Eternal Lover. Men have a perpetual longing to bring out this *Shakti* from the hidden depths of their own nature, and those of us who succeed in doing so at once clearly understand the meaning of the music coming to us from the Dark. He broke out singing:

"My flute, that was busy with its song,

Is silent now when we stand face to face.

My call went seeking you from sky to sky

When you lay hidden;

But now all my cry finds its smile

In the face of my beloved."

Listening to his allegories, I had forgotten that I was plain and simple Bimala. I was *Shakti*; also an embodiment of Universal joy. Nothing could fetter me, nothing was impossible for me; whatever I touched would gain new life. The world around me was a fresh creation of mine; for behold, before my heart's response had touched it, there had not been this wealth of gold in the Autumn sky! And this hero, this true servant of the country, this devotee of mine—this flaming intelligence, this burning energy, this shining genius—him also was I creating from moment to moment. Have I not seen how my presence pours fresh life into him time after time?

The other day Sandip begged me to receive a young lad, Amulya, an ardent disciple of his. In a moment I could see a new light flash out from the boy's eyes, and knew that he, too, had a vision of *Shakti* manifest, that my creative force had begun its work in his blood. "What sorcery is this of yours!" exclaimed Sandip next day. "Amulya is a boy no longer, the wick of his life is all ablaze. Who can hide your fire under your home-roof? Every one of them must be touched up by it, sooner or later, and when every lamp is alight what a grand carnival of a *Dewali* we shall have in the country!"

Blinded with the brilliance of my own glory I had decided to grant my devotee this boon. I was overweeningly confident that none could baulk me of what I really wanted. When I returned to my room after my talk with Sandip, I loosed my hair and tied it up over again. Miss Gilby had taught me a way of brushing it up from the neck and piling it in a knot over my head.

This style was a favourite one with my husband. "It is a pity," he once said, "that Providence should have chosen poor me, instead of poet Kalidas, for revealing all the wonders of a woman's neck. The poet would probably have likened it to a flower-stem; but I feel it to be a torch, holding aloft the black flame of your hair." With which he . . . but why, oh why, do I go back to all that?

I sent for my husband. In the old days I could contrive a hundred and one excuses, good or bad, to get him to come to me. Now that all this had stopped for days I had lost the art of contriving.

Panchu's wife has just died of a lingering consumption. Panchu must undergo a purification ceremony to cleanse himself of sin and to propitiate his community. The community has calculated and informed him that it will cost one hundred and twenty-three rupees.

"How absurd!" I cried, highly indignant. "Don't submit to this, Panchu. What can they do to you?"

Raising to me his patient eyes like those of a tired-out beast of burden, he said: "There is my eldest girl, sir, she will have to be married. And my poor wife's last rites have to be put through."

"Even if the sin were yours, Panchu," I mused aloud, "you have surely suffered enough for it already."

"That is so, sir," he naïvely assented. "I had to sell part of my land and mortgage the rest to meet the doctor's bills. But there is no escape from the offerings I have to make the Brahmins."

What was the use of arguing? When will come the time, I wondered, for the purification of the Brahmins themselves who can accept such offerings?

After his wife's illness and funeral, Panchu, who had been tottering on the brink of starvation, went altogether beyond his depth. In a desperate attempt to gain consolation of some sort he took to sitting at the feet of a wandering ascetic, and succeeded in acquiring philosophy enough to forget that his children went hungry. He kept himself steeped for a time in the idea that the world is vanity, and if of pleasure it has none, pain also is a delusion. Then, at last, one night he left his little ones in their tumble-down hovel, and started off wandering on his own account.

I knew nothing of this at the time, for just then a veritable ocean-churning by gods and demons was going on in my mind. Nor did my master tell me that he had taken Panchu's deserted children under his own roof and was caring for them, though alone in the house, with his school to attend to the whole day.

After a month Panchu came back, his ascetic fervour considerably worn off. His eldest boy and girl nestled up to him, crying: "Where have you been all this time, father?" His youngest boy filled his lap; his second girl leant over his back with her arms around his neck; and they all wept together. "O sir!" sobbed Panchu, at length, to my master. "I have not the power to give these little ones enough to eat—I am not free to run away from them. What has been my sin that I should be scourged so, bound hand and foot?"

In the meantime the thread of Panchu's little trade connections had snapped and he found he could not resume them. He clung on to the shelter of my master's roof, which had first received him on his return, and said not a word of going back home. "Look here, Panchu," my master was at last driven to say. "If you don't take care of your cottage, it will tumble down altogether. I will lend you some money with which you can do a bit of peddling and return it me little by little."

Panchu was not excessively pleased—was there then no such thing as charity on earth? And when my master asked him to write out a receipt for the money, he felt that this favour, demanding a return, was hardly worth having. My master, however, did not care to make an outward gift which would leave an inward obligation. To destroy self-respect is to destroy caste, was his idea.

After signing the note, Panchu's obeisance to my master fell off considerably in its reverence—the dust-taking was left out. It made my master smile; he asked nothing better than that courtesy should stoop less low. "Respect given and taken truly balances the account between man and man," was the way he put it, "but veneration is overpayment."

Panchu began to buy cloth at the market and peddle it about the village. He did not get much of cash payment, it is true, but what he could realize in kind, in the way of rice, jute, and other field produce, went towards settlement of his account. In two months" time he was able to pay back an instalment of my master's debt, and with it there was a corresponding reduction in the depth of his bow. He must have begun to feel that he had been revering as a saint a mere man, who had not even risen superior to the lure of lucre.

While Panchu was thus engaged, the full shock of the *Swadeshi* flood fell on him.

It was vacation time, and many youths of our village and its neighbourhood had come home from their schools and colleges. They attached themselves to Sandip's leadership with enthusiasm, and some, in their excess of zeal, gave up their studies altogether. Many of the boys had been free pupils of my school here, and some held college scholarships from me in Calcutta. They came up in a body, and demanded that I should banish foreign goods from my Suksar market.

I told them I could not do it.

They were sarcastic: "Why, Maharaja, will the loss be too much for you?"

I took no notice of the insult in their tone, and was about to reply that the loss would fall on the poor traders and their customers, not on me, when my master, who was present, interposed.

"Yes, the loss will be his—not yours, that is clear enough," he said.

"But for one's country . ."

"The country does not mean the soil, but the men on it," interrupted my master again. "Have you yet wasted so much as a glance on what was happening to them? But now you would dictate what salt they shall eat, what clothes they shall wear. Why should they put up with such tyranny, and why should we let them?"

"But we have taken to Indian salt and sugar and cloth ourselves."

"You may do as you please to work off your irritation, to keep up your fanaticism. You are well off, you need not mind the cost. The poor do not want to stand in your way, but you insist on their submitting to your compulsion. As it is, every moment of theirs is a life-and-death struggle for a bare living; you cannot even imagine the difference a few pice means to them—so little have you in common. You have spent your whole past in a superior compartment, and now you come down to use them as tools for the wreaking of your wrath. I call it cowardly."

They were all old pupils of my master, so they did not venture to be disrespectful, though they were quivering with indignation. They turned to me. "Will you then be the only one, Maharaja, to put obstacles in the way of what the country would achieve?"

"Who am I, that I should dare do such a thing? Would I not rather lay down my life to help it?"

The M.A. student smiled a crooked smile, as he asked: "May we enquire what you are actually doing to help?"

"I have imported Indian mill-made yarn and kept it for sale in my Suksar market, and also sent bales of it to markets belonging to neighbouring *zamindar*s."

"But we have been to your market, Maharaja," the same student exclaimed, "and found nobody buying this yarn."

"That is neither my fault nor the fault of my market. It only shows the whole country has not taken your vow."

"That is not all," my master went on. "It shows that what you have pledged yourselves to do is only to pester others. You want dealers, who have not taken your vow, to buy that yarn; weavers, who have not taken your vow, to make it up; then their wares eventually to be foisted on to consumers who, also, have not taken your vow. The method? Your clamour, and the *zamindars'* oppression. The result: all righteousness yours, all privations theirs!"

"And may we venture to ask, further, what your share of the privation has been?" pursued a science student.

"You want to know, do you?" replied my master. "It is Nikhil himself who has to buy up that Indian mill yarn; he has had to start a weaving school to get it woven; and to judge by his past brilliant business exploits, by the time his cotton fabrics leave the loom their cost will be that of cloth-of-gold; so they will only find a use, perhaps, as curtains for his drawing-room, even though their flimsiness may fail to screen him. When you get tired of your vow, you will laugh the loudest at their artistic effect. And if their workmanship is ever truly appreciated at all, it will be by foreigners."

I have known my master all my life, but have never seen him so agitated. I could see that the pain had been silently accumulating in his heart for some time, because of his surpassing love for me, and that his habitual self-possession had become secretly undermined to the breaking point.

"You are our elders," said the medical student. "It is unseemly that we should bandy words with you. But tell us, pray, finally, are you determined not to oust foreign articles from your market?"

"I will not," I said, "because they are not mine."

"Because that will cause you a loss!" smiled the M.A. student.

"Because he, whose is the loss, is the best judge," retorted my master.

With a shout of *Bande Mataram* they left us.

A few days later, my master brought Panchu round to me. His *zamindar*, it appeared, had fined him a hundred rupees, and was threatening him with ejectment.

"For what fault?" I enquired.

"Because," I was told, "he has been found selling foreign cloths. He begged and prayed Harish Kundu, his *zamindar*, to let him sell off his stock, bought with borrowed money, promising faithfully never to do it again; but the *zamindar* would not hear of it, and insisted on his burning the foreign stuff there and then, if he wanted to be let off. Panchu in his desperation blurted out defiantly: "I can't afford it! You are rich; why not buy it up and burn it?" This only made Harish Kundu red in the face as he shouted: "The scoundrel must be taught manners, give him a shoe-beating!" So poor Panchu got insulted as well as fined."

"What happened to the cloth?"

"The whole bale was burnt."

"Who else was there?"

"Any number of people, who all kept shouting *Bande Mataram*. Sandip was also there. He took up some of the ashes, crying: 'Brothers! This is the first funeral pyre lighted by your village in celebration of the last rites of foreign commerce. These are sacred ashes. Smear yourselves with them in token of your *Swadeshi* vow.'"

"Panchu," said I, turning to him, "you must lodge a complaint."

"No one will bear me witness," he replied.

"None bear witness?—Sandip! Sandip!"

Sandip came out of his room at my call. "What is the matter?" he asked.

"Won't you bear witness to the burning of this man's cloth?"

Sandip smiled. "Of course I shall be a witness in the case," he said. "But I shall be on the opposite side."

"What do you mean," I exclaimed, "by being a witness on this or that side? Will you not bear witness to the truth?"

"Is the thing which happens the only truth?"

"What other truths can there be?"

"The things that ought to happen! The truth we must build up will require a great deal of untruth in the process. Those who have made their way in the world have created truth, not blindly followed it."

"And so—"

"And so I will bear what you people are pleased to call false witness, as they have done who have created empires, built up social systems, founded religious organizations. Those who would rule do not dread untruths; the shackles of truth are reserved for those who will fall under their sway. Have you not read history? Do you not know that in the immense cauldrons, where vast political developments are simmering, untruths are the main ingredients?" "Political cookery on a large scale is doubtless going on, but—"

"Oh, I know! You, of course, will never do any of the cooking. You prefer to be one of those down whose throats the hotchpotch which is being cooked will be crammed. They will partition Bengal and say it is for your benefit. They will seal the doors of education and call it raising the standard. But you will always remain good boys, snivelling in your corners. We bad men, however, must see whether we cannot erect a defensive fortification of untruth."

"It is no use arguing about these things, Nikhil," my master interposed. "How can they who do not feel the truth within them, realize that to bring it out from its obscurity into the light is man's highest aim—not to keep on heaping material outside?"

Sandip laughed. "Right, sir!" said he. "Quite a correct speech for a schoolmaster. That is the kind of stuff I have read in books; but in the real world I have seen that man's chief business is the accumulation of outside material. Those who are masters in the art, advertise the biggest lies in their business, enter false accounts in their political ledgers with their broadest-pointed pens, launch their newspapers daily laden with untruths, and send preachers abroad to disseminate falsehood like flies carrying pestilential germs. I am a humble follower of these great ones. When I was attached to the Congress party I never hesitated to dilute ten per cent of truth with ninety per cent of untruth. And now, merely because I have ceased to belong to that party, I have not forgotten the basic fact that man's goal is not truth but success."

"True success," corrected my master.

"Maybe," replied Sandip, "but the fruit of true success ripens only by cultivating the field of untruth, after tearing up the soil and pounding it into dust. Truth grows up by itself like weeds and thorns, and only worms can expect to get fruit from it!" With this he flung out of the room.

My master smiled as he looked towards me. "Do you know, Nikhil," he said, "I believe Sandip is not irreligious—his religion is of the obverse side of truth, like the dark moon, which is still a moon, for all that its light has gone over to the wrong side."

"That is why," I assented, "I have always had an affection for him, though we have never been able to agree. I cannot contemn him, even now; though he has hurt me sorely, and may yet hurt me more."

"I have begun to realize that," said my master. "I have long wondered how you could go on putting up with him. I have, at times, even suspected you of weakness. I now see that though you two do not rhyme, your rhythm is the same."

"Fate seems bent on writing Paradise Lost in blank verse, in my case, and so has no use for a rhyming friend!" I remarked, pursuing his conceit.

"But what of Panchu?" resumed my master.

"You say Harish Kundu wants to eject him from his ancestral holding. Supposing I buy it up and then keep him on as my tenant?"

"And his fine?"

"How can the *zamindar* realize that if he becomes my tenant?"

"His burnt bale of cloth?"

"I will procure him another. I should like to see anyone interfering with a tenant of mine, for trading as he pleases!"

"I am afraid, sir," interposed Panchu despondently, "while you big folk are doing the fighting, the police and the law vultures will merrily gather round, and the crowd will enjoy the fun, but when it comes to getting killed, it will be the turn of only poor me!"

"Why, what harm can come to you?"

"They will burn down my house, sir, children and all!"

"Very well, I will take charge of your children," said my master. "You may go on with any trade you like. They shan't touch you."

That very day I bought up Panchu's holding and entered into formal possession. Then the trouble began.

Panchu had inherited the holding of his grandfather as his sole surviving heir. Everybody knew this. But at this juncture an aunt turned up from somewhere, with her boxes and bundles, her rosary, and a widowed niece. She ensconced herself in Panchu's home and laid claim to a life interest in all he had.

Panchu was dumbfounded. "My aunt died long ago," he protested.

In reply he was told that he was thinking of his uncle's first wife, but that the former had lost no time in taking to himself a second.

"But my uncle died before my aunt," exclaimed Panchu, still more mystified. "Where was the time for him to marry again?"

This was not denied. But Panchu was reminded that it had never been asserted that the second wife had come after the death of the first, but the former had been married by his uncle during the latter's lifetime. Not relishing the idea of living with a co-wife she had remained in her father's house till her husband's death, after which she had got religion and retired to holy Brindaban, whence she was now coming. These facts were well known to the officers of Harish Kundu, as well as to some of his tenants. And if the *zamindar*'s summons should be peremptory enough, even some of those who had partaken of the marriage feast would be forthcoming!

One afternoon, when I happened to be specially busy, word came to my office room that Bimala had sent for me. I was startled.

"Who did you say had sent for me?" I asked the messenger.

"The Rani Mother."

"The Bara Rani?"

"No, sir, the Chota Rani Mother."

The Chota Rani! It seemed a century since I had been sent for by her. I kept them all waiting there, and went off into the inner apartments. When I stepped into our room I had another shock of surprise to find Bimala there with a distinct suggestion of being dressed up. The room, which from persistent neglect had latterly acquired an air of having grown absent-minded, had regained something of its old order this afternoon. I stood there silently, looking enquiringly at Bimala.

She flushed a little and the fingers of her right hand toyed for a time with the bangles on her left arm. Then she abruptly broke the silence. "Look here! Is it right that ours should be the only market in all Bengal which allows foreign goods?"

"What, then, would be the right thing to do?" I asked.

"Order them to be cleared out!"

"But the goods are not mine."

"Is not the market yours?"

"It is much more theirs who use it for trade."

"Let them trade in Indian goods, then."

"Nothing would please me better. But suppose they do not?"

"Nonsense! How dare they be so insolent? Are you not . . ."

"I am very busy this afternoon and cannot stop to argue it out. But I must refuse to tyrannize."

"It would not be tyranny for selfish gain, but for the sake of the country."

"To tyrannize for the country is to tyrannize over the country. But that I am afraid you will never understand." With this I came away.

All of a sudden the world shone out for me with a fresh clearness. I seemed to feel it in my blood, that the Earth had lost the weight of its earthiness, and its daily task of sustaining life no longer appeared a burden, as with a wonderful access of power it whirled through space telling its beads of days and nights. What endless work, and withal what illimitable energy of freedom! None shall check it, oh, none can ever check it! From the depths of my being an uprush of joy, like a waterspout, sprang high to storm the skies.

I repeatedly asked myself the meaning of this outburst of feeling. At first there was no intelligible answer. Then it became clear that the bond against which I had been fretting inwardly, night and day, had broken. To my surprise I discovered that my mind was freed from all mistiness. I could see everything relating to Bimala as if vividly pictured on a camera screen. It was palpable that she had specially dressed herself up to coax that order out of me. Till that moment, I had never viewed Bimala's adornment as a thing apart from herself. But today the elaborate manner in which she had done up her hair, in the English fashion, made it appear a mere decoration. That which before had the mystery of her personality about it, and was priceless to me, was now out to sell itself cheap.

As I came away from that broken cage of a bedroom, out into the golden sunlight of the open, there was the avenue of bauhinias, along the gravelled path in front of my verandah, suffusing the sky with a rosy flush. A group of starlings beneath the trees were noisily chattering away. In the distance an empty bullock cart, with its nose on the ground, held up its tail aloft—one of its unharnessed bullocks grazing, the other resting on the grass, its eyes dropping for very comfort, while a crow on its back was pecking away at the insects on its body.

I seemed to have come closer to the heartbeats of the great earth in all the simplicity of its daily life; its warm breath fell on me with the perfume of the bauhinia blossoms; and an anthem, inexpressibly sweet, seemed to peal forth from this world, where I, in my freedom, live in the freedom of all else.

We, men, are knights whose quest is that freedom to which our ideals call us. She who makes for us the banner under which we fare forth is the true Woman for us. We must tear away the disguise of her who weaves our net of enchantment at home, and know her for what she is. We must beware of clothing her in the witchery of our own longings and imaginings, and thus allow her to distract us from our true quest.

Today I feel that I shall win through. I have come to the gateway of the simple; I am now content to see things as they are. I have gained freedom myself; I shall allow freedom to others. In my work will be my salvation.

I know that, time and again, my heart will ache, but now that I understand its pain in all its truth, I can disregard it. Now that I know it concerns only me, what after all can be its value? The suffering which belongs to all mankind shall be my crown.

Save me, Truth! Never again let me hanker after the false paradise of Illusion. If I must walk alone, let me at least tread your path. Let the drum-beats of Truth lead me to Victory.

Bimala sent for me that day, but for a time she could not utter a word; her eyes kept brimming up to the verge of overflowing. I could see at once that she had been unsuccessful with Nikhil. She had been so proudly confident that she would have her own way—but I had never shared her confidence. Woman knows man well enough where he is weak, but she is quite unable to fathom him where he is strong. The fact is that man is as much a mystery to woman as woman is to man. If that were not so, the separation of the sexes would only have been a waste of Nature's energy.

Ah pride, pride! The trouble was, not that the necessary thing had failed of accomplishment, but that the entreaty, which had cost her such a struggle to make, should have been refused. What a wealth of colour and movement, suggestion and deception, group themselves round this "me" and "mine" in woman. That is just where her beauty lies—she is ever so much more personal than man. When man was being made, the Creator was a schoolmaster—His bag full of commandments and principles; but when He came to woman, He resigned His headmastership and turned artist, with only His brush and paint-box.

When Bimala stood silently there, flushed and tearful in her broken pride, like a storm-cloud, laden with rain and charged with lightning, lowering over the horizon, she looked so absolutely sweet that I had to go right up to her and take her by the hand. It was trembling, but she did not snatch it away. "Bee," said I, "we two are colleagues, for our aims are one. Let us sit down and talk it over."

I led her, unresisting, to a seat. But strange! at that very point the rush of my impetuosity suffered an unaccountable check—just as the current of the mighty Padma, roaring on in its irresistible course, all of a sudden gets turned away from the bank it is crumbling by some trifling obstacle beneath the surface. When I pressed Bimala's hand my nerves rang music, like tuned-up strings; but the symphony stopped short at the first movement.

What stood in the way? Nothing singly; it was a tangle of a multitude of things—nothing definitely palpable, but only that unaccountable sense of obstruction. Anyhow, this much has become plain to me, that I cannot swear to what I really am. It is because I am such a mystery to my own mind that my attraction for myself is so strong! If once the whole of myself should become known to me, I would then fling it all away—and reach beatitude!

As she sat down, Bimala went ashy pale. She, too, must have realized what a crisis had come and gone, leaving her unscathed. The comet had passed by, but the brush of its burning tail had overcome her. To help her to recover herself I said: "Obstacles there will be, but let us fight them through, and not be down-hearted. Is not that best, Queen?"

Bimala cleared her throat with a little cough, but simply to murmur: "Yes."

"Let us sketch out our plan of action," I continued, as I drew a piece of paper and a pencil from my pocket.

I began to make a list of the workers who had joined us from Calcutta and to assign their duties to each. Bimala interrupted me before I was through, saying wearily: "Leave it now; I will join you again this evening" and then she hurried out of the room. It was evident she was not in a state to attend to anything. She must be alone with herself for a while—perhaps lie down on her bed and have a good cry!

When she left me, my intoxication began to deepen, as the cloud colours grow richer after the sun is down. I felt I had let the moment of moments slip by. What an awful coward I had been! She must have left me in sheer disgust at my qualms—and she was right!

While I was tingling all over with these reflections, a servant came in and announced Amulya, one of our boys. I felt like sending him away for the time, but he stepped in before I could make up my mind. Then we fell to discussing the news of the fights which were raging in different quarters over cloth and sugar and salt; and the air was soon clear of all fumes of intoxication. I felt as if awakened from a dream. I leapt to my feet feeling quite ready for the fray—Bande Mataram!

The news was various. Most of the traders who were tenants of Harish Kundu had come over to us. Many of Nikhil's officials were also secretly on our side, pulling the wires in our interest. The Marwari shopkeepers were offering to pay a penalty, if only allowed to clear their present stocks. Only some Mahomedan traders were still obdurate. One of them was taking home some German-made shawls for his family. These were confiscated and burnt by one of our village boys. This had given rise to trouble. We offered to buy him Indian woollen stuffs in their place. But where were cheap Indian woollens to be had? We could not very well indulge him in Cashmere shawls! He came and complained to Nikhil, who advised him to go to law. Of course Nikhil's men saw to it that the trial should come to nothing, even his law-agent being on our side!

The point is, if we have to replace burnt foreign clothes with Indian cloth every time, and on the top of that fight through a law-suit, where is the money to come from? And the beauty of it is that this destruction of foreign goods is increasing their demand and sending up the foreigner's profits—very like what happened to the fortunate shopkeeper whose chandeliers the nabob delighted in smashing, tickled by the tinkle of the breaking glass.

The next problem is—since there is no such thing as cheap and gaudy Indian woollen stuff, should we be rigorous in our boycott of foreign flannels and memos, or make an exception in their favour?

"Look here!" said I at length on the first point, "we are not going to keep on making presents of Indian stuff to those who have got their foreign purchases confiscated. The penalty is intended to fall on them, not on us. If they go to law, we must retaliate by burning down their granaries!—What startles you, Amulya? It is not the prospect of a grand illumination that delights me! You must remember, this is War. If you are afraid of causing suffering, go in for love-making, you will never do for this work!"

The second problem I solved by deciding to allow no compromise with foreign articles, in any circumstance whatever. In the good old days, when these gaily coloured foreign shawls were unknown, our peasantry used to manage well enough with plain cotton quilts—they must learn to do so again. They may not look as gorgeous, but this is not the time to think of looks.

Most of the boatmen had been won over to refuse to carry foreign goods, but the chief of them, Mirjan, was still insubordinate. "Could you not get his boat sunk?" I asked our manager here.

"Nothing easier, sir," he replied. "But what if afterwards I am held responsible?"

"Why be so clumsy as to leave any loophole for responsibility? However, if there must be any, my shoulders will be there to bear it."

Mirjan's boat was tied near the landing-place after its freight had been taken over to the market-place. There was no one on it, for the manager had arranged for some entertainment to which all had been invited. After dusk the boat, loaded with rubbish, was holed and set adrift. It sank in mid-stream.

Mirjan understood the whole thing. He came to me in tears to beg for mercy. "I was wrong, sir—" he began.

"What makes you realize that all of a sudden?" I sneered.

He made no direct reply. "The boat was worth two thousand rupees," he said. "I now see my mistake, and if excused this time I will never . . ." with which he threw himself at my feet.

I asked him to come ten days later. If only we could pay him that two thousand rupees at once, we could buy him up body and soul. This is just the sort of man who could render us immense service, if won over. We shall never be able to make any headway unless we can lay our hands on plenty of money.

As soon as Bimala came into the sitting-room, in the evening, I said as I rose up to receive her: "Queen! Everything is ready, success is at hand, but we must have money.

"Money? How much money?"

"Not so very much, but by hook or by crook we must have it!"

"But how much?"

"A mere fifty thousand rupees will do for the present."

Bimala blenched inwardly at the figure, but tried not to show it. How could she again admit defeat?

"Queen!" said I, "you only can make the impossible possible. Indeed you have already done so. Oh, that I could show you the extent of your achievement—then you would know it. But the time for that is not now. Now we want money!"

"You shall have it," she said.

I could see that the thought of selling her jewels had occurred to her. So I said: "Your jewels must remain in reserve. One can never tell when they may be wanted." And then, as Bimala stared blankly at me in silence, I went on: "This money must come from your husband's treasury."

Bimala was still more taken aback. After a long pause she said: "But how am Ito get his money?"

"Is not his money yours as well?"

"Ah, no!" she said, her wounded pride hurt afresh.

"If not," I cried, "neither is it his, but his country's, whom he has deprived of it, in her time of need!"

"But how am Ito get it?" she repeated.

"Get it you shall and must. You know best how. You must get it for Her to whom it rightfully belongs. *Bande Mataram*! These are the magic words which will open the door of his iron safe, break through the walls of his strong-room, and confound the hearts of those who are disloyal to its call. Say *Bande Mataram*, Bee!"

"*Bande Mataram*!"

We are men, we are kings, we must have our tribute. Ever since we have come upon the Earth we have been plundering her; and the more we claimed, the more she submitted. From primeval days have we men been plucking fruits, cutting down trees, digging up the soil, killing beast, bird and fish. From the bottom of the sea, from underneath the ground, from the very jaws of death, it has all been grabbing and grabbing and grabbing—no strong-box in Nature's store-room has been respected or left unrifled. The one delight of this Earth is to fulfil the claims of those who are men. She has been made fertile and beautiful and complete through her endless sacrifices to them. But for this, she would be lost in the wilderness, not knowing herself, the doors of her heart shut, her diamonds and pearls never seeing the light.

Likewise, by sheer force of our claims, we men have opened up all the latent possibilities of women. In the process of surrendering themselves to us, they have ever gained their true greatness. Because they had to bring all the diamonds of their happiness and the pearls of their sorrow into our royal treasury, they have found their true wealth. So for men to accept is truly to give: for women to give is truly to gain.

The demand I have just made from Bimala, however, is indeed a large one! At first I felt scruples; for is it not the habit of man's mind to be in purposeless conflict with itself? I thought I had imposed too hard a task. My first impulse was to call her back, and tell her I would rather not make her life wretched by dragging her into all these troubles. I forgot, for the moment, that it was the mission of man to be aggressive, to make woman's existence fruitful by stirring up disquiet in the depth of her passivity, to make the whole world blessed by churning up the immeasurable abyss of suffering! This is why man's hands are so strong, his grip so firm. Bimala had been longing with all her heart that I, Sandip, should demand of her some great sacrifice—should call her to her death. How else could she be happy? Had she not waited all these weary years only for an opportunity to weep out her heart—so satiated was she with the monotony of her placid happiness? And therefore, at the very sight of me, her heart's horizon darkened with the rain clouds of her impending days of anguish. If I pity her and save her from her sorrows, what then was the purpose of my being born a man?

The real reason of my qualms is that my demand happens to be for money. That savours of beggary, for money is man's, not woman's. That is why I had to make it a big figure. A thousand or two would have the air of petty theft. Fifty thousand has all the expanse of romantic brigandage. Ah, but riches should really have been mine! So many of my desires have had to halt, again and again, on the road to accomplishment simply for want of money. This does not become me! Had my fate been merely unjust, it could be forgiven—but its bad taste is unpardonable. It is not simply a hardship that a man like me should be at his wit's end to pay his house rent, or should have to carefully count out the coins for an Intermediate Class railway ticket—it is vulgar!

It is equally clear that Nikhil's paternal estates are a superfluity to him. For him it would not have been at all unbecoming to be poor. He would have cheerfully pulled in the double harness of indigent mediocrity with that precious master of his. I should love to have, just for once, the chance to fling about fifty thousand rupees in the service of my country and to the satisfaction of myself. I am a nabob born, and it is a great dream of mine to get rid of this disguise of poverty, though it be for a day only, and to see myself in my true character. I have grave misgivings, however, as to Bimala ever getting that fifty thousand rupees within her reach, and it will probably be only a thousand or two which will actually come to hand. Be it so. The wise man is content with half a loaf, or any fraction for that matter, rather than no bread. I must return to these personal reflections of mine later. News comes that I am wanted at once. Something has gone wrong . . .

It seems that the police have got a clue to the man who sank Mirjan's boat for us. He was an old offender. They are on his trail, but he should be too practised a hand to be caught blabbing. However, one never knows. Nikhil's back is up, and his manager may not be able to have things his own way.

"If I get into trouble, sir," said the manager when I saw him, "I shall have to drag you in!"

"Where is the noose with which you can catch me?" I asked.

"I have a letter of yours, and several of Amulya Babu's." I could not see that the letter marked "urgent" to which I had been hurried into writing a reply was wanted urgently for this purpose only! I am getting to learn quite a number of things.

The point now is, that the police must be bribed and hush-money paid to Mirjan for his boat. It is also becoming evident that much of the cost of this patriotic venture of ours will find its way as profit into the pockets of Nikhil's manager. However, I must shut my eyes to that for the present, for is he not shouting *Bande Mataram* as lustily as I am?

This kind of work has always to be carried on with leaky vessels which let as much through as they fetch in. We all have a hidden fund of moral judgement stored away within us, and so I was about to wax indignant with the manager, and enter in my diary a tirade against the unreliability of our countrymen. But, if there be a god, I must acknowledge with gratitude to him that he has given me a clear-seeing mind, which allows nothing inside or outside it to remain vague. 1 may delude others, but never myself. So I was unable to continue angry.

Whatever is true is neither good nor bad, but simply true, and that is Science. A lake is only the remnant of water which has not been sucked into the ground. Underneath the cult of *Bande Mataram*, as indeed at the bottom of all mundane affairs, there is a region of slime, whose absorbing power must be reckoned with. The manager will take what he wants; I also have my own wants. These lesser wants form a part of the wants of the great Cause—the horse must be fed and the wheels must be oiled if the best progress is to be made.

The long and short of it is that money we must have, and that soon. We must take whatever comes the readiest, for we cannot afford to wait. I know that the immediate often swallows up the ultimate; that the five thousand rupees of today may nip in the bud the fifty thousand rupees of tomorrow. But I must accept the penalty. Have I not often twitted Nikhil that they who walk in the paths of restraint have never known what sacrifice is? It is we greedy folk who have to sacrifice our greed at every step!

Of the cardinal sins of man, Desire is for men who are men—but Delusion, which is only for cowards, hampers them. Because delusion keeps them wrapped up in past and future, but is the very deuce for confounding their footsteps in the present. Those who are always straining their ears for the call of the remote, to the neglect of the call of the imminent, are like Sakuntala absorbed in the memories of her lover. The guest comes unheeded, and the curse descends, depriving them of the very object of their desire.

The other day I pressed Bimala's hand, and that touch still stirs her mind, as it vibrates in mine. Its thrill must not be deadened by repetition, for then what is now music will descend to mere argument. There is at present no room in her mind for the question "why?" So I must not deprive Bimala, who is one of those creatures for whom illusion is necessary, of her full supply of it.

As for me, I have so much else to do that I shall have to be content for the present with the foam of the wine cup of passion. O man of desire! Curb your greed, and practise your hand on the harp of illusion till you can bring out all the delicate nuances of suggestion. This is not the time to drain the cup to the dregs. Our work proceeds apace. But though we have shouted ourselves hoarse, proclaiming the Mussulmans to be our brethren, we have come to realize that we shall never be able to bring them wholly round to our side. So they must be suppressed altogether and made to understand that we are the masters. They are now showing their teeth, but one day they shall dance like tame bears to the tune we play.

"If the idea of a United India is a true one," objects Nikhil, "Mussulmans are a necessary part of it."

"Quite so," said I, "but we must know their place and keep them there, otherwise they will constantly be giving trouble."

"So you want to make trouble to prevent trouble?"

"What, then, is your plan?"

"There is only one well-known way of avoiding quarrels," said Nikhil meaningly.

I know that, like tales written by good people, Nikhil's discourse always ends in a moraL The strange part of it is that with all his familiarity with moral precepts, he still believes in them! He is an incorrigible schoolboy. His only merit is his sincerity. The mischief with people like him is that they will not admit the finality even of death, but keep their eyes always fixed on a hereafter.

I have long been nursing a plan which, if only I could carry it out, would set fire to the whole country. True patriotism will never be roused in our countrymen unless they can visualize the motherland. We must make a goddess of her. My colleagues saw the point at once. "Let us devise an appropriate image!" they exclaimed. "It will not do if you devise- it," I admonished them. "We must get one of the current images accepted as representing the country—the worship of the people must flow towards it along the deep-cut grooves of custom."

But Nikhil's needs must argue even about this. "We must not seek the help of illusions," he said to me some time ago,

"for what we believe to be the true cause."

"Illusions are necessary for lesser minds," I said, "and to this class the greater portion of the world belongs. That is why divinities are set up in every country to keep up the illusions of the people, for men are only too well aware of their weakness."

"No," he replied. "God is necessary to clear away our illusions. The divinities which keep them alive are false gods."

"What of that? If need be, even false gods must be invoked, rather than let the work suffer. Unfortunately for us, our illusions are alive enough, but we do not know how to make them serve our purpose. Look at the Brahmins. In spite of our treating them as demi-gods, and untiringly taking the dust of their feet, they are a force going to waste.

"There will always be a large class of people, given to grovelling, who can never be made to do anything unless they are bespattered with the dust of somebody's feet, be it on their heads or on their backs! What a pity if after keeping Brahmins saved up in our armoury for all these ages—keen and serviceable—they cannot be utilized to urge on this rabble in the time of our need."

But it is impossible to drive all this into Nikhil's head. He has such a prejudice in favour of truth—as though there exists such an objective reality! How often have I tried to explain to him that where untruth truly exists, there it is indeed the truth. This was understood in our country in the old days, and so they had the courage to declare that for those of little understanding untruth is the truth. For them, who can truly believe their country to be a goddess, her image will do duty for the truth. With our nature and our traditions we are unable to realize our country as she is, but we can easily bring ourselves to believe in her image. Those who want to do real work must not ignore this fact.

Nikhil only got excited. "Because you have lost the power of walking in the path of truth's attainment," he cried, "you keep waiting for some miraculous boon to drop from the skies! That is why when your service to the country has fallen centuries into arrears all you can think of is, to make of it an image and stretch out your hands in expectation of gratuitous favours."

"We want to perform the impossible," I said. "So our country needs must be made into a god."

"You mean you have no heart for possible tasks," replied Nikhil. "Whatever is already there is to be left undisturbed; yet there must be a supernatural result." "Look here, Nikhil," I said at length, thoroughly exasperated.

"The things you have been saying are good enough as moral lessons. These ideas have served their purpose, as milk for babes, at one stage of man's evolution, but will no longer do, now that man has cut his teeth.

"Do we not see before our very eyes how things, of which we never even dreamt of sowing the seed, are sprouting up on every side? By what power? That of the deity in our country who is becoming manifest. It is for the genius of the age to give that deity its image. Genius does not argue, it creates. I only give form to what the country imagines.

"I will spread it abroad that the goddess has vouchsafed me a dream. I will tell the Brahmins that they have been appointed her priests, and that their downfall has been due to their dereliction of duty in not seeing to the proper performance of her worship. Do you say I shall be uttering lies? No, say I, it is the truth—nay more, the truth which the country has so long been waiting to learn from my lips. If only I could get the opportunity to deliver my message, you would see the stupendous result."

"What I am afraid of," said Nikhil, "is, that my lifetime is limited and the result you speak of is not the final result. It will have after-effects which may not be immediately apparent."

"I only seek the result," said I, "which belongs to today."

"The result I seek," answered Nikhil, "belongs to all time."

Nikhil may have had his share of Bengal's greatest gift—imagination, but he has allowed it to be overshadowed and nearly killed by an exotic conscientiousness. Just look at the worship of Durga which Bengal has carried to such heights. That is one of her greatest achievements. I can swear that Durga is a political goddess and was conceived as the image of the *Shakti* of patriotism in the days when Bengal was praying to be delivered from Mussulman domination. What other province of India has succeeded in giving such wonderful visual expression to the ideal of its quest?

Nothing betrayed Nikhil's loss of the divine gift of imagination more conclusively than his reply to me. "During the Mussulman domination," he said, "the Maratha and the Sikh asked for fruit from the arms which they themselves took up. The Bengali contented himself with placing weapons in the hands of his goddess and muttering incantations to her; and as his country did not really happen to be a goddess the only fruit he got was the lopped-off heads of the goats and buffaloes of the sacrifice. The day that we seek the good of the country along the path of righteousness, He who is greater than our country will grant us true fruition."

The unfortunate part of it is that Nikhil's words sound so fine when put down on paper. My words, however, are not meant to be scribbled on paper, but to be scored into the heart of the country. The Pandit records his Treatise on Agriculture in printer's ink; but the cultivator at the point of his plough impresses his endeavour deep in the soil.

When I next saw Bimala I pitched my key high without further ado. "Have we been able," I began, "to believe with all our heart in the god for whose worship we have been born all these millions of years, until he actually made himself visible to us?

"How often have I told you," I continued, "that had I not seen you I never would have known all my country as One. I know not yet whether you rightly understand me. The gods are invisible only in their heaven—on earth they show themselves to mortal men."

Bimala looked at me in a strange kind of way as she gravely replied: "Indeed I understand you, Sandip." This was the first time she called me plain Sandip.

"Krishna," I continued, "whom Arjuna ordinarily knew only as the driver of his chariot, had also His universal aspect, of which, too, Arjuna had a vision one day, and that day he saw the Truth. I have seen your Universal Aspect in my country. The Ganges and the Brahmaputra are the chains of gold that wind round and round your neck; in the woodland fringes on the distant banks of the dark waters of the river, I have seen your collyrium-darkened eyelashes; the changeful sheen of your *sari* moves for me in the play of light and shade amongst the swaying shoots of green corn; and the blazing summer heat, which makes the whole sky lie gasping like a red-tongued lion in the desert, is nothing but your cruel radiance.

"Since the goddess has vouchsafed her presence to her votary in such wonderful guise, it is for me to proclaim her worship throughout our land, and then shall the country gain new life. 'Your image make we in temple after temple.' But this our people have not yet fully realized. So I would call on them in your name and offer for their worship an image from which none shall be able to withhold belief. Oh give me this boon, this power."

Bimala's eyelids drooped and she became rigid in her seat like a figure of stone. Had I continued she would have gone off into a trance. When I ceased speaking she opened wide her eyes, and murmured with fixed gaze, as though still dazed: "O Traveller in the path of Destruction! Who is there that can stay your progress? Do I not see that none shall stand in the way of your desires? Kings shall lay their crowns at your feet; the wealthy shall hasten to throw open their treasure for your acceptance; those who have nothing else shall beg to be allowed to offer their lives. O my king, my god! What you have seen in me I know not, but I have seen the immensity of your grandeur in my heart. Who am I, what am I, in its presence? Ah, the awful power of Devastation! Never shall I truly live till it kills me utterly! I can bear it no longer, my heart is breaking!" Bimala slid down from her seat and fell at my feet, which she clasped, and then she sobbed and sobbed and sobbed.

This is hypnotism indeed—the charm which can subdue the world! No materials, no weapons—but just the delusion of irresistible suggestion. Who says "Truth shall Triumph"?" Delusion shall win in the end. The Bengali understood this when he conceived the image of the ten-handed goddess astride her lion, and spread her worship in the land. Bengal must now create a new image to enchant and conquer the world. *Bande Mataram*!

I gently lifted Bimala back into her chair, and lest reaction should set in, I began again without losing time: "Queen! The Divine Mother has laid on me the duty of establishing her worship in the land. But, alas, 1 am poor!"

Bimala was still flushed, her eyes clouded, her accents thick, as she replied: "You poor? Is not all that each one has yours? What are my caskets full of jewellery for? Drag away from me all my gold and gems for your worship. I have no use for them!" Once before Bimala had offered up her ornaments. I am not usually in the habit of drawing lines, but I felt I had to draw the line there. I know why I feel this hesitation. It is for man to give ornaments to woman; to take them from her wounds his manliness.

But I must forget myself. Am I taking them? They are for the Divine Mother, to be poured in worship at her feet. Oh, but it must be a grand ceremony of worship such as the country has never beheld before. It must be a landmark in our history. It shall be my supreme legacy to the Nation. Ignorant men worship gods. I, Sandip, shall create them.

But all this is a far cry. What about the urgent immediate? At least three thousand is indispensably necessary—five thousand would do roundly and nicely. But how on earth am I to mention money after the high flight we have just taken? And yet time is precious!

I crushed all hesitation under foot as I jumped up and made my plunge: "Queen! Our purse is empty, our work about to stop!" Bimala winced. I could see she was thinking of that impossible fifty thousand rupees. What a load she must have been carrying within her bosom, struggling under it, perhaps, through sleepless nights! What else had she with which to express her loving worship? Debarred from offering her heart at my feet, she hankers to make this sum of money, so hopelessly large for her, the bearer of her imprisoned feelings. The thought of what she must have gone through gives me a twinge of pain; for she is now wholly mine. The wrench of plucking up the plant by the roots is over. It is now only careful tending and nurture that is needed.

"Queen!" said I, "that fifty thousand rupees is not particularly wanted just now. I calculate that, for the present, five thousand or even three will serve."

The relief made her heart rebound. "I shall fetch you five thousand," she said in tones which seemed like an outburst of song—the song which Radhika of the Vaishnava lyrics sang:

For my lover will I bind in my hair

The flower which has no equal in the three worlds!

—it is the same tune, the same song: five thousand will I bring! That flower will I bind in my hair!

The narrow restraint of the flute brings out this quality of song. I must not allow the pressure of too much greed to flatten out the reed, for then, as I fear, music will give place to the questions "Why?" "What is the use of so much?" "How am I to get it?"—not a word of which will rhyme with what Radhika sang! So, as I was saying, illusion alone is real—it is the flute itself; while truth is but its empty hollow. Nikhil has of late got a taste of that pure emptiness—one can see it in his face, which pains even me. But it was Nikhil's boast that he wanted the Truth, while mine was that I would never let go illusion from my grasp. Each has been suited to his taste, so why complain?

To keep Bimala's heart in the rarefied air of idealism, I cut short all further discussion over the five thousand rupees. I reverted to the demon-destroying goddess and her worship. When was the ceremony to be held and where? There is a great annual fair at Ruimari, within Nikhil's estates, where hundreds of thousands of pilgrims assemble. That would be a grand place to inaugurate the worship of our goddess!

Bimala waxed intensely enthusiastic. This was not the burning of foreign cloth or the people's granaries, so even Nikhil could have no objection—so thought she. But I smiled inwardly. How little these two persons, who have been together, day and night, for nine whole years, know of each other! They know something perhaps of their home life, but when it comes to outside concerns they are entirely at sea. They had cherished the belief that the harmony of the home with the outside was perfect. Today they realize to their cost that it is too late to repair their neglect of years, and seek to harmonize them now.

What does it matter? Let those who have made the mistake learn their error by knocking against the world. Why need I bother about their plight? For the present I find it wearisome to keep Bimala soaring much longer, like a captive balloon, in regions ethereal. I had better get quite through with the matter in hand.

When Bimala rose to depart and had neared the door I remarked in my most casual manner: "So, about the money . . ."

Bimala halted and faced back as she said: "On the expiry of the month, when our personal allowances become due . . ."

"That, I am afraid, would be much too late."

"When do you want it then?"

"Tomorrow.

"Tomorrow you shall have it."

NIKHIL'S STORY

Paragraph and letters against me have begun to come out in the local papers; cartoons and lampoons are to follow, I am told. Jets of wit and humour are being splashed about, and the lies thus scattered are convulsing the whole country. They know that the monopoly of mud-throwing is theirs, and the innocent passer-by cannot escape unsoiled.

They are saying that the residents in my estates, from the highest to the lowest, are in favour of *Swadeshi*, but they dare not declare themselves, for fear of me. The few who have been brave enough to defy me have felt the full rigour of my persecution. I am in secret league with the police, and in private communication with the magistrate, and these frantic efforts of mine to add a foreign title of my own earning to the one I have inherited, will not, it is opined, go in vain.

On the other hand, the papers are full of praise for those devoted sons of the motherland, the Kundu and the Chakravarti *zamindars*. If only, say they, the country had a few more of such staunch patriots, the mills of Manchester would have, had to sound their own dirge to the tune of *Bande Mataram*.

Then comes a letter in blood-red ink, giving a list of the traitorous *zamindars* whose treasuries have been burnt down because of their failing to support the Cause. Holy Fire, it goes on to say, has been aroused to its sacred function of purifying the country; and other agencies are also at work to see that those who are not true sons of the motherland do cease to encumber her lap. The signature is an obvious *nom-de-plume*.

I could see that this was the doing of our local students. So I sent for some of them and showed them the letter.

The B.A. student gravely informed me that they also had heard that a band of desperate patriots had been formed who would stick at nothing in order to clear away all obstacles to the success of *Swadeshi*.

"If," said I, "even one of our countrymen succumbs to these overbearing desperadoes, that will indeed be a defeat for the country!"

"We fail to follow you, Maharaja," said the history student.

"'Our country," I tried to explain, "has been brought to death's door through sheer fear—from fear of the gods down to fear of the police; and if you set up, in the name of freedom, the fear of some other bogey, whatever it may be called; if you would raise your victorious standard on the cowardice of the country by means of downright oppression, then no true lover of the country can bow to your decision."

"Is there any country, sir," pursued the history student, "where submission to Government is not due to fear?"

"The freedom that exists in any country," I replied, "may be measured by the extent of this reign of fear. Where its threat is confined to those who would hurt or plunder, there the Government may claim to have freed man from the violence of man. But if fear is to regulate how people are to dress, where they shall trade, or what they must eat, then is man's freedom of will utterly ignored, and manhood destroyed at the root."

"Is not such coercion of the individual will seen in other countries too?" continued the history student.

"Who denies it?" I exclaimed. "But in every country man has destroyed himself to the extent that he has permitted slavery to flourish."

"Does it not rather show," interposed a Master of Arts, "that trading in slavery is inherent in man—a fundamental fact of his nature?"

"Sandip Babu made the whole thing clear," said a graduate. "He gave us the example of Harish Kundu, your neighbouring *zamindar*. From his estates you cannot ferret out a single ounce of foreign salt. Why? Because he has always ruled with an iron hand. In the case of those who are slaves by nature, the lack of a strong master is the greatest of all calamities."

"Why, sir!" chimed in an undergraduate, "have you not heard of the obstreperous tenant of Chakravarti, the other *zamindar* close by—how the law was set on him till he was reduced to utter destitution? When at last he was left with nothing to eat, he started out to sell his wife's silver ornaments, but no one dared buy them. Then Chakravarti's manager offered him five rupees for the lot. They were worth over thirty, but he had to accept or starve. After taking over the bundle from him the manager coolly said that those five rupees would be credited towards his rent! We felt like having nothing more to do with Chakravarti or his manager after that, but Sandip Babu told us that if we threw over all the live people, we should have only dead bodies from the burning-grounds to carry on the work with! These live men, he pointed out, know what they want and how to get it—they are born rulers. Those who do not know how to desire for themselves, must live in accordance with, or die by virtue of, the desires of such as these. Sandip Babu contrasted them—Kundu and Chakravarti—with you, Maharaja. You, he said, for all your good intentions, will never succeed in planting *Swadeshi* within your territory."

"It is my desire," I said, "to plant something greater than *Swadeshi*. I am not after dead logs but living trees—and these will take time to grow."

"I am afraid, sir," sneered the history student, "that you will get neither log nor tree. Sandip Babu rightly teaches that in order to get, you must snatch. This is taking all of us some time to learn, because it runs counter to what we were taught at school. I have seen with my own eyes that when a rent-collector of Harish Kundu's found one of the tenants with nothing which could be sold up to pay his rent, he was made to sell his young wife!

Buyers were not wanting, and the *zamindar*'s demand was satisfied. I tell you, sir, the sight of that man's distress prevented my getting sleep for nights together! But, feel it as I did, this much I realized, that the man who knows how to get the money he is out for, even by selling up his debtor's wife, is a better man than I am. I confess it is beyond me—I am a weakling, my eyes fill with tears. If anybody can save our country it is these Kundus and these Chakravartis and their officials!"

I was shocked beyond words. "If what you say be true," I cried, "I clearly see that it must be the one endeavour of my life to save the country from these same Kundus and Chakravartis and officials. The slavery that has entered into our very bones is breaking out, at this opportunity, as ghastly tyranny. You have been so used to submit to domination through fear, you have come to believe that to make others submit is a kind of religion. My fight shall be against this weakness, this atrocious cruelty!" These things, which are so simple to ordinary folk, get so twisted in the minds of our B.A.'s and M.A.'s, the only purpose of whose historical quibbles seems to be to torture the truth!

I am worried over Panchu's sham aunt. It will be difficult to disprove her, for though witnesses of a real event may be few or even wanting, innumerable proofs of a thing that has not happened can always be marshalled. The object of this move is, evidently, to get the sale of Panchu's holding to me set aside. Being unable to find any other way out of it, I was thinking of allowing Panchu to hold a permanent tenure in my estates and building him a cottage on it. But my master would not have it. I should not give in to these nefarious tactics so easily, he objected, and offered to attend to the matter himself.

"You, sir!" I cried, considerably surprised.

"Yes, I," he repeated.

I could not see, at all clearly, what my master could do to counteract these legal machinations. That evening, at the time he usually came to me, he did not turn up. On my making inquiries, his servant said he had left home with a few things packed in a small trunk, and some bedding, saying he would be back in a few days. I thought he might have sallied forth to hunt for witnesses in Panchu's uncle's village. In that case, however, I was. sure that his would be a hopeless quest . . .

During the day I forget myself in my work. As the late autumn afternoon wears on, the colours of the sky become turbid, and so do the feelings of my mind. There are many in this world whose minds dwell in brick-built houses—they can afford to ignore the thing called the outside. But my mind lives under the trees in the open, directly receives upon itself the messages borne by the free winds, and responds from the bottom of its heart to all the musical cadences of light and darkness. While the day is bright and the world in the pursuit of its numberless tasks crowds around, then it seems as if my life wants nothing else. But when the colours of the sky fade away and the blinds are drawn down over the windows of heaven, then my heart tells me that evening falls just for the purpose of shutting out the world, to mark the time when the darkness must be filled with the One. This is the end to which earth, sky, and waters conspire, and I cannot harden myself against accepting its meaning. So when the gloaming deepens over the world, like the gaze of the dark eyes of the beloved, then my whole being tells me that work alone cannot be the truth of life, that work is not the be-all and the end-all of man, for man is not simply a serf—even though the serfdom be of the True and the Good.

Alas, Nikhil, have you for ever parted company with that self of yours who used to be set free under the starlight, to plunge into the infinite depths of the night's darkness after the day's work was done? How terribly alone is he, who misses companionship in the midst of the multitudinousness of life.

The other day, when the afternoon had reached the meeting-point of day and night, I had no work, nor the mind for work, nor was my master there to keep me company. With my empty, drifting heart longing to anchor on to something, I traced my steps towards the inner gardens. I was very fond of chrysanthemums and had rows of them, of all varieties, banked up in pots against one of the garden walls. When they were in flower, it looked like a wave of green breaking into iridescent foam. It was some time since I had been to this part of the grounds, and I was beguiled into a cheerful expectancy at the thought of meeting my chrysanthemums after our long separation.

As I went in, the full moon had just peeped over the wall, her slanting rays leaving its foot in deep shadow. It seemed as if she had come a-tiptoe from behind, and clasped the darkness over the eyes, smiling mischievously. When I came near the bank of chrysanthemums, I saw a figure stretched on the grass in front. My heart gave a sudden thud. The figure also sat up with a start at my footsteps.

What was to be done next? I was wondering whether it would do to beat a precipitate retreat. Bimala, also, was doubtless casting about for some way of escape. But it was as awkward to go as to stay! Before I could make up my mind, Bimala rose, pulled the end of her *sari* over her head, and walked off towards the inner apartments.

This brief pause had been enough to make real to me the cruel load of Bimala's misery. The plaint of my own life vanished from me in a moment. I called out: "Bimala!"

She started and stayed her steps, but did not turn back. I went round and stood before her. Her face was in the shade, the moonlight fell on mine. Her eyes were downcast, her hands clenched.

"Bimala," said I, "why should I seek to keep you fast in this closed cage of mine? Do I not know that thus you cannot but pine and droop?"

She stood still, without raising her eyes or uttering a word.

"I know," I continued, "that if I insist on keeping you shackled my whole life will be reduced to nothing but an iron chain. What pleasure can that be to me?"

She was still silent.

"So," I concluded, "I tell you, truly, Bimala, you are free. Whatever I may or may not have been to you, I refuse to be your fetters." With which I came away towards the outer apartments.

No, no, it was not a generous impulse, nor indifference. I had simply come to understand that never would I be free until I could set free. To try to keep Bimala as a garland round my neck, would have meant keeping a weight hanging over my heart. Have I not been praying with all my strength, that if happiness may not be mine, let it go; if grief needs must be my lot, let it come; but let me not be kept in bondage. To clutch hold of that which is untrue as though it were true, is only to throttle oneself. May I be saved from such self-destruction.

When I entered my room, I found my master waiting there. My agitated feelings were still heaving within me. "Freedom, sir," I began unceremoniously, without greeting or inquiry, "freedom is the biggest thing for man. Nothing can be compared to it—nothing at all!"

Surprised at my outburst, my master looked up at me in silence.

"One can understand nothing from books," I went on. "We read in the scriptures that our desires are bonds, fettering us as well as others. But such words, by themselves, are so empty. It is only when we get to the point of letting the bird out of its cage that we can realize how free the bird has set us. Whatever we cage, shackles us with desire whose bonds are stronger than those of iron chains. I tell you, sir, this is just what the world has failed to understand. They all seek to reform something outside themselves. But reform is wanted only in one's own desires, nowhere else, nowhere else!"

"We think," he said, "that we are our own masters when we get in our hands the object of our desire—but we are really our own masters only when we are able to cast out our desires from our minds."

"When we put all this into words, sir," I went on, "it sounds like some bald-headed injunction, but when we realize even a little of it we find it to be *amrita*—which the gods have drunk and become immortal. We cannot see Beauty till we let go our hold of it. It was Buddha who conquered the world, not Alexander—this is untrue when stated in dry prose—oh when shall we be able to sing it? When shall all these most intimate truths of the universe overflow the pages of printed books and leap out in a sacred stream like the Ganges from the Gangotrie?"

I was suddenly reminded of my master's absence during the last few days and of my ignorance as to its reason. I felt somewhat foolish as I asked him: "And where have you been all this while, sir?"

"Staying with Panchu," he replied.

"Indeed!" I exclaimed. "Have you been there all these days?"

"Yes. I wanted to come to an understanding with the woman who calls herself his aunt. She could hardly be induced to believe that there could be such an odd character among the gentlefolk as the one who sought their hospitality. When she found I really meant to stay on, she began to feel rather ashamed of herself. 'Mother,' said I, 'you are not going to get rid of me, even if you abuse me! And so long as I stay, Panchu stays also. For you see, do you not, that I cannot stand by and see his motherless little ones sent out into the streets?'

"She listened to my talks in this strain for a couple of days without saying yes or no. This morning I found her tying up her bundles. 'We are going back to Brindaban,' she said. 'Let us have our expenses for the journey.' I knew she was not going to Brindaban, and also that the cost of her journey would be substantial. So I have come to you."

"The required cost shall be paid," I said.

"The old woman is not a bad sort," my master went on musingly. "Panchu was not sure of her caste, and would not let her touch the water-jar, or anything at all of his. So they were continually bickering. When she found I had no objection to her touch, she looked after me devotedly. She is a splendid cook!

"But all remnants of Panchu's respect for me vanished! To the last he had thought that I was at least a simple sort of person. But here was I, risking my caste without a qualm to win over the old woman for my purpose. Had I tried to steal a march on her by tutoring a witness for the trial, that would have been a different matter. Tactics must be met by tactics. But stratagem at the expense of orthodoxy is more than he can tolerate!

"Anyhow, I must stay on a few days at Panchu's even after the woman leaves, for Harish Kundu may be up to any kind of devilry. He has been telling his satellites that he was content to have furnished Panchu with an aunt, but I have gone the length of supplying him with a father. He would like to see, now, how many fathers of his can save him!"

"We may or may not be able to save him," I said; "but if we should perish in the attempt to save the country from the thousand-and-one snares—of religion, custom and selfishness—which these people are busy spreading, we shall at least die happy."

Who could have thought that so much would happen in this one life? I feel as if I have passed through a whole series of births, time has been flying so fast, I did not feel it move at all, till the shock came the other day.

I knew there would be words between us when I made up my mind to ask my husband to banish foreign goods from our market. But it was my firm belief that I had no need to meet argument by argument, for there was magic in the very air about me. Had not so tremendous a man as Sandip fallen helplessly at my feet, like a wave of the mighty sea breaking on the shore? Had I called him? No, it was the summons of that magic spell of mine. And Amulya, poor dear boy, when he first came to me—how the current of his life flushed with colour, like the river at dawn! Truly have I realized how a goddess feels when she looks upon the radiant face of her devotee.

With the confidence begotten of these proofs of my power, I was ready to meet my husband like a lightning-charged cloud. But what was it that happened? Never in all these nine years have I seen such a far-away, distraught look in his eyes—like the desert sky—with no merciful moisture of its own, no colour reflected, even, from what it looked upon. I should have been so relieved if his anger had flashed out! But I could find nothing in him which I could touch. I felt as unreal as a dream—a dream which would leave only the blackness of night when it was over.

In the old days I used to be jealous of my sister-in-law for her beauty. Then I used to feel that Providence had given me no power of my own, that my whole strength lay in the love which my husband had bestowed on me. Now that I had drained to the dregs the cup of power and could not do without its intoxication, I suddenly found it dashed to pieces at my feet, leaving me nothing to live for.

How feverishly I had sat to do my hair that day. Oh, shame, shame on me, the utter shame of it! My sister-in-law, when passing by, had exclaimed: "Aha, Chota Rani! Your hair seems ready to jump off. Don't let it carry your head with it."

And then, the other day in the garden, how easy my husband found it to tell me that he set me free! But can freedom—empty freedom—be given and taken so easily as all that? It is like setting a fish free in the sky—for how can I move or live outside the atmosphere of loving care which has always sustained me?

When I came to my room today, I saw only furniture—only the bedstead, only the looking-glass, only the clothes-rack—not the all-pervading heart which used to be there, over all. Instead of it there was freedom, only freedom, mere emptiness! A dried-up watercourse with all its rocks and pebbles laid bare. No feeling, only furniture!

When I had arrived at a state of utter bewilderment, wondering whether anything true was left in my life, and whereabouts it could be, I happened to meet Sandip again. Then life struck against life, and the sparks flew in the same old way. Here was truth—impetuous truth—which rushed in and overflowed all bounds, truth which was a thousand times truer than the Bara Rani with her maid, Thako and her silly songs, and all the rest of them who talked and laughed and wandered about . . .

"Fifty thousand!" Sandip had demanded.

"What is fifty thousand?" cried my intoxicated heart. "You shall have it!"

How to get it, where to get it, were minor points not worth troubling over. Look at me. Had I not risen, all in one moment, from my nothingness to a height above everything? So shall all things come at my beck and call. I shall get it, get it, get it—there cannot be any doubt.

Thus had I come away from Sandip the other day. Then as I looked about me, where was it—the tree of plenty? Oh, why does this outer world insult the heart so?

And yet get it I must; how, I do not care; for sin there cannot be. Sin taints only the weak; I with my *Shakti* am beyond its reach. Only a commoner can be a thief, the king conquers and takes his rightful spoil . . . I must find out where the treasury is; who takes the money in; who guards it.

I spent half the night standing in the outer verandah peering at the row of office buildings. But how to get that fifty thousand rupees out of the clutches of those iron bars? If by some *mantram* I could have made all those guards fall dead in their places, I would not have hesitated—so pitiless did I feel!

But while a whole gang of robbers seemed dancing a war-dance within the whirling brain of its Rani, the great house of the Rajas slept in peace. The gong of the watch sounded hour after hour, and the sky overhead placidly looked on.

At last I sent for Amulya.

"Money is wanted for the Cause," I told him. "Can you not get it out of the treasury?"

"Why not?" said he, with his chest thrown out.

Alas! had I not said "Why not?" to Sandip just in the same way? The poor lad's confidence could rouse no hopes in my mind.

"How will you do it?" I asked.

The wild plans he began to unfold would hardly bear repetition outside the pages of a penny dreadful.

"No, Amulya," I said severely, "you must not be childish."

"Very well, then," he said, "let me bribe those watchmen."

"Where is the money to come from?"

"I can loot the bazar," he burst out, without blenching.

"Leave all that alone. I have my ornaments, they will serve.

"But," said Amulya, "it strikes me that the cashier cannot be bribed. Never mind, there is another and simpler way."

"What is that?"

"Why need you hear it? It is quite simple."

"Still, I should like to know."

Amulya fumbled in the pocket of his tunic and pulled out, first a small edition of the Gita, which he placed on the table—and then a little pistol, which he showed me, but said nothing further.

Horror! It did not take him a moment to make up his mind to kill our good old cashier! To look at his frank, open face one would not have thought him capable of hurting a fly, but how different were the words which came from his mouth. It was clear that the cashier's place in the world meant nothing real to him; it was a mere vacancy, lifeless, feelingless, with only stock phrases from the Gita—*Who kills the body kills naught!*

"Whatever do you mean, Amulya?" I exclaimed at length. "Don't you know that the dear old man has got a wife and children and that he is . . ."

"Where are we to find men who have no wives and children?" he interrupted. "Look here, Maharani, the thing we call pity is, at bottom, only pity for ourselves. We cannot bear to wound our own tender instincts, and so we do not strike at all—pity indeed! The height of cowardice!"

To hear Sandip's phrases in the mouth of this mere boy staggered me. So delightfully, lovably immature was he—of that age when the good may still be believed in as good, of that age when one really lives and grows. The Mother in me awoke.

For myself there was no longer good or bad—only death, beautiful alluring death. But to hear this stripling calmly talk of murdering an inoffensive old man as the right thing to do, made me shudder all over. The more clearly I saw that there was no sin in his heart, the more horrible appeared to me the sin of his words. I seemed to see the sin of the parents visited on the innocent child.

The sight of his great big eyes shining with faith and enthusiasm touched me to the quick. He was going, in his fascination, straight to the jaws of the python, from which, once in, there was no return. How was he to be saved? Why does not my country become, for once, a real Mother—clasp him to her bosom and cry out: "Oh, my child, my child, what profits it that you should save me, if so it be that I should fail to save you?"

I know, I know, that all Power on earth waxes great under compact with Satan. But the Mother is there, alone though she be, to contemn and stand against this devil's progress. The Mother cares not for mere success, however great—she wants to give life, to save life. My very soul, today, stretches out its hands in yearning to save this child.

A while ago I suggested robbery to him. Whatever I may now say against it will be put down to a woman's weakness. They only love our weakness when it drags the world in its toils!

"You need do nothing at all, Amulya, I will see to the money," I told him finally. When he had almost reached the door, I called him back.

"Amulya," said I, "I am your elder sister. Today is not the Brothers' Day according to the calendar, but all the days in the year are really Brothers' Days. My blessing be with you: may God keep you always."

These unexpected words from my lips took Amulya by surprise. He stood stock-still for a time. Then, coming to himself, he prostrated himself at my feet in acceptance of the relationship and did me reverence. When he rose his eyes were full of tears... O little brother mine! I am fast going to my death—let me take all your sin away with me. May no taint from me ever tarnish your innocence! I said to him: "Let your offering of reverence be that pistol!"

"What do you want with it, sister?"

"I will practise death."

"Right, sister. Our women, also, must know how to die, to deal death!" with which Amulya handed me the pistol. The radiance of his youthful countenance seemed to tinge my life with the touch of a new dawn. I put away the pistol within my clothes. May this reverence-offering be the last resource in my extremity . . .

The door to the mother's chamber in my woman's heart once opened, I thought it would always remain open. But this pathway to the supreme good was closed when the mistress took the place of the mother and locked it again. The very next day I saw Sandip; and madness, naked and rampant, danced upon my heart.

What was this? Was this, then, my truer self? Never! I had never before known this shameless, this cruel one within me. The snake-charmer had come, pretending to draw this snake from within the fold of my garment—but it was never there, it was his all the time. Some demon has gained possession of me, and what I am doing today is the play of his activity—it has nothing to do with me.

This demon, in the guise of a god, had come with his ruddy torch to call me that day, saying: "I am your Country. I am your Sandip. I am more to you than anything else of yours. *Bande Mataram*!" And with folded hands I had responded: "You are my religion. You are my heaven. Whatever else is mine shall be swept away before my love for you. *Bande Mataram*!"

Five thousand is it? Five thousand it shall be! You want it tomorrow? Tomorrow you shall have it! In this desperate orgy, that gift of five thousand shall be as the foam of wine—and then for the riotous revel!

The immovable world shall sway under our feet, fire shall flash from our eyes, a storm shall roar in our ears, what is or is not in front shall become equally dim. And then with tottering footsteps we shall plunge to our death—in a moment all fire will be extinguished, the ashes will be scattered, and nothing will remain behind.

For a time I was utterly at a loss to think of any way of getting that money. Then, the other day, in the light of intense excitement, suddenly the whole picture stood out clear before me.

Every year my husband makes a reverence-offering of six thousand rupees to my sister-in-law at the time of the Durga Puja. Every year it is deposited in her account at the bank in Calcutta. This year the offering was made as usual, but it has not yet been sent to the bank, being kept meanwhile in an iron safe, in a corner of the little dressing-room attached to our bedroom.

Every year my husband takes the money to the bank himself. This year he has not yet had an opportunity of going to town. How could I fail to see the hand of Providence in this? The money has been held up because the country wants it—who could have the power to take it away from her to the bank? And how can I have the power to refuse to take the money? The goddess revelling in destruction holds out her blood-cup crying: "Give me drink. I am thirsty." I will give her my own heart's blood with that five thousand rupees. Mother, the loser of that money will scarcely feel the loss, but me you will utterly ruin! Many a time, in the old days, have I inwardly called the Senior Rani a thief, for I charged her with wheedling money out of my trusting husband. After her husband's death, she often used to make away with things belonging to the estate for her own use. This I used to point out to my husband, but he remained silent. I would get angry and say: "If you feel generous, make gifts by all means, but why allow yourself to be robbed?"

Providence must have smiled, then, at these complaints of mine, for tonight I am on the way to rob my husband's safe of my sister-in-law's money. My husband's custom was to let his keys remain in his pockets when he took off his clothes for the night, leaving them in the dressing-room. I picked out the key of the safe and opened it. The slight sound it made seemed to wake the whole world! A sudden chill turned my hands and feet icy cold, and I shivered all over.

There was a drawer inside the safe. On opening this I found the money, not in currency notes, but in gold rolled up in paper. I had no time to count out what I wanted. There were twenty rolls, all of which I took and tied up in a corner of my *sari*.

What a weight it was. The burden of the theft crushed my heart to the dust. Perhaps notes would have made it seem less like thieving, but this was all gold.

After I had stolen into my room like a thief, it felt like my own room no longer. All the most precious rights which I had over it vanished at the touch of my theft. I began to mutter to myself, as though telling *mantrams: Bande Mataram, Bande Mataram*, my Country, my golden Country, all this gold is for you, for none else!

But in the night the mind is weak. I came back into the bedroom where my husband was asleep, closing my eyes as I passed through, and went off to the open terrace beyond, on which I lay prone, clasping to my breast the end of the *sari* tied over the gold. And each one of the rolls gave me a shock of pain.

The silent night stood there with forefinger upraised. I could not think of my house as separate from my country: I had robbed my house, I had robbed my country. For this sin my house had ceased to be mine, my country also was estranged from me. Had I died begging for my country, even unsuccessfully, that would have been worship, acceptable to the gods. But theft is never worship—how then can I offer this gold? Ah me! I am doomed to death myself, must I desecrate my country with my impious touch? The way to put the money back is closed to me. I have not the strength to return to the room, take again that key, open once more that safe—I should swoon on the threshold of my husband's door. The only road left now is the road in front. Neither have I the strength deliberately to sit down and count the coins. Let them remain behind their coverings: I cannot calculate. There was no mist in the winter sky. The stars were shining brightly. If, thought I to myself, as I lay out there, I had to steal these stars one by one, like golden coins, for my country—these stars so carefully stored up in the bosom of the darkness—then the sky would be blinded, the night widowed for ever, and my theft would rob the whole world. But was not also this very thing I had done a robbing of the whole world—not only of money, but of trust, of righteousness?

I spent the night lying on the terrace. When at last it was morning, and I was sure that my husband had risen and left the room, then only with my shawl pulled over my head, could I retrace my steps towards the bedroom. My sister-in-law was about, with her brass pot, watering her plants. When she saw me passing in the distance she cried: "Have you heard the news, Chota Rani?"

I stopped in silence, all in a tremor. It seemed to me that the rolls of sovereigns were bulging through the shawl. I feared they would burst and scatter in a ringing shower, exposing to all the servants of the house the thief who had made herself destitute by robbing her own wealth.

"Your band of robbers," she went on, "have sent an anonymous message threatening to loot the treasury."

I remained as silent as a thief.

"I was advising Brother Nikhil to seek your protection," she continued banteringly. "Call off your minions, Robber Queen!

We will offer sacrifices to your *Bande Mataram* if you will but save us. What doings there are these days!—but for the Lord's sake, spare our house at least from burglary."

I hastened into my room without reply. I had put my foot on quicksand, and could not now withdraw it. Struggling would only send me down deeper.

If only the time would arrive when I could hand over the money to Sandip! I could bear it no longer, its weight was breaking through my very ribs.

It was still early when I got word that Sandip was awaiting me. Today I had no thought of adornment. Wrapped as I was in my shawl, I went off to the outer apartments. As I entered the sitting-room I saw Sandip and Amulya there, together. All my dignity, all my honour, seemed to run tingling through my body from head to foot and vanish into the ground. I should have to lay bare a woman's uttermost shame in sight of this boy! Could they have been discussing my deed in their meeting place? Had any vestige of a veil of decency been left for me?

We women shall never understand men. When they are bent on making a road for some achievement, they think nothing of breaking the heart of the world into pieces to pave it for the progress of their chariot.

When they are mad with the intoxication of creating, they rejoice in destroying the creation of the Creator. This heart-breaking shame of mine will not attract even a glance from their eyes. They have no feeling for life itself—all their eagerness is for their object. What am I to them but a meadow flower in the path of a torrent in flood?

What good will this extinction of me be to Sandip? Only five thousand rupees? Was not I good for something more than only five thousand rupees? Yes, indeed! Did I not learn that from Sandip himself, and was I not able in the light of this knowledge to despise all else in my world? I was the giver of light, of life, of *Shakti*, of immortality—in that belief, in that joy, I had burst all my bounds and come into the open. Had anyone then fulfilled for me that joy, I should have lived in my death. I should have lost nothing in the loss of my all.

Do they want to tell me now that all this was false? The psalm of my praise which was sung so devotedly, did it bring me down from my heaven, not to make heaven of earth, but only to level heaven itself with the dust?

"The money, Queen?" said Sandip with his keen glance full on my face.

Amulya also fixed his gaze on me. Though not my own mother's child, yet the dear lad is brother to me; for mother is mother all the world over. With his guileless face, his gentle eyes, his innocent youth, he looked at me. And I, a woman—of his mother's sex—how could I hand him poison, just because he asked for it?

"The money, Queen!" Sandip's insolent demand rang in my ears. For very shame and vexation I felt I wanted to fling that gold at Sandip's head. I could hardly undo the knot of my *sari*, my fingers trembled so. At last the paper rolls dropped on the table.

Sandip's face grew black . . . He must have thought that the rolls were of silver . . . What contempt was in his looks. What utter disgust at incapacity.

It was almost as if he could have struck me! He must have suspected that I had come to parley with him, to offer to compound his claim for five thousand rupees with a few hundreds. There was a moment when I thought he would snatch up the rolls and throw them out of the window, declaring that he was no beggar, but a king claiming tribute.

"Is that all?" asked Amulya with such pity welling up in his voice that I wanted to sob out aloud. I kept my heart tightly pressed down, and merely nodded my head. Sandip was speechless. He neither touched the rolls, nor uttered a sound.

My humiliation went straight to the boy's heart. With a sudden, feigned enthusiasm he exclaimed: "It's plenty. It will do splendidly. You have saved us." With which he tore open the covering of one of the rolls.

The sovereigns shone out. And in a moment the black covering seemed to be lifted from Sandip's countenance also. His delight beamed forth from his features. Unable to control his sudden revulsion of feeling, he sprang up from his seat towards me. What he intended I know not. I flashed a lightning glance towards Amulya—the colour had left the boy's face as at the stroke of a whip. Then with all my strength I thrust Sandip from me. As he reeled back his head struck the edge of the marble table and he dropped on the floor. There he lay awhile, motionless. Exhausted with my effort, I sank back on my seat.

Amulya's face lightened with a joyful radiance. He did not even turn towards Sandip, but came straight up, took the dust of my feet, and then remained there, sitting on the floor in front of me. O my little brother, my child!

This reverence of yours is the last touch of heaven left in my empty world! I could contain myself no longer, and my tears flowed fast. I covered my eyes with the end of my *sari*, which I pressed to my face with both my hands, and sobbed and sobbed. And every time that I felt on my feet his tender touch trying to comfort me my tears broke out afresh.

After a little, when I had recovered myself and taken my hands from my face, I saw Sandip back at the table, gathering up the sovereigns in his handkerchief, as if nothing had happened. Amulya rose to his seat, from his place near my feet, his wet eyes shining.

Sandip coolly looked up at my face as he remarked: "It is six thousand."

"What do we want with so much, Sandip Babu?" cried Amulya. "Three thousand five hundred is all we need for our work."

"Our wants are not for this one place only," Sandip replied. "We shall want all we can get."

"That may be," said Amulya. "But in future I undertake to get you all you want. Out of this, Sandip Babu, please return the extra two thousand five hundred to the Maharani."

Sandip glanced enquiringly at me.

"No, no," I exclaimed. "I shall never touch that money again. Do with it as you will."

"Can man ever give as woman can?" said Sandip, looking towards Amulya.

"They are goddesses!" agreed Amulya with enthusiasm.

"We men can at best give of our power," continued Sandip. "But women give themselves. Out of their own life they give birth, out of their own life they give sustenance. Such gifts are the only true gifts." Then turning to me, "Queen!" said he, "if what you have given us had been only money I would not have touched it. But you have given that which is more to you than life itself!"

There must be two different persons inside men. One of these in me can understand that Sandip is trying to delude me; the other is content to be deluded. Sandip has power, but no strength of righteousness. The weapon of his which rouses up life smites it again to death. He has the unfailing quiver of the gods, but the shafts in them are of the demons.

Sandip's handkerchief was not large enough to hold all the coins. "Queen," he asked, "can you give me another?" When I gave him mine, he reverently touched his forehead with it, and then suddenly kneeling on the floor he made me an obeisance. "Goddess!" he said, "it was to offer my reverence that I had approached you, but you repulsed me, and rolled me in the dust. Be it so, I accept your repulse as your boon to me, I raise it to my head in salutation!" with which he pointed to the place where he had been hurt.

Had I then misunderstood him? Could it be that his outstretched hands had really been directed towards my feet? Yet, surely, even Amulya had seen the passion that flamed out of his eyes, his face. But Sandip is such an adept in setting music to his chant of praise that I cannot argue; I lose my power of seeing truth; my sight is clouded over like an opium-eater's eyes. And so, after all, he gave me back twice as much in return for the blow I had dealt him—the wound on his head ended by making me bleed at heart. When I had received Sandip's obeisance my theft seemed to gain a dignity, and the gold glittering on the table to smile away all fear of disgrace, all stings of conscience.

Like me Amulya also was won back. His devotion to Sandip, which had suffered a momentary check, blazed up anew. The flower-vase of his mind filled once more with offerings for the worship of Sandip and me.

His simple faith shone out of his eyes with the pure light of the morning star at dawn. After I had offered worship and received worship my sin became radiant. And as Amulya looked on my face he raised his folded hands in salutation and cried *Bande Mataram*! I cannot expect to have this adoration surrounding me for ever; and yet this has come to be the only means of keeping alive my self-respect.

I can no longer enter my bedroom. The bedstead seems to thrust out a forbidding hand, the iron safe frowns at me. I want to get away from this continual insult to myself which is rankling within me.

I want to keep running to Sandip to hear him sing my praises. There is just this one little altar of worship which has kept its head above the all-pervading depths of my dishonour, and so I want to cleave to it night and day; for on whichever side I step away from it, there is only emptiness.

Praise, praise, I want unceasing praise. I cannot live if my wine-cup be left empty for a single moment. So, as the very price of my life, I want Sandip of all the world, today.

When my husband nowadays comes in for his meals I feel I cannot sit before him; and yet it is such a shame not to be near him that I feel I cannot do that either. So I seat myself where we cannot look at each other's face. That was how I was sitting the other day when the Bara Rani came and joined us.

"It is all very well for you, brother," said she, "to laugh away these threatening letters. But they do frighten me so. Have you sent off that money you gave me to the Calcutta bank?"

"No, I have not yet had the time to get it away," my husband replied.

"You are so careless, brother dear, you had better look out..."

"But it is in the iron safe right inside the inner dressing-room," said my husband with a reassuring smile.

"What if they get in there? You can never tell!"

"If they go so far, they might as well carry you off too!"

"Don't you fear, no one will come for poor me. The real attraction is in your room! But joking apart, don't run the risk of keeping money in the room like that."

"They will be taking along the Government revenue to Calcutta in a few days now; I will send this money to the bank under the same escort."

"Very well. But see you don't forget all about it, you are so absent-minded."

"Even if that money gets lost, while in my room, the loss cannot be yours, Sister Rani."

"Now, now, brother, you will make me very angry if you talk in that way. Was I making any difference between yours and mine? What if your money is lost, does not that hurt me? If Providence has thought fit to take away my all, it has not left me insensible to the value of the most devoted brother known since the days of Lakshman."

"Well, Junior Rani, are you turned into a wooden doll? You have not spoken a word yet. Do you know, brother, our Junior Rani thinks I try to flatter you. If things came to that pass I should not hesitate to do so, but I know my dear old brother does not need it!"

Thus the Senior Rani chattered on, not forgetting now and then to draw her brother's attention to this or that special delicacy amongst the dishes that were being served. My head was all the time in a whirl. The crisis was fast coming. Something must be done about replacing that money. And as I kept asking myself what could be done, and how it was to be done, the unceasing patter of my sister-in-law's words seemed more and more intolerable.

What made it all the worse was, that nothing could escape my sister-in-law's keen eyes. Every now and then she was casting side glances towards me. What she could read in my face I do not know, but to me it seemed that everything was written there only too plainly.

Then I did an infinitely rash thing. Affecting an easy, amused laugh I said: "All the Senior Rani's suspicions, I see, are reserved for me—her fears of thieves and robbers are only a feint."

The Senior Rani smiled mischievously. "You are right, sister mine. A woman's theft is the most fatal of all thefts. But how can you elude my watchfulness? Am I a man, that you should hoodwink me?"

"If you fear me so," I retorted, "let me keep in your hands all I have, as security. If I cause you loss, you can then repay yourself."

"Just listen to her, our simple little Junior Rani!" she laughed back, turning to my husband. "Does she not know that there are losses which no security can make good, either in this world or in the next?"

My husband did not join in our exchange of words. When he had finished, he went off to the outer apartments, for nowadays he does not take his mid-day rest in our room.

All my more valuable jewels were in deposit in the treasury in charge of the cashier. Still what I kept with me must have been worth thirty or forty thousand. I took my jewel-box to the Bara Rani's room and opened it out before her, saying: "I leave these with you, sister. They will keep you quite safe from all worry."

The Bara Rani made a gesture of mock despair. "You positively astound me, Chota Rani!" she said. "Do you really suppose I spend sleepless nights for fear of being robbed by you?"

"What harm if you did have a wholesome fear of me? Does anybody know anybody else in this world?"

"You want to teach me a lesson by trusting me? No, no! I am bothered enough to know what to do with my own jewels, without keeping watch over yours. Take them away, there's a dear, so many prying servants are about."

I went straight from my sister-in-law's room to the sitting-room outside, and sent for Amulya. With him Sandip came along too. I was in a great hurry, and said to Sandip: "If you don't mind, I want to have a word or two with Amulya. Would you. . ."

Sandip smiled a wry smile. "So Amulya and I are separate in your eyes? If you have set about to wean him from me, I must confess I have no power to retain him."

I made no reply, but stood waiting.

"Be it so," Sandip went on. "Finish your special talk with Amulya. But then you must give me a special talk all to myself too, or it will mean a defeat for me.

I can stand everything, but not defeat. My share must always be the lion's share. This has been my constant quarrel with Providence. I will defeat the Dispenser of my fate, but not take defeat at his hands." With a crushing look at Amulya, Sandip walked out of the room.

"Amulya, my own little brother, you must do one thing for me," I said.

"I will stake my life for whatever duty you may lay on me, sister."

I brought out my jewel-box from the folds of my shawl and placed it before him. "Sell or pawn these," I said, "and get me six thousand rupees as fast as ever you can."

"No, no, Sister Rani," said Amulya, touched to the quick. "Let these jewels be. I will get you six thousand all the same."

"Oh, don't be silly," I said impatiently. "There is no time for any nonsense. Take this box. Get away to Calcutta by the night train. And bring me the money by the day after tomorrow positively."

Amulya took a diamond necklace out of the box, held it up to the light and put it back gloomily.

"I know," I told him, "that you will never get the proper price for these diamonds, so I am giving you jewels worth about thirty thousand. I don't care if they all go, but I must have that six thousand without fail."

"Do you know, Sister Rani," said Amulya, "I have had a quarrel with Sandip Babu over that six thousand rupees he took from you? I cannot tell you how ashamed I felt. But Sandip Babu would have it that we must give up even our shame for the country. That may be so.

But this is somehow different. I do not fear to die for the country, to kill for the country—that much *Shakti* has been given me. But I cannot forget the shame of having taken money from you. There Sandip Babu is ahead of me. He has no regrets or compunctions. He says we must get rid of the idea that the money belongs to the one in whose box it happens to be—if we cannot, where is the magic of *Bande Mataram*?"

Amulya gathered enthusiasm as he talked on. He always warms up when he has me for a listener. "The Gita tells us," he continued, "that no one can kill the soul. Killing is a mere word. So also is the taking away of money. Whose is the money? No one has created it. No one can take it away with him when he departs this life, for it is no part of his soul.

Today it is mine, tomorrow my son's, the next day his creditor's. Since, in fact, money belongs to no one, why should any blame attach to our patriots if, instead of leaving it for some worthless son, they take it for their own use?"

When I hear Sandip's words uttered by this boy, I tremble all over. Let those who are snake-charmers play with snakes; if harm comes to them, they are prepared for it. But these boys are so innocent, all the world is ready with its blessing to protect them.

They play with a snake not knowing its nature, and when we see them smilingly, trustfully, putting their hands within reach of its fangs, then we understand how terribly dangerous the snake is. Sandip is right when he suspects that though I, for myself, may be ready to die at his hands, this boy I shall wean from him and save.

"So the money is wanted for the use of your patriots?" I questioned with a smile.

"Of course it is!" said Amulya proudly. "Are they not our kings? Poverty takes away from their regal power. Do you know, we always insist on Sandip Babu travelling First Class? He never shirks kingly honours—he accepts them not for himself, but for the glory of us all.

The greatest weapon of those who rule the world, Sandip Babu has told us, is the hypnotism of their display. To take the vow of poverty would be for them not merely a penance—it would mean suicide."

At this point Sandip noiselessly entered the room. I threw my shawl over the jewel-case with a rapid movement.

"The special-talk business not yet over?" he asked with a sneer in his tone.

"Yes, we've quite finished," said Amulya apologetically. "It was nothing much."

"No, Amulya," I said, "we have not quite finished."

"So exit Sandip for the second time, I suppose?" said Sandip.

"If you please."

"And as to Sandip's re-entry .

"Not today. I have no time."

"I see!" said Sandip as his eyes flashed. "No time to waste, only for special talks!"

Jealousy! Where the strong man shows weakness, there the weaker sex cannot help beating her drums of victory. So I repeated firmly: "I really have no time."

Sandip went away looking black. Amulya was greatly perturbed. "Sister Rani," he pleaded, "Sandip Babu is annoyed."

"He has neither cause nor right to be annoyed," I said with some vehemence. "Let me caution you about one thing, Amulya. Say nothing to Sandip Babu about the sale of my jewels—on your life."

"No, I will not."

"Then you had better not delay any more. You must get away by tonight's train."

Amulya and I left the room together. As we came out on the verandah Sandip was standing there. I could see he was waiting to waylay Amulya. To prevent that I had to engage him. "What is it you wanted to tell me, Sandip Babu?" I asked.

"I have nothing special to say—mere small talk. And since you have not the time . . "

"I can give you just a little."

By this time Amulya had left. As we entered the room Sandip asked: "What was that box Amulya carried away?"

The box had not escaped his eyes. I remained firm. "If I could have told you, it would have been made over to him in your presence!"

"So you think Amulya will not tell me?"

"No, he will not."

Sandip could not conceal his anger any longer. You think you will gain the mastery over me?" he blazed out.

"That shall never be. Amulya, there, would die a happy death if I deigned to trample him under foot. I will never, so long as I live, allow you to bring him to your feet!"

Oh, the weak! the weak! At last Sandip has realized that he is weak before me! That is why there is this sudden outburst of anger.

He has understood that he cannot meet the power that I wield, with mere strength. With a glance I can crumble his strongest fortifications. So he must needs resort to bluster. I simply smiled in contemptuous silence.

At last have I come to a level above him. I must never lose this vantage ground; never descend lower again. Amidst all my degradation this bit of dignity must remain to me!

"I know," said Sandip, after a pause, "it was your jewel-case."

"You may guess as you please," said I, "but you will get nothing out of me.

"So you trust Amulya more than you trust me? Do you know that the boy is the shadow of my shadow, the echo of my echo—that he is nothing if I am not at his side?"

"Where he is not your echo, he is himself, Amulya. And that is where I trust him more than I can trust your echo!"

"You must not forget that you are under a promise to render up all your ornaments to me for the worship of the Divine Mother. In fact your offering has already been made."

"Whatever ornaments the gods leave to me will be offered up to the gods. But how can I offer those which have been stolen away from me?"

"Look here, it is no use your trying to give me the slip in that fashion. Now is the time for grim work. Let that work be finished, then you can make a display of your woman's wiles to your heart's content—and I will help you in your game."

The moment I had stolen my husband's money and paid it to Sandip, the music that was in our relations stopped. Not only did I destroy all my own value by making myself cheap, but Sandip's powers, too, lost scope for their full play. You cannot employ your marksmanship against a thing which is right in your grasp.

So Sandip has lost his aspect of the hero; a tone of low quarrelsomeness has come into his words. Sandip kept his brilliant eyes fixed full on my face till they seemed to blaze with all the thirst of the mid-day sky.

Once or twice he fidgeted with his feet, as though to leave his seat, as if to spring right on me. My whole body seemed to swim, my veins throbbed, the hot blood surged up to my ears; I felt that if I remained there, I should never get up at all. With a supreme effort I tore myself off the chair, and hastened towards the door.

From Sandip's dry throat there came a muffled cry: "Whither would you flee, Queen?" The next moment he left his seat with a bound to seize hold of me. At the sound of footsteps outside the door, however, he rapidly retreated and fell back into his chair. I checked my steps near the bookshelf, where I stood staring at the names of the books.

As my husband entered the room, Sandip exclaimed: "I say, Nikhil, don't you keep Browning among your books here?

I was just telling Queen Bee of our college club. Do you remember that contest of ours over the translation of those lines from Browning? You don't?

"She should never have looked at me,

If she meant I should not love her,

There are plenty . . . men you call such,

I suppose . . . she may discover

All her soul to, if she pleases,

And yet leave much as she found them:

But I'm not so, and she knew it

When she fixed me, glancing round them.

"I managed to get together the words to render it into Bengali, somehow, but the result was hardly likely to be a 'joy forever' to the people of Bengal. I really did think at one time that I was on the verge of becoming a poet, but Providence was kind enough to save me from that disaster.

Do you remember old Dakshina? If he had not become a Salt Inspector, he would have been a poet. I remember his rendering to this day . . .

"No, Queen Bee, it is no use rummaging those bookshelves. Nikhil has ceased to read poetry since his marriage—perhaps he has no further need for it. But I suppose 'the fever fit of poesy', as the Sanskrit has it, is about to attack me again."

"I have come to give you a warning, Sandip," said my husband.

"About the fever fit of poesy?"

My husband took no notice of this attempt at humour. "For some time," he continued, "Mahomedan preachers have been about stirring up the local Mussulmans. They are all wild with you, and may attack you any moment."

"Are you come to advise flight?"

"I have come to give you information, not to offer advice."

"Had these estates been mine, such a warning would have been necessary for the preachers, not for me. If, instead of trying to frighten me, you give them a taste of your intimidation, that would be worthier both of you and me. Do you know that your weakness is weakening your neighbouring *zamindars* also?"

"I did not offer you my advice, Sandip. I wish you, too, would refrain from giving me yours. Besides, it is useless. And there is another thing I want to tell you. You and your followers have been secretly worrying and oppressing my tenantry. I cannot allow that any longer. So I must ask you to leave my territory."

"For fear of the Mussulmans, or is there any other fear you have to threaten me with?"

"There are fears the want of which is cowardice. In the name of those fears, I tell you, Sandip, you must go. In five days I shall be starting for Calcutta. I want you to accompany me. You may of course stay in my house there—to that there is no objection."

"All right, I have still five days" time then. Meanwhile, Queen Bee, let me hum to you my song of parting from your honey-hive. Ah! you poet of modern Bengal! Throw open your doors and let me plunder your words.

The theft is really yours, for it is my song which you have made your own—let the name be yours by all means, but the song is mine." With this Sandip struck up in a deep, husky voice, which threatened to be out of tune, a song in the Bhairavi mode:

"In the springtime of your kingdom, my Queen,

Meetings and partings chase each other in their endless hide and seek,

And flowers blossom in the wake of those that droop and die in the shade.

In the springtime of your kingdom, my Queen,

My meeting with you had its own songs,

But has not also my leave-taking any gift to offer you?

That gift is my secret hope, which I keep hidden in the

shadows of your flower garden,

That the rains of July may sweetly temper your fiery June."

His boldness was immense—boldness which had no veil, but was naked as fire. One finds no time to stop it: it is like trying to resist a thunderbolt: the lightning flashes: it laughs at all resistance.

I left the room. As I was passing along the verandah towards the inner apartments, Amulya suddenly made his appearance and came and stood before me.

"Fear nothing, Sister Rani," he said. "I am off tonight and shall not return unsuccessful."

"Amulya," said I, looking straight into his earnest, youthful face, "I fear nothing for myself, but may I never cease to fear for you."

Amulya turned to go, but before he was out of sight I called him back and asked: "Have you a mother, Amulya?"

"I have."

"A sister?"

"No, I am the only child of my mother. My father died when I was quite little."

"Then go back to your mother, Amulya."

"But, Sister Rani, I have now both mother and sister."

"Then, Amulya, before you leave tonight, come and have your dinner here."

"There won't be time for that. Let me take some food for the journey, consecrated with your touch."

"What do you specially like, Amulya?"

"If I had been with my mother I should have had lots of Poush cakes. Make some for me with your own hands, Sister Rani!"

4

TAGORE AND HIS POEMS

A reader conversant with the high points of ancient Sanskrit literature and medieval Bengali literature as well as English literature from Spenser to Swinburne on the one hand, and the monotheistic Upanishadic Hinduism and Christianity as practised in the 19th century (with its concomitant Puritanism) on the other, will realise that Tagore's poetic and lyrical imagination had three major aspects: devotion to the Upanishadic Brahman - formless, attributeless, yet all-pervasive; an abiding enchantment with nature, specifically the natural scenes of the lower Gangetic plains, richly varying through the cycle of the seasons; and last, but perhaps the most powerful - an intense yearning for romantic love. The informed Bengali reader can, with a little effort, trace the roots of the poetic style which he developed to the emotional need to express these and the influence of the literary sources cited above.

Those who, like Rothenstein and Yeats did not have a close acquaintance with Classical Sanskrit literature and Bengali poetic literature from Kalidasa to Michael Madhusudan Dutt, inclusive of the Vaishnava poets, and the prose of Bankim Chandra Chatterjee are and were unlikely to be in a position to appreciate, even to a modest extent, the nuances of word, idiom and imagery which constitute the characteristic style of Tagore.

THE FUNDAMENTAL CONFUSION

The role that Vaishnava poetry played in Tagore's artistic development was formidable; one cannot do better than to quote him in this context: "If you ask what gave me boldness when I was young I should say that one thing was my early acquaintance with the old 'Vaishnava' poems of Bengal, full of freedom in meter and expression. I think I was only twelve when these poems first began to be reprinted. I surreptitiously obtained copies from the desks of my elders. . . I must. . . admit that the greater part of these lyrics was erotic and not quite suited to a boy just about to reach his teens, but my imagination was completely occupied with the beauty of their forms and the music of their words and their breath, heavily laden with voluptuousness, passed over my mind without distracting it."

To Yeats, Rothenstein, Pound and their associates, these origins of Tagore's poetic imagination and emotional life were largely unknown; it was, therefore, possible, and perhaps imperative, for them to accept him as a quasi-saint whose spiritual quests were aided rather than retarded by a tamely sentimental view of romantic love, in line with Christian morality.

Yet Vaishnava verses like their ancient Sanskrit predecessors, in their spirit, were the most un-Christian literary compositions conceivableAmiya Chakravarty, himselfa competent poet and Tagore's one-time literary secretary felt obliged to add the following words, in a note, with reference to the passage quoted above: "The erotic tendency of some Vaishnava poetry, especially in connection with degenerate forms of the cult of Radha and Krishna had aroused opposition among the more sober-minded Hindus." This must not be treated as an insignificant footnote; it refers, in fact to a problem which plagued Tagore throughout his life, which I shall now have to address.

Imbued as he was with the densely sensual spirit and imageries of Vaishnava poetry, yet embedded in the Puritanical educated elite of 19th century Bengal, the daunting dilemma that Tagore faced was that of creating a style for himself through which passionate romantic love could be portrayed in a sensitive, appealing and varied manner without offending the moral sensibilities of the age, which were formed in the main, by the general mood of the Bengal renaissance.

In the English romantic poets, Tagore found a world in which love and emotions directly or indirectly connected to it, were expressed in an entirely different idiom; one which in its exquisite poignancy and delight was in consonance with a more spiritual, and less corporeal conception of amorous relations than was to be met with in the ancient Sanskritic and the medieval Vaishnavite literature.

It has been affirmed or conjectured by Tagorean writers that Tagore created for himself a personal deity, whom he addressed by the second person singular. Yet his religious beliefs and indeed that of his father were based fundamentally on the Upanishadic Brahman who, being non-anthropomorphic, could not be addressed directly by human beings. But the Christian Almighty cast his influence on the monotheism of Brahmoism and being anthropomorphic could be addressed freely in song and poetry. The synthesis or intermixture of these two entities resulted in a deity who was formless and not susceptible of idol worship, yet could be the object of devotional songs and poetry making liberal use of the crucial second person singular.

In Tagore's imagination, a female beloved and a male deity often merged with each other. He composed some songs in such a manner as to leave room for dual interpretations. An example of this device is: *Tomaare-i kariaachhi jIbaner-o dhrubataaraa* ("It is you whom I have chosen as the pole-star guiding my life. . . ") which appears in the section of *Gitabitan* titled Romantic Love (*Prem*), yet is included in the collection of monotheistic devotional songs Brahma-sangit. Significantly, the neo-Hindu celibate monk and missionary Swami Vivekaananda used to sing this song, one of his favourites. Though the second person singular was originally meant to represent an amorous beloved, in the Swami's conception, it certainly referred to the deity, for effusions of romantic love were strongly inimical to the ascetic spirit of the monastic order to which he belonged.

It is not difficult to find a typical example of the converse device — romantic or even quasi-erotic imageries pervading a devotional song included in the section of the *Gitabitan* titled 'Worship'(*Puja*): It appears as Item 20 in *Gitanjali* : "On the day when the lotus bloomed, alas, my mind was straying, and I knew it not".

Perhaps few readers are able to sing this song which, to my knowledge, has been commercially recorded by only one senior artiste: "*Yedin phuTlo kamal kichhu-i jaani naai*". If the Bengali reader surveys this song in its entirety, recalls or listens to at least one faithful rendition of it and if possible hums the tune, he or she will intuitively grasp the mood and will recognise an element of indirect, subtle and tempered sensuality in it. It must be noticed that there is no mention of the deity whatsoever in this song: the poet speaks of himself, a lotus recently bloomed and the wistfulness that it evokes in his mind.

Numerous other examples may be located to this interchangeability and intermingling of religious and romantic devotion, of deity and beloved. However, for many songs such an interchangeability was not possible, and an indiscriminate oscillation between the two could only impair their mood and appeal.

But Tagore knew that sensuous imageries were likely to offend Euro-American moral sensibilities, and as we have seen in one example he scrupulously deleted all reference to the sense of touch and indeed, any allusion that might suggest or evoke unChristian shades of sensuous emotions. To this matter I shall have to return later in the essay. The peculiar handling of the dilemma pervades the descriptions of the cycle of the seasons, too, which make their own contributions to the incomprehensibilty of Tagore's lyrics for Western readers.

The role played by climate in Tagore's songs, therefore, have now to be considered. Monsoon was Tagore's favourite; but this is a misleadingly simplistic statement. What permeated the majority of Tagore's songs on nature is specifically the monsoon in the lower Gangetic plains. I do not believe that inhabitants of, say, Punjab, Kashmir or Goa, not to speak of the Western world, could ever be able to appreciate the character of Tagore's musical treatment of the characteristic features of monsoon therein: the dense and lush foliage; the tumultuous thundershowers; the merging of forest, field, river and sky into a single continuum of watery mass; and the primordial drama of the rain-bearing clouds which, centuries ago, had provoked Kalidasa to compose some of the most bewitchingly beautiful verse in Sanskrit literature. *Gitanjali* offers several lyrics based on scenes of monsoon. It must be kept in mind that moods of monsoon pervade large stretches in the *Gitabitan* and is not limited to the section titled Monsoon (*Barshhaa*).

Item 22 of *Gitanjali* is as follows : 'In the deep shadows of the rainy July, with secret steps, thou walkest, silent as night, eluding all watchers.' This is the translation of song no. 94 of the section of the *Gitabitan* titled Monsoon (p463): *"aaji sraaban ghana gahan mohe, gopan taba charan phele/nishaar mata, nIrab ohe, sabaar diThi e.Daye ele."*

The Bengali reader, upon contrasting the original and the translation will discern a perceptible difference in mood and atmosphere: the original pertains to the natural scenes in the Bengal monsoon that we have discussed; the translation is constrained to deal with a rainy season that is geographically unspecified, for Tagore has to speak to an English-speaking readership that is widely dispersed over more than one continent. The Western reader is unable to fix his or her mind firmly to any specific set of experiences characteristic of some specific region: this inevitably impairs or hinders the imagination and blurs the impact of the lyric on the mind. The English romantic poets made allusions to natural scenes of England which, however, were better known to readers in the Westernized parts of the Orient, especially, educated Indians, since through a formidable literature read and assimilated in early life, an indirect familiarity with English scenes had been accomplished.

But a discrepancy that is far more serious is one that is so subtle as to almost elude notice : the second person singular in the original is, as usual, a beloved; or else, the song would have been placed in the section of the *Gitabitan* titled 'Worship' (*Puja*). The word *helaa* (neglect or indifference) has been repeatedly used in the love songs of *Gitabitan* to describe an attitude particularly excruciating for the forlorn yearner after love. The last line of the original is "*samukh diye swapanasama jeyo naa more helaay Thele*"; in the translation one finds "do not pass by like a dream". The last two words "*helaay Thele*" (neglectfully evade or dismiss) have been expunged. Why? In the English translation the beloved of the original had had to be transformed or transmuted into a rather vaguely delineated entity, formed perhaps partially upon a personification of the deity: and a benevolent godhead is not supposed to forsake or neglect human beings in the manner in which a beloved might his or her lover. The poignant yearning expressed in the last line of the original is therefore enfeebled in the semi-devotionalised translation. The confusion is repeated in the next item (no. 23) of the *Gitanjali* :

> *"Art thou abroad on this stormy night on thy journey of love, my friend?"*

"*Aaji jha.Der raate tomaar abhisaar paraansakhaa bandhu he aamaar*"

The relatively innocent 'journey of love' represents *abhisaara* - the clandestine nocturnal prowl or jaunt of the lover who has a tryst with his beloved. Comparison of the last stanzas of the original and the translation shows a distinct alteration of the mood; for, though in the union of love there is uncertainty, in the communion with the deity, given sufficient devotion, there is none. Once again, Tagore had veered from his original mood, with the tastes of the West uppermost in his mind.

In his songs, Tagore often alluded to things more easily palpable, and when he set himself the task of translating them, he had to resort to devices even more disruptive than we have hitherto discussed, as the following citation illustrates: (Item 74, *Gitanjali*)

> *"The day is no more, the shadow is upon the earth. It is time I go to the stream to fill my pitcher." This is song No. 84,* Gitabitan, *p. 306 "Aar naa-i re belaa naamlo chhaayaa dharanite / Ebaar chal re ghaaTe kalaskhaani bhare nite".*

In the second stanza of the translation, we find "In the lonely lane there is no passerby, the wind is up, the ripples are rampant in the river." The Bengali original: "*Ekhan bijan pathe kare naa keu aasa-jaaoyaa, ore, premnadite uThechhe Dheu, utal haaoyaa.*"

Premnadi (literally, river of love) has been translated as merely 'river'. Unbeknownst to many this song is based upon an old feature of rural Bengali society (for these observations I am indebted to the late Nirad C. Chaudhuri). When family women went to the adjoining river or pond to fill their pitchers, there often prowled by the wayside, and near the *ghats*, prospective or performing paramours waiting for a meeting with them. Few would fail to guess what such meetings resulted in. So irresistible was the appeal of such practices that folklore had received their imprint, social censure notwithstanding and Tagore had made a delicately nuanced and discreetly indirect reference to it in this song to create a pall of vague and languid amorousness hanging in the evening air. But in the English translation he had to alter the mood to make it suit Western moral demands; hence, river of love (figuratively, the emotion of love envisioned as a river, susceptible to ripples and waves) had to be curtailed to mere 'river'.

From the discussion above, there is no room for doubt as to who the last sentence of the song refers to : "There at the fording in the little boat the unknown man plays upon his lute." The Bengali original obviously belongs to the section of the *Gitabitan* titled Romantic Love (*Prem*).

Yet Yeats takes an unwarranted religious view of the item : ". . . a man sitting in a boat upon a river river playing upon a lute, . . . is God Himself!" And the misapprehension was not rectified by Tagore, perhaps understandingly. Another curious contrast is also in line with our present theme: use of the word '*maayaa*' in its Sanskrit form, untranslated into English, (in item #71, *Gitanjali*), yet the ommission of the word "*leelaa*" and substitution of the word "pleasure" in its place (item #1 "Thou hast made me endless, such is thy pleasure" - "*Aamaare tumi asheshh korechho, emani leelaa taba*").

The word '*maayaa*' is spiritual, or even mystical, and free of erotic connotations; therefore it was left unstranslated; but "*leelaa*", referring to the playful dalliance of Lord Krishna with the voluptuous cowherd girls, had to be sanitized by the disappointing and misleading translation "pleasure".

A similar analysis of several other songs of *Gitanjali*, on similar lines, can be carried out by any Bengali reader who is conversant with the Bengali originals. I believe I have given enough examples to show that Tagore's poetic and lyrical imagination had foundations which often bordered on the voluptuary, and in this his spirit was moved by ancient Sanskrit verse and especially *Vaishnava* poetry, in which his mind had been steeped from early adolescence onward.

The songs of *Gitabitan* on love and nature have virtually nothing to do with the Christian model of piety and asceticism and Yeats's projection of Tagore as primarily a religious poet in the Christian mould was almost entirely erroneous. It is in vain that he alludes to the writing of European saints of the Renaissance in his discussion of Tagore's lyrics.

It is here that all the major shortcomings of *Gitanjali* lie, rather than in such faulty, and sometimes risible, translations such as "I sit like a beggar maid, drawing my skirt over my face, . . . ". An unnecessary and unfair amount of censure has been heaped on Tagore for literal faults in translations. Unfortunately, so urgently eager was Tagore on entering the Western world of letters, that he made no effort to rectify Yeats's misconceptions; Tagore himself could have persuaded Yeats to be less sentimentally effusive and more realistic and true to the actual spirit of his songs in his Introduction to the *Gitanjali*; he did not. In this, intellectually if not morally, he was in error. Though Yeats's cloyingly laudatory introduction induced the West to take *Gitanjali* very seriously, at least initially, in the end it was this error which made an incurable confusion of ideas the basis of Tagore's image in the West.

RELIGION

If there is one word that can describe Tagore's principal capital when he proceeded to the West, it is 'religion'. It is finally as a religious missionary that the West accepted him. Even his first patrons were struck by the religious spirit of his poetry : Sturge Moore wrote to a friend: "Yeats and Rothenstein had a Bengalee poet on view during the last days I was in London. I was first privileged to see him in Yeats's rooms and then to hear a translation of his poems made by himself and read by Yeats in Rothenstein's drawing room. His unique subject is 'the love of God'. When I told Yeats that I found his poetry preposterously optimistic he said "Ah, you see, he is absorbed in God. "

But religion in Europe and America meant Christianity; and we have seen how Tagore had tailored and doctored the mood of his lyrics and poems to suit Christian expectations. To be sure, Christianity was very much on his mind when he embarked upon his voyage to Europe in 1912. In his address to the inmates of his school at *Santiniketan* titled "On the Eve of Departure", he said,

"There is no dearth in Europe of heroic souls who stand firmly against th tyranny of the mighty. Such upright men do not hesitate to take sides with alien peoples in far-off lands and suffer in their account. Who indeed are the friends of the Indians seeking self-government for their country ?. . . They are the knights who have undertaken to defend the weak. They tread in the hard path of Christ, stained with the blood of the divine leader who took the sorrows of the world upon himself to save the soul of man and to lead him from darkness into light. Deep within the heart of Europe that light still shines." One can clearly notice that his interest in Christianity was intimately bound-up with nationalistic political considerations.

He wrote: 'Many have asked me, "Why do you want to travel in Europe?" and he remarked in this address, "I have not known how to answer them."' The rest of the address is a long-winded justification of his voyage; but nowhere does he say that his interests were literary; poetry is not discussed.

One might begin to suspect that his journey to Europe and his publication of the English *Gitanjali* constituted the first deliberate step towards acquiring a Western image which would provide him with a political standing in the emerging nation. Without Western recognition, he realised, the whole of India would never take seriously the political views of one who was a mere poet confined to the cultural milieu of Bengal.

It was Yeats's fulsome Introduction to the English *Gitanjali* that set the stage for the emergence of Tagore as a religious prophet in the West, very much in the Christian mould. He observes, "Since the Renaissance the writing of European saints — however familiar their metaphor and the general structure of their thought — has ceased to hold our attention. He goes on to mention St. Bernard, the Book of Revelation, a Kempis, John of the Cross and St. Francis in his Introduction.

And very significantly, Yeats observes, ". . . yet we are not moved because of its strangeness, but because we have met our own image, . . . "

Gradually, a notion developed in the West that his verse demonstrates that Christianity had permeated the lives of millions in India, thus Westernizing it religiously; and that he was at the vanguard of this conversion. Harriet Monroe, in whose residence in Chicago Tagore spent a few weeks, in her memoirs described *Gitanjali* as "those sacred songs of praise which were chanted everywhere in his native India."

That certain sections of the Christian establishment too held a similar view is shown by the following citation from the Baptist Times, February 2, 1914 :

"The poems of Rabindranath Tagore are valuable for their performance, but still more valuable for the promise they afford of a coming dawn. We have been waiting anxiously for some indication of the effect of Christian ideas on a truly representative Hindu mind. Here, surely, is the person we have been longing for — one sent before the chariot of the Lord to make His path straight. And when we remember that this poet's every word is eagerly caught up by waiting millions, may we venture to assert that the new, the Christian India, is already at the door?" The Christian India, however, is yet to emerge.

LATER REACTIONS

I have now to deal with the later reactions to Tagore's work in the West. Ezra Pound, one of the coterie of poets who first championed Tagore in the West, later bitterly rejected

Tagore's religious themes purveyed to the West through poetry. Romain Rolland, too, was critical of Tagore's preaching tours. Greene, the ruthless realist, remarked in 1937: "As for Rabindranath Tagore, I cannot believe that anyone but Mr. Yeats can still take his poems very seriously." (He was, of course, referring to the West.) But already in 1935, even this last eminent admirer of Tagore had lost his patience with him: an irritated Yeats thundered in a letter to Rothenstein in 1935 : "Damn Tagore. We got out three good books, Sturge Moore and I, and then, because he thought it more important to see and know English than to be a great poet, he brought out sentimental rubbish and wrecked his reputation. Tagore does not know English, no Indian knows English. Nobody can write with music and style in a language not learned in childhood and ever since the language of his thought."

The works of Nirad C. Chaudhuri and R. K. Narayan have conclusively disproved the misguided verdict: ". . . no Indian knows English. "Yet Yeats's annoyance with Tagore has to be accorded the attention that it deserves. It is amusing to observe the contrast of this quotation and the fulsome introduction to the *Gitanjali*.

Unfortunately, the honest and starkly expressed observations of a fair number of eminent intellectuals of the West in respect of Tagore were made in private correspondences which have been published much after the initial Western ballyhoo about Tagore. D. H Lawrence saw the unreal nature of the prevailing Western attitude towards Tagore, based on ignorance of the East, and wrote to Russell's mistress Lady Ottoline Morrell in May 1916: ". . . this fraud of looking up to them — this wretched worship-of-Tagore attitude — is disgusting."

Harsh words. But true, unfortunately.

Bertrand Russell was even more trenchant in his appraisal of Tagore the lecturing spiritualist. In a letter to Lady Ottoline, dated June 19, 1913, he wrote: "Here I am back from Tagore's lecture, after walking most of the way home. It was unmitigated rubbish - cut-and-dried conventional stuff about the river becoming one with the ocean and man becoming one with *Brahma*. . . "

Later, when asked his opinion of a letter Tagore wrote him on the essence of religion, he curtly wrote; ". . . His talk about the infinite is vague nonsense. The sort of language that is admired by many Indians unfortunately does not, in fact, mean anything at all."

My heart goes out to those disciples of Tagore who are hurt by these sincere yet strong words of Russell; but I know too much about Russell to be able to dismiss this assertion as one based on incomprehension.

It becomes evident, then, that quite a few Western intellectuals could see through the essential unreality of Tagore's Western image; yet the private expressions of their perceptions did not become known publicly during Tagore's lifetime, perhaps mercifully.

But the tragedy is that Tagore was at his highest in his songs, especially the descriptive ones, based on natural scenes and the cycle of the seasons, and it is precisely his music to which the West is necessarily deaf. It is in his songs of nature and love that Tagore expresses his true sensual self, which he felt compelled in the last decade of his life to express to a large extent in a rather unusual manner in his paintings.

PROSE AND PAINTINGS

Tagore's novels and other prose works enjoyed a transient reputation in the West. His play 'The Post Office' was widely appreciated; and surprisingly, the anthologies of his works that have been published so far contain more prose than poetry. His lectures and letters do not present the difficulties of translations that his poetry and songs do, and this is one reason they feature profusely in these collections. Tagore remarked in 1930, 'My poetry is for my countrymen, my paintings are my gift to the West. 'His latest biographers state, "The best of the paintings— several hundred — are powerfully appealing (and suggestive of the untranslatable delicacies in the poetry.)". Actually, his paintings were a rather belated outlet for feelings which he could never clearly express in his songs and poetry, given the limitations of the style which he assumed rather early in life. There is a pagan element in some of them, which set them apart from all his verbal creations. However, the greater part of Tagore's Western image is based on his poems and lyrics, and had become fixed within a decade of the publication of *'Gitanjali.* '

POLITICS AND NATIONALISM

Once Tagore acquired an image in the West, those in Bengal who were previously censorious of his work suddenly began to hold him in esteem, leaders such as Gandhi sought his comradeship. He had achieved his objective. Thereby he quickly acquired a nationalistic image which held sway all over India, and eventually he allowed himself to be viewed as a religio-political leader of a stature almost comparable to Gandhi. This image, which had its origins in his Western image, further reinforced the latter, through nationalistic propaganda. All major Indian political leaders felt called upon to comment on his life and work; of these judgments we examine only the most salient, made by the most eminent.

Dr. Sarvepalli Radhakrishnan who, being a Tamil, did not possess a knowledge of Tagore's work comparable to that possessed by any ordinary educated Bengali, summarised Tagore's oeuvre as follows:

"In all Rabindranath's work three features are striking : (1) The ultimateness of spiritual values to be obtained by inward honesty and cultivation of inner life; (2) the futility of mere negation or renunciation and the need for a holy or a whole development of life; and (3) the positive attitude of sympathy for all, even the lowly and the lost. It is a matter for satisfaction to find an Indian leader insisting on these real values of life at a time when so many old things are crumbling away and a thousand new ones are springing up."

This verdict almost defies comment; so vast is its scope, and so vague is the sense in which the words have been used, that one might employ this very summary in characterising the work not of Tagore but of any one amongst Gandhi, Vivekananda and Aurobindo Ghose. No Westerner, who has not read Tagore, can guess from this statement that he was primarily a composer of Bengali songs and poetry.

Jawaharlal Nehru's judgment is, of course, frankly political, and he too was unable to read even a single page of *Gitabitaan* in the original Bengali : ". . . Rabindranath Tagore has given to our nationalism the outlook of internationalism and has enriched it with art and music and the magic of his words, so that it has become the full-blooded emblem of INDIA'S awakened spirit." (Emphasis mine)

Perhaps Nehru the intellectual (as opposed to the politician) had the perspicacity to see, though he found it imprudent to state, that it was far easier for Tagore to reach out to the Bengali-speaking people of (the erstwhile) East Pakistan through his songs and thereby become an emblem, whether full-blooded or not, of its awakening spirit, which was to lead to the creation of Bangladesh merely seven years after his decease, than to enthrall entire populations of the speakers of Tamil, Telugu, Kannada, Malayalam, Marathi, Gujarati et al who, knowing no Bengali, had no access to his songs and poetry at all.

And Gandhi proclaimed, "I regard the poet as a sentinel warning us against the approach of enemies called Bigotry, Lethargy, Intolerance, Ignorance, Inertia and other memebers of that brood." From all this emerges an image of a religio-political leader, always on the road, addressing hortatory speeches and sermons to great masses of people; its superficiality can be seen by any educated Bengali.

But if such be the utterances of non-Bengali Indians who, on account of their exalted political positions, were naturally taken seriously in the West, one can hardly blame Westerners alone for creating a grandiosely false image of Tagore.

THE MAN HIMSELF

An author who has made bold to claim that the Western image of Tagore is ersatz will perhaps be expected to set forth an account of his true identity, undistorted and unaberrated.

The fact of the matter, unfortunately, is that Tagore's temperament was essentially unsuited to an active public or political life; he was fundamentally a loner whose creative energies found their ideal expression in solitude.

Though he was aggressively litigious - he had been engaged in furious lawsuits over property with several of his siblings (inclusive of his once-beloved Jyotirindranath) and even when on his deathbed in 1941, was involved in a legal battle with his only surviving sibling Barnakumari (who was at that time about 90) - he was not emotionally equipped to withstand the wear and tear of public censure and ridicule to which every politician and active public person is inevitably subject; poets seldom are.

Here I must let the man speak for himself. When he was thirty-one, he wrote: "Intimacy with men is absolutley intolerable to me. Unless I have plenty of room around myself I cannot stretch my limbs, settle down and unpack my mind. I pray that mankind may prosper, but they should not jostle me. . . "

Again, when he was thirty-two he wrote, speaking of his mind: "It is only when it gets a little solitude that it can muse to its heart's content, look round itself, and express its feelings in all their meanderings exactly as it pleases."

Chaudhuri rightly states, "It is from this Tagore that his greatest literary achievement came out. He is at his greatest as a writer when he is speaking as a lone soul with a lone voice to lone souls."

As for romantic love, the exultant eroticism of ancient and medieval Sanskrit literature provided him with imageries, but the mood of his songs of love are often, if not always, of sorrow and despair. Throughout his life he yearned in vain for an idealised form of romantic love, and this failure caused him intense anguish till his last days. His songs express it in a delicate manner with which many Bengalis, similarly deprived, can identify their feelings.

Out of a plethora of songs as examples, I choose only one:

"You are indeed my heart's desire,

I have nothing and no one in this world except you.

I shall lose myself in my separation from you, and thereby live in you

Through long days, long nights, long months, and long years.

If you love someone else, and never come back,

May you get all that you seek,

And I bear all the sorrow that there may be. "

But it was his profound love of nature that enabled him to save his soul. Once again, we must let the man speak for himself:

"I feel that once upon a time I was at one with the rest of the earth, that grass grew green upon me, that the autumn sun fell on me and under its rays the warm scent of youth wafted from every pore of my far-flung evergreen body. As my waters and mountains lay spread out through every land, dumbly soaking up the radiance of a cloudless sky, an elixir of life and joy was inarticulately secreted from the immensity of my being. So it is that my feelings seem to be those of our ancient planet, ever germinant and efflorescent, shuddering with sun-kissed delight. The current of my consciousness streams through each blade of grass, each sucking root, each sappy vein, and breaks out in the waving fields of corn and in the rustling leaves of the palms."

One man, his solitude, his yearnings for love, and his love of nature — all experienced and expressed through a highly sensuous musical and poetic intuition : this is the essential Tagore.

CONCLUSION

That his image in the West was a brittle fabric of appreciation based on incomprehension had of course become clear to him, if it had not been evident right from the beginning. But the very Bengalis whose harsh censure and ridicule had pained him and against whom he had hit out time and again were not susceptible to the misinterpretations to which the

West was prone; the Bengalis sang his songs spontaneously and with genuine passion, in celebration of the seasons, of love and even of religion. Inasmuch as he had been at perfect harmony with Bengal, its rivers, verdant fields and villages, his songs, especially the seasonal ones, had an enduring character free from all temporary literary or religious fads and fashions, and consequently merged with the life of the Bengali mind completely. He remarked in his last days that the fate of his poems and stories was uncertain, but his songs had indeed found a lasting lodgment in the hearts of Bengalis. Bengal, in the end, was his true home, as it had been at the dawn of his life.

But what did the West gain from him? I shall have to quote Alex Aronson :

> *"A great scholar would expound the philosophy of Rabindranath in terms of metaphysics and mysticism; a politician would elucidate his position in European politics; litterateurs would establish comparisons and parallels; and priests of various denominations would exalt or debase his spiritual message. Everyone of them had his own axe to grind, and Rabindranath became a useful and innocent tool which they knew how to handle for their own ulterior purposes. So it came about that he was unknowingly made to represent certain tendencies in the party-politics of various nations, that his name was freely used for the sake of either appeasing or inflaming national hatred, and that the various religious or pseudo-racial denominations used him for their own ends. The litterateurs were often uncritical and outrageously condescending. In addition to all this an atmosphere of sensationalism was being created around him symptomatic of the loss of mental equilibrium, and perhaps also of the loss of all beliefs in the West."*
>
> *". . . Rabindranaths's voice when it was heard in Europe evoked (in Mathew arnold's words about Shelley) "a vision of beauty and radiance, indeed, but availing nothing, effecting nothing."*

Indeed, now that we approach the centenary of Tagore's first encounter with the West, and find feeble voices still shrieking in order to continue projecting an ersatz Western image of the poet based on incomprehension and academic sensationalism, what profound religious faith, what luminous truth about humanity, is being upheld by his Western champions?

We might well wonder.

THE YEAR 1400

A hundred years from today who are you, sitting, reading a poem of mine, under curiosity's sway - a hundred years from today?

Not the least portion of this young spring's morning bliss, neither blossom nor birdsong, nor any of its scarlet splashes can I drench in passion and despatch to your hands a hundred years hence!

Yet do this, please: unlatch your south-faced door, just sit at your window for once; basking in fantasy, eyes on the far horizon, figure out if you can: how one day a hundred years back roving delights in a free fall from a heavenly region had touched all that there was - the infant Phalgun day, utterly free, was frenzied, all agog, while borne on brisk wings, the south wind pollen-scent-brushed had suddenly arrived and in a flash dyed the earth with all youth's hues a hundred years before your day.

There lived then a poet, ebullient of spirit, his heart steeped in song, who wanted to open his words like so many flowers with so much passion one day a hundred years back.

A hundred years from today who is the new poet whose songs flow through your homes?

To him I convey this springtime's gladsome greetings.

May my vernal song find its echo for a moment in your spring day in the throbbing of your hearts, in the buzzing of your bees, in the rustling of your leaves a hundred years from today.

5

TAGORE'S VIEW OF INDIA

Rabindranath Tagore, who died in 1941 at the age of eighty, is a towering figure in the millennium-old literature of Bengal. Anyone who becomes familiar with this large and flourishing tradition will be impressed by the power of Tagore's presence in Bangladesh and in India. His poetry as well as his novels, short stories, and essays are very widely read, and the songs he composed reverberate around the eastern part of India and throughout Bangladesh. In contrast, in the rest of the world, especially in Europe and America, the excitement that Tagore's writings created in the early years of the twentieth century has largely vanished. The enthusiasm with which his work was once greeted was quite remarkable. *Gitanjali,* a selection of his poetry for which he was awarded the Nobel Prize in Literature in 1913, was published in English translation in London in March of that year, and had been reprinted ten times by November, when the award was announced. But he is not much read now in the West, and already by 1937, Graham Greene was able to say: "As for Rabindranath Tagore, I cannot believe that anyone but Mr. Yeats can still take his poems very seriously."

THE MYSTIC

The contrast between Tagore's commanding presence in Bengali literature and culture, and his near-total eclipse in the rest of the world, is perhaps less interesting than the distinction between the view of Tagore as a deeply relevant and many-sided contemporary thinker in Bangladesh and India, and his image in the West as a repetitive and remote spiritualist. Graham Greene had, in fact, gone on to explain that he associated Tagore "with what Chesterton calls 'the bright pebbly eyes' of the Theosophists." Certainly, an air of mysticism played some part in the "selling" of Rabindranath Tagore to the West by Yeats, Ezra Pound, and his other early champions. Even Anna Akhmatova, one of Tagore's few later admirers (who translated his poems into Russian in the mid-1960s), talks of "that mighty flow of poetry which takes its strength from Hinduism as from the Ganges, and is called Rabindranath Tagore."

CULTURAL CONFLUENCE

Rabindranath did come from a Hindu family—one of the landed gentry who owned estates mostly in what is now Bangladesh. But whatever wisdom there might be in Akhmatova's invoking of Hinduism and the Ganges, it did not prevent the largely Muslim citizens of Bangladesh from having a deep sense of identity with Tagore and his ideas. Nor did it stop the newly independent Bangladesh from choosing one of Tagore's songs—the "Amar Sonar Bangla" which means "my golden Bengal"—as its national anthem. This must be very confusing to those who see the contemporary world as a "clash of civilizations"—with "the Muslim civilization," "the Hindu civilization," and "the Western civilization," each forcefully confronting the others. They would also be confused by Rabindranath Tagore's own description of his Bengali family as the product of "a confluence of three cultures: Hindu, Mohammedan, and British".

Rabindranath's grandfather, Dwarkanath, was well known for his command of Arabic and Persian, and Rabindranath grew up in a family atmosphere in which a deep knowledge of Sanskrit and ancient Hindu texts was combined with an understanding of Islamic traditions as well as Persian literature. It is not so much that Rabindranath tried to produce—or had an interest in producing—a "synthesis" of the different religions (as the great Moghul emperor Akbar tried hard to achieve) as that his outlook was persistently non-sectarian, and his writings—some two hundred books—show the influence of different parts of the Indian cultural background as well as of the rest of the world.

ABODE OF PEACE

Most of his work was written at Santiniketan (Abode of Peace), the small town that grew around the school he founded in Bengal in 1901, and he not only conceived there an imaginative and innovative system of education, but through his writings and his influence on students and teachers, he was able to use the school as a base from which he could take a major part in India's social, political, and cultural movements.

The profoundly original writer, whose elegant prose and magical poetry Bengali readers know well, is not the sermonizing spiritual guru admired—and then rejected—in London. Tagore was not only an immensely versatile poet; he was also a great short story writer, novelist, playwright, essayist, and composer of songs, as well as a talented painter whose pictures, with their mixture of representation and abstraction, are only now beginning to receive the acclaim that they have long deserved. His essays, moreover, ranged over literature, politics, culture, social change, religious beliefs, philosophical analysis, international relations, and much else.

The coincidence of the fiftieth anniversary of Indian independence with the publication of a selection of Tagore's letters by Cambridge University Press , brought Tagore's ideas and reflections to the fore, which makes it important to examine what kind of leadership in thought and understanding he provided in the Indian subcontinent in the first half of this century.

GANDHI AND TAGORE

Since Rabindranath Tagore and Mohandas Gandhi were two leading Indian thinkers in the twentieth century, many commentators have tried to compare their ideas. On learning of Rabindranath's death, Jawaharlal Nehru, then incarcerated in a British jail in India, wrote in his prison diary for August 7, 1941:

> *"Gandhi and Tagore. Two types entirely different from each other, and yet both of them typical of India, both in the long line of India's great men ... It is not so much because of any single virtue but because of the* tout ensemble, *that I felt that among the world's great men today Gandhi and Tagore were supreme as human beings. What good fortune for me to have come into close contact with them."*

Romain Rolland was fascinated by the contrast between them, and when he completed his book on Gandhi, he wrote to an Indian academic, in March 1923: "I have finished my *Gandhi,* in which I pay tribute to your two great river-like souls, overflowing with divine spirit, Tagore and Gandhi." The following month, he recorded in his diary an account of some of the differences between Gandhi and Tagore written by Reverend C.F. Andrews, the English clergyman and public activist who was a close friend of both men (and whose important role in Gandhi's life in South Africa as well as India is well portrayed in Richard Attenborough's film Gandhi [1982]). Andrews described to Rolland a discussion between Tagore and Gandhi, at which he was present, on subjects that divided them:

> *"The first subject of discussion was idols; Gandhi defended them, believing the masses incapable of raising themselves immediately to abstract ideas. Tagore cannot bear to see the people eternally treated as a child. Gandhi quoted the great things achieved in Europe by the flag as an idol; Tagore found it easy to object, but Gandhi held his ground, contrasting European flags bearing eagles, etc., with his own, on which he has put a spinning wheel. The second point of discussion was nationalism, which Gandhi defended. He said that one must go through nationalism to reach internationalism, in the same way that one must go through war to reach peace."*

Tagore greatly admired Gandhi but he had many disagreements with him on a variety of subjects, including nationalism, patriotism, the importance of cultural exchange, the role of rationality and of science, and the nature of economic and social development. These differences, I shall argue, have a clear and consistent pattern, with Tagore pressing for more room for reasoning, and for a less traditionalist view, a greater interest in the rest of the world, and more respect for science and for objectivity generally.

Rabindranath knew that he could not have given India the political leadership that Gandhi provided, and he was never stingy in his praise for what Gandhi did for the nation (it was, in fact, Tagore who popularized the term "Mahatma"—great soul—as a description of Gandhi). And yet each remained deeply critical of many things that the other stood for. That Mahatma Gandhi has received incomparably more attention outside India and also within much of India itself makes it important to understand "Tagore's side" of the Gandhi-Tagore debates.

In his prison diary, Nehru wrote: "Perhaps it is as well that [Tagore] died now and did not see the many horrors that are likely to descend in increasing measure on the world and on India. He had seen enough and he was infinitely sad and unhappy." Toward the end of his life, Tagore was indeed becoming discouraged about the state of India, especially as its normal burden of problems, such as hunger and poverty, was being supplemented by politically organized incitement to "communal" violence between Hindus and Muslims. This conflict would lead in 1947, six years after Tagore's death, to the widespread killing that took place during partition; but there was much gore already during his declining days. In December 1939, he wrote to his friend Leonard Elmhirst, the English philanthropist and social reformer who had worked closely with him on rural reconstruction in India (and who had gone on to found the Dartington Hall Trust in England and a progressive school at Dartington that explicitly invoked Rabindranath's educational ideals):

> *"It does not need a defeatist to feel deeply anxious about the future of millions who, with all their innate culture and their peaceful traditions are being simultaneously subjected to hunger, disease, exploitations foreign and indigenous, and the seething discontents of communalism."*

How would Tagore have viewed the India of today? Would he see progress there, or wasted opportunity, perhaps even a betrayal of its promise and conviction? And, on a wider subject, how would he react to the spread of cultural separatism in the contemporary world?

EAST AND WEST

Given the vast range of his creative achievements, perhaps the most astonishing aspect of the image of Tagore in the West is its narrowness; he is recurrently viewed as "the great mystic from the East," an image with a putative message for the West, which some would welcome, others dislike, and still others find deeply boring. To a great extent this Tagore was the West's own creation, part of its tradition of message-seeking from the East, particularly from India, which—as Hegel put it—had "existed for millennia in the imagination of the Europeans." Friedrich Schlegel, Schelling, Herder, and Schopenhauer were only a few of the thinkers who followed the same pattern. They theorized, at first, that India was the source of superior wisdom. Schopenhauer at one stage even argued that the New Testament "must somehow be of Indian origin: this is attested by its completely Indian ethics, which transforms morals into asceticism, its pessimism, and its avatar," in "the person of Christ." But then they rejected their own theories with great vehemence, sometimes blaming India for not living up to their unfounded expectations.

We can imagine that Rabindranath's physical appearance—handsome, bearded, dressed in non-Western clothes—may, to some extent, have encouraged his being seen as a carrier of exotic wisdom. Yasunari Kawabata, the first Japanese Nobel Laureate in Literature, treasured memories from his middle-school days of "this sage-like poet":

> *His white hair flowed softly down both sides of his forehead; the tufts of hair under the temples also were long like two beards, and linking up with the hair on his cheeks, continued into his beard, so that he gave an impression, to the boy I was then, of some ancient Oriental wizard.*

That appearance would have been well-suited to the selling of Tagore in the West as a quintessentially mystical poet, and it could have made it somewhat easier to pigeonhole him. Commenting on Rabindranath's appearance, Frances Cornford told William Rothenstein, "I can now imagine a powerful and gentle Christ, which I never could before." Beatrice Webb, who did not like Tagore and resented what she took to be his "quite obvious dislike of all that the Webbs stand for" (there is, in fact, little evidence that Tagore had given much thought to this subject), said that he was "beautiful to look at" and that "his speech has the perfect intonation and slow chant-like moderation of the dramatic saint." Ezra Pound and W. B. Yeats, among others, first led the chorus of adoration in the Western appreciation of Tagore, and then soon moved to neglect and even shrill criticism. The contrast between Yeats's praise of his work in 1912 ("These lyrics...display in their thought a world I have dreamed of all my life long," "the work of a supreme culture") and his denunciation in 1935 ("Damn Tagore") arose partly from the inability of Tagore's many-sided writings to fit into the narrow box in which Yeats wanted to place—and keep—him. Certainly, Tagore did write a huge amount, and published ceaselessly, even in English (sometimes in indifferent English translation), but Yeats was also bothered, it is clear, by the difficulty of fitting Tagore's later writings into the image Yeats had presented to the West. Tagore, he had said, was the product of "a whole people, a whole civilization, immeasurably strange to us," and yet "we have met our own image,...or heard, perhaps for the first time in literature, our voice as in a dream."

Yeats did not totally reject his early admiration (as Ezra Pound and several others did), and he included some of Tagore's early poems in *The Oxford Book of Modern Verse,* which he edited in 1936. Yeats also had some favorable things to say about Tagore's prose writings. His censure of Tagore's later poems was reinforced by his dislike of Tagore's own English translations of his work ("Tagore does not know English, no Indian knows English," Yeats explained), unlike the English version of *Gitanjali* which Yeats had himself helped to prepare. Poetry is, of course, notoriously difficult to translate, and anyone who knows Tagore's poems in their original Bengali cannot feel satisfied with any of the translations (made with or without Yeats's help). Even the translations of his prose works suffer, to some extent, from distortion. E.M. Forster noted, in a review of a translation of one of Tagore's great Bengali novels, *The Home and the World,* in 1919: "The theme is so beautiful," but the charms have "vanished in translation," or perhaps "in an experiment that has not quite come off."

Tagore himself played a somewhat bemused part in the boom and bust of his English reputation. He accepted the extravagant praise with much surprise as well as pleasure, and then received denunciations with even greater surprise, and barely concealed pain. Tagore was sensitive to criticism, and was hurt by even the most far-fetched accusations, such as the charge that he was getting credit for the work of Yeats, who had "rewritten" Gitanjali. (This charge was made by a correspondent for The Times, Sir Valentine Chirol, whom E.M. Forster once described as "an old Anglo-Indian reactionary hack.") From time to time Tagore also protested the crudity of some of his overexcited advocates. He wrote to C.F. Andrews in 1920: "These people...are like drunkards who are afraid of their lucid intervals."

GOD AND OTHERS

Yeats was not wrong to see a large religious element in Tagore's writings. He certainly had interesting and arresting things to say about life and death. Susan Owen, the mother of Wilfred Owen, wrote to Rabindranath in 1920, describing her last conversations with her son before he left for the war which would take his life. Wilfred said goodbye with "those wonderful words of yours—beginning at 'When I go from hence, let this be my parting word.'" When Wilfred's pocket notebook was returned to his mother, she found "these words written in his dear writing—with your name beneath."

The idea of a direct, joyful, and totally fearless relationship with God can be found in many of Tagore's religious writings, including the poems of *Gitanjali.* From India's diverse religious traditions he drew many ideas, both from ancient texts and from popular poetry. But "the bright pebbly eyes of the Theosophists" do not stare out of his verses. Despite the archaic language of the original translation of *Gitanjali,* which did not, I believe, help to preserve the simplicity of the original, its elementary humanity comes through more clearly than any complex and intense spirituality:

Leave this chanting and singing and telling of beads! Whom dost thou worship in this lonely dark corner of a temple with doors all shut?

Open thine eyes and see thy God is not before thee!

He is there where the tiller is tilling the hard ground and where the pathmaker is breaking stones. He is with them in sun and in shower, and his garment is covered with dust.

An ambiguity about religious experience is central to many of Tagore's devotional poems, and makes them appeal to readers irrespective of their beliefs; but excessively detailed interpretation can ruinously strip away that ambiguity. This applies particularly to his many poems which combine images of human love and those of pious devotion. Tagore writes:

I have no sleep to-night. Ever and again I open my door and look out on the darkness, my friend!

I can see nothing before me. I wonder where lies thy path!

By what dim shore of the ink-black river, by what far edge of the frowning forest, through what mazy depth of gloom, art thou threading thy course to come to see me, my friend?

I suppose it could be helpful to be told, as Yeats hastens to explain, that "the servant or the bride awaiting the master's home-coming in the empty house" is "among the images of the heart turning to God." But in Yeats's considerate attempt to make sure that the reader does not miss the "main point," something of the enigmatic beauty of the Bengali poem is lost - even what had survived the antiquated language of the English translation. Tagore certainly had strongly held religious beliefs (of an unusually nondenominational kind), but he was interested in a great many other things as well and had many different things to say about them.

Some of the ideas he tried to present were directly political, and they figure rather prominently in his letters and lectures. He had practical, plainly expressed views about nationalism, war and peace, cross-cultural education, freedom of the mind, the importance of rational criticism, the need for openness, and so on. His admirers in the West, however, were tuned to the more otherworldly themes which had been emphasized by his first Western patrons. People came to his public lectures in Europe and America, expecting ruminations on grand, transcendental themes; when they heard instead his views on the way public leaders should behave, there was some resentment, particularly (as E.P. Thompson reports) when he delivered political criticism "at $700 a scold."

Reasoning in Freedom

For Tagore it was of the highest importance that people be able to live, and reason, in freedom. His attitudes toward politics and culture, nationalism and internationalism, tradition and modernity, can all be seen in the light of this belief. Nothing, perhaps, expresses his values as clearly as a poem in *Gitanjali:*

> *Where the mind is without fear and the head is held high;*
>
> *Where knowledge is free;*
>
> *Where the world has not been broken up into fragments by narrow domestic walls; ...*
>
> *Where the clear stream of reason has not lost its way into the dreary desert sand of dead habit; ...*
>
> *Into that heaven of freedom, my Father, let my country awake.*

Rabindranath's qualified support for nationalist movements—and his opposition to the unfreedom of alien rule—came from this commitment. So did his reservations about patriotism, which, he argued, can limit both the freedom to engage ideas from outside "narrow domestic walls" and the freedom also to support the causes of people in other countries. Rabindranath's passion for freedom underlies his firm opposition to unreasoned traditionalism, which makes one a prisoner of the past (lost, as he put it, in "the dreary desert sand of dead habit").

Tagore illustrates the tyranny of the past in his amusing yet deeply serious parable "Kartar Bhoot" ("The Ghost of the Leader"). As the respected leader of an imaginary land is about to die, his panic-stricken followers request him to stay on after his death to instruct them on what to do. He consents. But his followers find their lives are full of rituals and constraints on everyday behavior and are not responsive to the world around them. Ultimately, they request the ghost of the leader to relieve them of his domination, when he informs them that he exists only in their minds.

Tagore's deep aversion to any commitment to the past that could not be modified by contemporary reason extended even to the alleged virtue of invariably keeping past promises. On one occasion when Mahatma Gandhi visited Tagore's school at Santiniketan, a young woman got him to sign her autograph book. Gandhi wrote: "Never make a promise in haste. Having once made it fulfill it at the cost of your life." When he saw this entry, Tagore became agitated.

He wrote in the same book a short poem in Bengali to the effect that no one can be made "a prisoner forever with a chain of clay." He went on to conclude in English, possibly so that Gandhi could read it too, "Fling away your promise if it is found to be wrong."

Tagore had the greatest admiration for Mahatma Gandhi as a person and as a political leader, but he was also highly skeptical of Gandhi's form of nationalism and his conservative instincts regarding the country's past traditions. He never criticized Gandhi personally. In the 1938 essay, "Gandhi the Man," he wrote:

Great as he is as a politician, as an organizer, as a leader of men, as a moral reformer, he is greater than all these as a man, because none of these aspects and activities limits his humanity. They are rather inspired and sustained by it.

And yet there is a deep division between the two men. Tagore was explicit about his disagreement:

> *We who often glorify our tendency to ignore reason, installing in its place blind faith, valuing it as spiritual, are ever paying for its cost with the obscuration of our mind and destiny. I blamed Mahatmaji for exploiting this irrational force of credulity in our people, which might have had a quick result [in creating] a superstructure, while sapping the foundation. Thus began my estimate of Mahatmaji, as the guide of our nation, and it is fortunate for me that it did not end there.*

But while it "did not end there," that difference of vision was a powerful divider. Tagore, for example, remained unconvinced of the merit of Gandhi's forceful advocacy that everyone should spin at home with the "charka," the primitive spinning wheel. For Gandhi this practice was an important part of India's self-realization. "The spinning-wheel gradually became," as his biographer B.R. Nanda writes, "the center of rural uplift in the Gandhian scheme of Indian economics." Tagore found the alleged economic rationale for this scheme quite unrealistic. As Romain Rolland noted, Rabindranath "never tires of criticizing the charka." In this economic judgment, Tagore was probably right. Except for the rather small specialized market for high-quality spun cloth, it is hard to make economic sense of hand-spinning, even with wheels less primitive than Gandhi's charka. Hand-spinning as a widespread activity can survive only with the help of heavy government subsidies. However, Gandhi's advocacy of the charka was not based only on economics. He wanted everyone to spin for "thirty minutes every day as a sacrifice," seeing this as a way for people who are better off to identify themselves with the less fortunate. He was impatient with Tagore's refusal to grasp this point:

> The poet lives for the morrow, and would have us do likewise.... "Why should I, who have no need to work for food, spin?" may be the question asked. Because I am eating what does not belong to me. I am living on the spoliation of my countrymen. Trace the source of every coin that finds its way into your pocket, and you will realise the truth of what I write.

Every one must spin. Let Tagore spin like the others. Let him burn his foreign clothes; that is the duty today. God will take care of the morrow.

If Tagore had missed something in Gandhi's argument, so did Gandhi miss the point of Tagore's main criticism. It was not only that the charka made little economic sense, but also, Tagore thought, that it was not the way to make people reflect on anything: "The charka does not require anyone to think; one simply turns the wheel of the antiquated invention endlessly, using the minimum of judgment and stamina."

CELIBACY AND PERSONAL LIFE

Tagore and Gandhi's attitudes toward personal life were also quite different. Gandhi was keen on the virtues of celibacy, theorized about it, and, after some years of conjugal life, made a private commitment—publicly announced—to refrain from sleeping with his wife. Rabindranath's own attitude on this subject was very different, but he was gentle about their disagreements:

> *[Gandhiji] condemns sexual life as inconsistent with the moral progress of man, and has a horror of sex as great as that of the author of* The Kreutzer Sonata, *but, unlike Tolstoy, he betrays no abhorrence of the sex that tempts his kind. In fact, his tenderness for women is one of the noblest and most consistent traits of his character, and he counts among the women of his country some of his best and truest comrades in the great movement he is leading.*

Tagore's personal life was, in many ways, an unhappy one. He married in 1883, lost his wife in 1902, and never remarried. He sought close companionship, which he did not always get (perhaps even during his married life—he wrote to his wife, Mrinalini: "If you and I could be comrades in all our work and in all our thoughts it would be splendid, but we cannot attain all that we desire"). He maintained a warm friendship with, and a strong Platonic attachment to, the literature-loving wife, Kadambari, of his elder brother, Jyotirindranath. He dedicated some poems to her before his marriage, and several books afterward, some after her death (she committed suicide, for reasons that are not fully understood, at the age of twenty-five, four months after Rabindranath's wedding). Much later in life, during his tour of Argentina in 1924-1925, Rabindranath came to know the talented and beautiful Victoria Ocampo, who later became the publisher of the literary magazine *Sur*. They became close friends, but it appears that Rabindranath deflected the possibility of a passionate relationship into a confined intellectual one. His friend Leonard Elmhirst, who accompanied Rabindranath on his Argentine tour, wrote:

Besides having a keen intellectual understanding of his books, she was in love with him—but instead of being content to build a friendship on the basis of intellect, she was in a hurry to establish that kind of proprietary right over him which he absolutely would not brook.

Ocampo and Elmhirst, while remaining friendly, were both quite rude in what they wrote about each other. Ocampo's book on Tagore (of which a Bengali translation was made from the Spanish by the distinguished poet and critic Shankha Ghosh) is primarily concerned with Tagore's writings but also discusses the pleasures and difficulties of their relationship, giving quite a different account from Elmhirst's, and never suggesting any sort of proprietary intentions.

Victoria Ocampo, however, makes it clear that she very much wanted to get physically closer to Rabindranath: "Little by little he [Tagore] partially tamed the young animal, by turns wild and docile, who did not sleep, dog-like, on the floor outside his door, simply because it was not done." Rabindranath, too, was clearly very much attracted to her. He called her "Vijaya" (the Sanskrit equivalent of Victoria), dedicated a book of poems to her, Purabi—an "evening melody," and expressed great admiration for her mind ("like a star that was distant"). In a letter to her he wrote, as if to explain his own reticence:

> *When we were together, we mostly played with words and tried to laugh away our best opportunities to see each other clearly ... Whenever there is the least sign of the nest becoming a jealous rival of the sky [,] my mind, like a migrant bird, tries to take ... flight to a distant shore.*

Five years later, during Tagore's European tour in 1930, he sent her a cable: "Will you not come and see me." She did. But their relationship did not seem to go much beyond conversation, and their somewhat ambiguous correspondence continued over the years. Written in 1940, a year before his death at eighty, one of the poems in Sesh Lekha ("Last Writings"), seems to be about her: "How I wish I could once again find my way to that foreign land where waits for me the message of love!/... Her language I knew not, but what her eyes said will forever remain eloquent in its anguish." However indecisive, or confused, or awkward Rabindranath may have been, he certainly did not share Mahatma Gandhi's censorious views of sex. In fact, when it came to social policy, he advocated contraception and family planning while Gandhi preferred abstinence.

EDUCATIONAL IDEAS

Rabindranath Tagore's role in the innovation of educational ideas has been eclipsed by his fame as a poet. He was a pioneer in the field of education. For the last forty years of his life he was content to be a schoolmaster in humble rural surroundings, even when he had achieved fame such as no Indian had known before. He was one of the first, in India, to think out for himself and put in practice principles of education which have now become commonplace of educational theory, if not yet of practice.

Today we all know that what the child imbibes at home and in school is far more important than what he studies at college, that the teaching is more easily and naturally communicated through the child's mother-tongue than through an alien medium, that learning through activity is more real than through the written word, that wholesome education consists in training of all the senses along with the mind instead of cramming the brain with memorized knowledge, that culture is something much more than academic knowledge.

But few of Rabindranath's countrymen took notice of him when he made his first experiments in education in 1901 with less than half a dozen pupils. A poet's whim, thought most of them. Even today few of his countrymen understand the significance of these principles in their national life. The schoolmaster is still the most neglected member of our community, despite the fact that Rabindranath attached more merit to what he taught to children in his school than to the Hibbert lectures he delivered before the distinguished audience at Oxfoard.

Mahatma Gandhi adopted the scheme of teaching through crafts many years after Rabindranath had worked it out at Santiniketan. In fact the Mahatma imported his first teachers for his basic School from Santiniketan.

If Rabindranath had done nothing else, what he did at Santiniketan and Sriniketan would be sufficient to rank him as one of the India's greatest nation-builders.

With the years, Rabindranath had won the world and the world in turn had won him. He sought his home everywhere in the world and would bring the world to his home. And so the little school for children at Santiniketan became a world university, Visva-Bharati, a centre for Indian Culture, a seminary for Eastern Studies and a meeting-place of the East and West. The poet selected for its motto an ancient Sanskrit verse, *Yatra visvam bhavatieka nidam*, which means, "Where the whole world meets in a single nest."

"Visva-Bharati", he declared, " *represents India where she has her wealth of mind which is for all. Visva-Bharati acknowledges India's obligation to offer to others the hospitality of her best culture and India's right to accept from others their best.*"

In 1940 a year before he died, he put a letter in Gandhi's hand, *"Visva-Bharati is like a vessel which is carrying the cargo of my life's best treasure , and I hope it may claim special care from my countrymen for its preservation."*

SCIENCE AND THE PEOPLE

Gandhi and Tagore severely clashed over their totally different attitudes toward science. In January 1934, Bihar was struck by a devastating earthquake, which killed thousands of people. Gandhi, who was then deeply involved in the fight against untouchability (the barbaric system inherited from India's divisive past, in which "lowly people" were kept at a physical distance), extracted a positive lesson from the tragic event. "A man like me," Gandhi argued, "cannot but believe this earthquake is a divine chastisement sent by God for our sins"—in particular the sins of untouchability. "For me there is a vital connection between the Bihar calamity and the untouchability campaign."

Tagore, who equally abhorred untouchability and had joined Gandhi in the movements against it, protested against this interpretation of an event that had caused suffering and death to so many innocent people, including children and babies. He also hated the epistemology implicit in seeing an earthquake as caused by ethical failure. "It is," he wrote, "all the more unfortunate because this kind of unscientific view of [natural] phenomena is too readily accepted by a large section of our countrymen."

The two remained deeply divided over their attitudes toward science. However, while Tagore believed that modern science was essential to the understanding of physical phenomena, his views on epistemology were interestingly heterodox.

He did not take the simple "realist" position often associated with modern science. The report of his conversation with Einstein, published in The New York Times in 1930, shows how insistent Tagore was on interpreting truth through observation and reflective concepts.

To assert that something is true or untrue in the absence of anyone to observe or perceive its truth, or to form a conception of what it is, appeared to Tagore to be deeply questionable. When Einstein remarked, "If there were no human beings any more, the Apollo Belvedere no longer would be beautiful?" Tagore simply replied, "No." Going further—and into much more interesting territory—Einstein said, "I agree with regard to this conception of beauty, but not with regard to truth." Tagore's response was: "Why not? Truth is realized through men."

Tagore's epistemology, which he never pursued systematically, would seem to be searching for a line of reasoning that would later be elegantly developed by Hilary Putnam, who has argued: "Truth depends on conceptual schemes and it is nonetheless 'real truth.'" Tagore himself said little to explain his convictions, but it is important to take account of his heterodoxy, not only because his speculations were invariably interesting, but also because they illustrate how his support for any position, including his strong interest in science, was accompanied by critical scrutiny.

NATIONALISM AND COLONIALISM

Tagore was predictably hostile to communal sectarianism (such as a Hindu orthodoxy that was antagonistic to Islamic, Christian, or Sikh perspectives). But even nationalism seemed to him to be suspect. Isaiah Berlin summarizes well Tagore's complex position on Indian nationalism:

> *Tagore stood fast on the narrow causeway, and did not betray his vision of the difficult truth. He condemned romantic overattachment to the past, what he called the tying of India to the past "like a sacrificial goat tethered to a post," and he accused men who displayed it - they seemed to him reactionary - of not knowing what true political freedom was, pointing out that it is from English thinkers and English books that the very notion of political liberty was derived. But against cosmopolitanism he maintained that the English stood on their own feet, and so must Indians. In 1917 he once more denounced the danger of 'leaving everything to the unalterable will of the Master,' be he brahmin or Englishman.*

The duality Berlin points to is well reflected also in Tagore's attitude toward cultural diversity. He wanted Indians to learn what is going on elsewhere, how others lived, what they valued, and so on, while remaining interested and involved in their own culture and heritage. Indeed, in his educational writings the need for synthesis is strongly stressed. It can also be found in his advice to Indian students abroad.

In 1907 he wrote to his son-in-law Nagendranath Gangulee, who had gone to America to study agriculture:

> *To get on familiar terms with the local people is a part of your education. To know only agriculture is not enough; you must know America too. Of course if, in the process of knowing America, one begins to lose one's identity and falls into the trap of becoming an Americanised person contemptuous of everything Indian, it is preferable to stay in a locked room.*

Tagore was strongly involved in protest against the Raj on a number of occasions, most notably in the movement to resist the 1905 British proposal to split in two the province of Bengal, a plan that was eventually withdrawn following popular resistance. He was forthright in denouncing the brutality of British rule in India, never more so than after the Amritsar massacre of April 13, 1919, when 379 unarmed people at a peaceful meeting were gunned down by the army, and two thousand more were wounded. Between April 23 and 26, Rabindranath wrote five agitated letters to C.F. Andrews, who himself was extremely disturbed, especially after he was told by a British civil servant in India that thanks to this show of strength, the "moral prestige" of the Raj had "never been higher."

A month after the massacre, Tagore wrote to the Viceroy of India, asking to be relieved of the knighthood he had accepted four years earlier:

> *The disproportionate severity of the punishments inflicted upon the unfortunate people and the methods of carrying them out, we are convinced, are without parallel in the history of civilized governments, barring some conspicuous exceptions, recent and remote. Considering that such treatment has been meted out to a population, disarmed and resourceless, by a power which has the most terribly efficient organisation for destruction of human lives, we must strongly assert that it can claim no political expediency, far less moral justification.... The universal agony of indignation roused in the hearts of our people has been ignored by our rulers - possibly congratulating themselves for imparting*

what they imagine as salutary lessons.... I for my part want to stand, shorn of all special distinctions, by the side of those of my countrymen who for their so-called insignificance are liable to suffer a degradation not fit for human beings.

Both Gandhi and Nehru expressed their appreciation of the important part Tagore took in the national struggle. It is fitting that after independence, India chose a song of Tagore ("Jana Gana Mana Adhinayaka," which can be roughly translated as "the leader of people's minds") as its national anthem. Since Bangladesh would later choose another song of Tagore ("Amar Sonar Bangla") as its national anthem, he may be the only one ever to have authored the national anthems of two different countries.

Tagore's criticism of the British administration of India was consistently strong and grew more intense over the years. This point is often missed, since he made a special effort to dissociate his criticism of the Raj from any denigration of British—or Western—people and culture. Mahatma Gandhi's well-known quip in reply to a question, asked in England, on what he thought of Western civilization ("It would be a good idea") could not have come from Tagore's lips. He would understand the provocations to which Gandhi was responding - involving cultural conceit as well as imperial tyranny. D.H. Lawrence supplied a fine example of the former: "I become more and more surprised to see how far higher, in reality, our European civilization stands than the East, Indian and Persian, ever dreamed of.... This fraud of looking up to them—this wretched worship-of-Tagore attitude is disgusting." But, unlike Gandhi, Tagore could not, even in jest, be dismissive of Western civilization.

Even in his powerful indictment of British rule in India in 1941, in a lecture which he gave on his last birthday, and which was later published as a pamphlet under the title *Crisis in Civilization,* he strains hard to maintain the distinction between opposing Western imperialism and rejecting Western civilization. While he saw India as having been "smothered under the dead weight of British administration" (adding "another great and ancient civilization for whose recent tragic history the British cannot disclaim responsibility is China"), Tagore recalls what India has gained from "discussions centred upon Shakespeare's drama and Byron's poetry and above all...the large-hearted liberalism of nineteenth-century English politics." The tragedy, as Tagore saw it, came from the fact that what "was truly best in their own civilization, the upholding of dignity of human relationships, has no place in the British administration of this country." "If in its place they have established, baton in hand, a reign of 'law and order,' or in other words a policeman's rule, such a mockery of civilization can claim no respect from us."

PATRIOTISM AND ITS CRITICS

Rabindranath rebelled against the strongly nationalist form that the independence movement often took, and this made him refrain from taking a particularly active part in contemporary politics. He wanted to assert India's right to be independent without denying the importance of what India could learn—freely and profitably—from abroad. He was afraid that a rejection of the West in favor of an indigenous Indian tradition was not only limiting in itself; it could easily turn into hostility to other influences from abroad, including Christianity, which came to parts of India by the fourth century; Judaism, which came through Jewish immigration shortly after the fall of Jerusalem, as did Zoroastrianism through Parsi immigration later on (mainly in the eighth century), and, of course—and most importantly—Islam, which has had a very strong presence in India since the tenth century.

Tagore's criticism of patriotism is a persistent theme in his writings. As early as 1908, he put his position succinctly in a letter replying to the criticism of Abala Bose, the wife of a great Indian scientist, Jagadish Chandra Bose: "Patriotism cannot be our final spiritual shelter; my refuge is humanity. I will not buy glass for the price of diamonds, and I will never allow patriotism to triumph over humanity as long as I live." His novel *Ghare Baire* (The Home and the World) has much to say about this theme. In the novel, Nikhil, who is keen on social reform, including women's liberation, but cool toward nationalism, gradually loses the esteem of his spirited wife, Bimala, because of his failure to be enthusiastic about anti-British agitations, which she sees as a lack of patriotic commitment. Bimala becomes fascinated with Nikhil's nationalist friend Sandip, who speaks brilliantly and acts with patriotic militancy, and she falls in love with him. Nikhil refuses to change his views: "I am willing to serve my country; but my worship I reserve for Right which is far greater than my country. To worship my country as a god is to bring a curse upon it."

As the story unfolds, Sandip becomes angry with some of his countrymen for their failure to join the struggle as readily as he thinks they should ("Some Mohamedan traders are still obdurate"). He arranges to deal with the recalcitrants by burning their meager trading stocks and physically attacking them. Bimala has to acknowledge the connection between Sandip's rousing nationalistic sentiments and his sectarian - and ultimately violent-actions. The dramatic events that follow (Nikhil attempts to help the victims, risking his life) include the end of Bimala's political romance.

This is a difficult subject, and Satyajit Ray's beautiful film of *The Home and the World* brilliantly brings out the novel's tensions, along with the human affections and disaffections of the story. Not surprisingly, the story has had many detractors, not just among dedicated nationalists in India. Georg Lukács found Tagore's novel to be "a petit bourgeois yarn of the shoddiest kind," "at the intellectual service of the British police," and "a contemptible caricature of Gandhi." It would, of course, be absurd to think of Sandip as Gandhi, but the novel gives a "strong and gentle" warning, as Bertolt Brecht noted in his diary, of the corruptibility of nationalism, since it is not even-handed. Hatred of one group can lead to hatred of others, no matter how far such feeling may be from the minds of large-hearted nationalist leaders like Mahatma Gandhi.

ADMIRATION AND CRITICISM OF JAPAN

Tagore's reaction to nationalism in Japan is particularly telling. As in the case of India, he saw the need to build the self-confidence of a defeated and humiliated people, of people left behind by developments elsewhere, as was the case in Japan before its emergence during the nineteenth century. At the beginning of one of his lectures in Japan in 1916 ("Nationalism in Japan"), he observed that "the worst form of bondage is the bondage of dejection, which keeps men hopelessly chained in loss of faith in themselves."

Tagore shared the admiration for Japan widespread in Asia for demonstrating the ability of an Asian nation to rival the West in industrial development and economic progress. He noted with great satisfaction that Japan had "in giant strides left centuries of inaction behind, overtaking the present time in its foremost achievement." For other nations outside the West, he said, Japan "has broken the spell under which we lay in torpor for ages, taking it to be the normal condition of certain races living in certain geographical limits."

But then Tagore went on to criticize the rise of a strong nationalism in Japan, and its emergence as an imperialist nation. Tagore's outspoken criticisms did not please Japanese audiences and, as E.P. Thompson wrote, "the welcome given to him on his first arrival soon cooled." Twenty-two years later, in 1937, during the Japanese war on China, Tagore received a letter from Rash Behari Bose, an anti-British Indian revolutionary then living in Japan, who sought Tagore's approval for his efforts there on behalf of Indian independence, in which he had the support of the Japanese government. Tagore replied:

> *Your cable has caused me many restless hours, for it hurts me very much to have to ignore your appeal. I wish you had asked for my cooperation in a cause against which my spirit did not protest. I know, in making this appeal, you counted on my great regard for the Japanese for I, along with the rest of Asia, did once admire and look up to Japan and did once fondly hope that in Japan Asia had at last discovered its challenge to the West, that Japan's new strength would be consecrated in safeguarding the culture of the East against alien interests. But Japan has not taken long to betray that rising hope and repudiate all that seemed*

> *significant in her wonderful, and, to us symbolic, awakening, and has now become itself a worse menace to the defenceless peoples of the East.*

How to view Japan's position in the Second World War was a divisive issue in India. After the war, when Japanese political leaders were tried for war crimes, the sole dissenting voice among the judges came from the Indian judge, Radhabinod Pal, a distinguished jurist. Pal dissented on various grounds, among them that no fair trial was possible in view of the asymmetry of power between the victor and the defeated. Ambivalent feelings in India toward the Japanese military aggression, given the unacceptable nature of British imperialism, possibly had a part in predisposing Pal to consider a perspective different from that of the other judges. More tellingly, Subhas Chandra Bose (no relation of Rash Behari Bose), a leading nationalist, made his way to Japan during the war via Italy and Germany after escaping from a British prison; he helped the Japanese to form units of Indian soldiers, who had earlier surrendered to the advancing Japanese army, to fight on the Japanese side as the "Indian National Army." Rabindranath had formerly entertained great admiration for Subhas Bose as a dedicated nonsectarian fighter for Indian independence. But their ways would have parted when Bose's political activities took this turn, although Tagore was dead by the time Bose reached Japan.

Tagore saw Japanese militarism as illustrating the way nationalism can mislead even a nation of great achievement and promise. In 1938 Yone Noguchi, the distinguished poet and friend of Tagore (as well as of Yeats and Pound), wrote to Tagore, pleading with him to change his mind about Japan. Rabindranath's reply, written on September 12, 1938, was altogether uncompromising:

> *It seems to me that it is futile for either of us to try to convince the other, since your faith in the infallible right of Japan to bully other Asiatic nations into line with your Government's policy is not shared by me.... Believe me, it is sorrow and shame, not anger, that prompt me to write to you. I suffer intensely not only*

because the reports of Chinese suffering batter against my heart, but because I can no longer point out with pride the example of a great Japan.

He would have been much happier with the postwar emergence of Japan as a peaceful power. Then, too, since he was not free of egotism, he would also have been pleased by the attention paid to his ideas by the novelist Yasunari Kawabata and others.

INTERNATIONAL CONCERNS

Tagore was not invariably well-informed about international politics. He allowed himself to be entertained by Mussolini in a short visit to Italy in May-June 1926, a visit arranged by Carlo Formichi, professor of Sanskrit at the University of Rome. When he asked to meet Benedetto Croce, Formichi said, "Impossible! Impossible!" Mussolini told him that Croce was "not in Rome." When Tagore said he would go "wherever he is," Mussolini assured him that Croce's whereabouts were unknown.

Such incidents, as well as warnings from Romain Rolland and other friends, should have ended Tagore's flirtation with Mussolini more quickly than it did. But only after he received graphic accounts of the brutality of Italian fascism from two exiles, Gaetano Salvemini and Gaetano Salvadori, and learned more of what was happening in Italy, did he publicly denounce the regime, publishing a letter to the *Manchester Guardian* in August. The next month, Popolo d'Italia, the magazine edited by Benito Mussolini's brother, replied: "Who cares? Italy laughs at Tagore and those who brought this unctuous and insupportable fellow in our midst."

With his high expectations of Britain, Tagore continued to be surprised by what he took to be a lack of official sympathy for international victims of aggression. He returned to this theme in the lecture he gave on his last birthday, in 1941:

While Japan was quietly devouring North China, her act of wanton aggression was ignored as a minor incident by the veterans of British diplomacy. We have also

> *witnessed from this distance how actively the British statesmen acquiesced in the destruction of the Spanish Republic.*

But distinguishing between the British government and the British people, Rabindranath went on to note "with admiration how a band of valiant Englishmen laid down their lives for Spain."

Tagore's view of the Soviet Union has been a subject of much discussion. He was widely read in Russia. In 1917 several Russian translations of *Gitanjali* (one edited by Ivan Bunin, later the first Russian Nobel Laureate in Literature) were available, and by the late 1920s many of the English versions of his work had been rendered into Russian by several distinguished translators. Russian versions of his work continued to appear: Boris Pasternak translated him in the 1950s and 1960s.

When Tagore visited Russia in 1930, he was much impressed by its development efforts and by what he saw as a real commitment to eliminate poverty and economic inequality. But what impressed him most was the expansion of basic education across the old Russian empire. In Letters from Russia, written in Bengali and published in 1931, he unfavorably compares the acceptance of widespread illiteracy in India by the British administration with Russian efforts to expand education:

> *In stepping on the soil of Russia, the first thing that caught my eye was that in education, at any rate, the peasant and the working classes have made such enormous progress in these few years that nothing comparable has happened even to our highest classes in the course of the last hundred and fifty years.... The people here are not at all afraid of giving complete education even to Turcomans of distant Asia; on the contrary, they are utterly in earnest about it.*

When parts of the book were translated into English in 1934, the under-secretary for India stated in Parliament that it was "calculated by distortion of the facts to bring the British

Administration in India into contempt and disrepute," and the book was then promptly banned. The English version would not be published until after independence.

EDUCATION AND FREEDOM

The British Indian administrators were not, however, alone in trying to suppress Tagore's reflections on Russia. They were joined by Soviet officials. In an interview with *Izvestia* in 1930, Tagore sharply criticized the lack of freedom that he observed in Russia:

> *I must ask you: Are you doing your ideal a service by arousing in the minds of those under your training anger, class-hatred, and revengefulness against those whom you consider to be your enemies?... Freedom of mind is needed for the reception of truth; terror hopelessly kills it.... For the sake of humanity I hope you may never create a vicious force of violence, which will go on weaving an interminable chain of violence and cruelty.... You have tried to destroy many of the other evils of [the czarist] period. Why not try to destroy this one also?*

The interview was not published in *Izvestia* until 1988—nearly sixty years later. Tagore's reaction to the Russia of 1930 arose from two of his strongest commitments: his uncompromising belief in the importance of "freedom of mind" (the source of his criticism of the Soviet Union), and his conviction that the expansion of basic education is central to social progress (the source of his praise, particularly in contrast to British-run India). He identified the lack of basic education as the fundamental cause of many of India's social and economic afflictions:

> *In my view the imposing tower of misery which today rests on the heart of India has its sole foundation in the absence of education. Caste divisions, religious conflicts, aversion to work, precarious economic conditions - all centre on this single factor.*

It was on education (and on the reflection, dialogue, and communication that are associated with it), rather than on, say, spinning "as a sacrifice" ("the charka does not require anyone to think"), that the future of India would depend.

Tagore was concerned not only that there be wider opportunities for education across the country (especially in rural areas where schools were few), but also that the schools themselves be more lively and enjoyable. He himself had dropped out of school early, largely out of boredom, and had never bothered to earn a diploma. He wrote extensively on how schools should be made more attractive to boys and girls and thus more productive. His own co-educational school at Santiniketan had many progressive features. The emphasis here was on self-motivation rather than on discipline, and on fostering intellectual curiosity rather than competitive excellence.

Much of Rabindranath's life was spent in developing the school at Santiniketan. The school never had much money, since the fees were very low. His lecture honoraria, "$700 a scold," went to support it, as well as most of his Nobel Prize money. The school received no support from the government, but did get help from private citizens—even Mahatma Gandhi raised money for it.

The dispute with Mahatma Gandhi on the Bihar earthquake touched on a subject that was very important to Tagore: the need for education in science as well as in literature and the humanities. At Santiniketan, there were strong "local" elements in its emphasis on Indian traditions, including the classics, and in the use of Bengali rather than English as the language of instruction. At the same time there were courses on a great variety of cultures, and study programs devoted to China, Japan, and the Middle East. Many foreigners came to Santiniketan to study or teach, and the fusion of studies seemed to work.

I am partial to seeing Tagore as an educator, having myself been educated at Santiniketan. The school was unusual in many different ways, such as the oddity that classes, excepting those requiring a laboratory, were held outdoors (whenever the weather permitted). No matter what we thought of Rabindranath's belief that one gains from being in a natural setting while learning (some of us argued about this theory), we typically found the experience of outdoor schooling extremely attractive and pleasant. Academically, our school was not particularly exacting (often we did not have any examinations at all), and it could not, by the usual academic standards, compete with some of the better schools in Calcutta. But there was something remarkable about the ease with which class discussions could move from Indian traditional literature to contemporary as well as classical Western thought, and then to the culture of China or Japan or elsewhere. The school's celebration of variety was also in sharp contrast with the cultural conservatism and separatism that has tended to grip India from time to time.

The cultural give and take of Tagore's vision of the contemporary world has close parallels with the vision of Satyajit Ray, also an alumnus of Santiniketan who made several films based on Tagore's stories. Ray's words about Santiniketan in 1991 would have greatly pleased Rabindranath:

INDIA TODAY

At the fiftieth anniversary of Indian independence, the reckoning of what India had or had not achieved in this half century was a subject of considerable interest: "What has been the story of those first fifty years?" (as Shashi Tharoor asked in his balanced, informative, and highly readable account of *India: From Midnight to the Millennium*). If Tagore were to see the India of today, more than half a century after independence, nothing perhaps would shock him so much as the continued illiteracy of the masses. He would see this as a total betrayal of what the nationalist leaders had promised during the struggle for independence—a promise that had figured even in Nehru's rousing speech on the eve of independence in August 1947 (on India's "tryst with destiny").

In view of his interest in childhood education, Tagore would not be consoled by the extraordinary expansion of university education, in which India sends to its universities six times as many people per unit of population as does China. Rather, he would be stunned that, in contrast to East and

Southeast Asia, including China, half the adult population and two thirds of Indian women remain unable to read or write. Statistically reliable surveys indicate that even in the late 1980s, nearly half of the rural girls between the ages of twelve and fourteen did not attend any school for a single day of their lives.

This state of affairs is the result of the continuation of British imperial neglect of mass education, which has been reinforced by India's traditional elitism, as well as upper-class-dominated contemporary politics (except in parts of India such as Kerala, where anti-upper-caste movements have tended to concentrate on education as a great leveller). Tagore would see illiteracy and the neglect of education not only as the main source of India's continued social backwardness, but also as a great constraint that restricts the possibility and reach of economic development in India (as his writings on rural development forcefully make clear). Tagore would also have strongly felt the need for a greater commitment—and a greater sense of urgency—in removing endemic poverty.

At the same time, Tagore would undoubtedly find some satisfaction in the survival of democracy in India, in its relatively free press, and in general from the "freedom of mind" that post-independence Indian politics has, on the whole, managed to maintain. He would also be pleased by the fact noted by the historian E.P. Thompson (whose father Edward Thompson had written one of the first major biographies of Tagore:

> *All the convergent influences of the world run through this society: Hindu, Moslem, Christian, secular; Stalinist, liberal, Maoist, democratic socialist, Gandhian. There is not a thought that is being thought in the West or East that is not active in some Indian mind.*

Tagore would have been happy also to see that the one governmental attempt to dispense generally with basic liberties and political and civil rights in India, in the 1970s, when Prime Minister Indira Gandhi (ironically, herself a former student at Santiniketan) declared an "emergency," was overwhelmingly rejected by the Indian voters, leading to the precipitate fall of her government.

Rabindranath would also see that the changes in policy that have eliminated famine since independence had much to do with the freedom to be heard in a democratic India. In Tagore's play *Raja O Rani* ("The King and the Queen"), the sympathetic Queen eventually rebels against the callousness of state policy toward the hungry. She begins by inquiring about the ugly sounds outside the palace, only to be told that the noise is coming from "the coarse, clamorous crowd who howl unashamedly for food and disturb the sweet peace of the palace." The Viceregal office in India could have taken a similarly callous view of Indian famines, right up to the easily preventable Bengal famine of 1943, just before independence, which killed between two and three million people. But a government in a multi-party democracy, with elections and free newspapers, cannot any longer dismiss the noise from "the coarse, clamorous crowd."

Unlike Gandhi, Rabindranath would not resent the development of modern industries in India, or the acceleration of technical progress, since he did not want India to be shackled to the turning of "the wheel of an antiquated invention." Tagore was concerned that people not be dominated by machines, but he was not opposed to making good use of modern technology. "The mastery over the machine," he wrote in *Crisis in Civilization,* "by which the British have consolidated their sovereignty over their vast empire, has been kept a sealed book, to which due access has been denied to this helpless country." Rabindranath had a deep interest in the environment - he was particularly concerned about deforestation and initiated a "festival of tree-planting" (vriksha-ropana) as early as 1928. He would want increased private and government commitments to environmentalism; but he would not derive from this position a general case against modern industry and technology.

VIEWS ON CULTURAL SEPARATION

Rabindranath would be shocked by the growth of cultural separatism in India, as elsewhere. The "openness" that he valued so much is certainly under great strain right now - in many countries. Religious fundamentalism still has a relatively small following in India; but various factions seem to be doing their best to increase their numbers. Certainly religious sectarianism has had much success in some parts of India (particularly in the west and the north). Tagore would see the expansion of religious sectarianism as being closely associated with an artificially separatist view of culture.

He would have strongly resisted defining India in specifically Hindu terms, rather than as a "confluence" of many cultures. Even after the partition of 1947, India is still the third- largest Muslim country in the world, with more Muslims than in Bangladesh, and nearly as many as in Pakistan. Only Indonesia has substantially more followers of Islam. Indeed, by pointing to the immense heterogeneousness of India's cultural background and its richly diverse history, Tagore had argued that the "idea of India" itself militated against a culturally separatist view—"against the intense consciousness of the separateness of one's own people from others."

Tagore would also oppose the cultural nationalism that has recently been gaining some ground in India, along with an exaggerated fear of the influence of the West. He was uncompromising in his belief that human beings could absorb quite different cultures in constructive ways:

> *Whatever we understand and enjoy in human products instantly becomes ours, wherever they might have their origin. I am proud of my humanity when I can acknowledge the poets and artists of other countries as my own. Let me feel with unalloyed gladness that all. the great glories of man are mine. Therefore it hurts me deeply when the cry of rejection rings loud against the West in my country with the clamour that Western education can only injure us.*

In this context, it is important to emphasize that Rabindranath was not short of pride in India's own heritage, and often spoke about it. He lectured at Oxford, with evident satisfaction, on the importance of India's religious ideas—quoting both from ancient texts and from popular poetry (such as the verses of the sixteenth-century Muslim poet Kabir). In 1940, when he was given an honorary doctorate by Oxford

University, in a ceremony arranged at his own educational establishment in Santiniketan ("In Gangem Defluit Isis," Oxford helpfully explained), to the predictable "volley of Latin" Tagore responded "by a volley of Sanskrit," as Marjorie Sykes, a Quaker friend of Rabindranath, reports. Her cheerful summary of the match, "India held its own," was not out of line with Tagore's pride in Indian culture. His welcoming attitude to Western civilization was reinforced by this confidence: he did not see India's culture as fragile and in need of "protection" from Western influence.

In India, he wrote, "circumstances almost compel us to learn English, and this lucky accident has given us the opportunity of access into the richest of all poetical literatures of the world." There seems to me much force in Rabindranath's argument for clearly distinguishing between the injustice of a serious asymmetry of power (colonialism being a prime example of this) and the importance nevertheless of appraising Western culture in an open-minded way, in colonial and postcolonial territories, in order to see what uses could be made of it.

Rabindranath insisted on open debate on every issue, and distrusted conclusions based on a mechanical formula, no matter how attractive that formula might seem in isolation (such as "This was forced on us by our colonial masters - we must reject it," "This is our tradition—we must follow it," "We have promised to do this—we must fulfill that promise," and so on). The question he persistently asks is whether we have reason enough to want what is being proposed, taking everything into account. Important as history is, reasoning has to go beyond the past. It is in the sovereignty of reasoning—fearless reasoning in freedom—that we can find Rabindranath Tagore's lasting voice.

Devotio Humana: Rabindranath's Love Poems Revisited

Rabindranath Tagore's (1861-1941) reputation as a *rishi* (saint), *mahamanab* (superman), or *gurudeb* (divine mentor) has created a haze and a halo through which we can neither recognize the concrete human being of flesh and blood nor appreciate his emotional sensibilities in their proper perspectives. As such, a number of critics such as Ajitkumar

Chakravarti, Srikumar Banerjee, Mohitlal Majumdar, or Charuchandra Banerjee either refused to consider the direct influence of the human experiences, especially his relationships with various women, on some of Rabindranath's greatest lyrical pieces, or considered any attempt to probe into them irrelevant, irreverent, or irresponsible. However, the distinguished Tagore scholar Pramathanath Bishi provided an explanation for his claim that Rabindranath's poems and lyrics dealing with love lack human intimacy. A distinct signature of Tagore's love poems, Bishi goes on, is that they reveal sadness, disappointment, and compassion rather than passion, euphoria, or tumult of the heart.

If we pay heed to Buddhadeva Bose and Sankha Ghosh's sensible suggestion to read Rabindranath's poetry *qua* poetry *(kabitar uddeshe kabita)* and try not to analyze it either insisting on the contexts and causes of his works or ignoring their human and historical but emphasizing spiritual or philosophical dimensions, we would readily realize that he truly was what another great poet of his day, though hailing from an earlier generation, Walt Whitman of America (1819-92), wrote in a celebrated poem: "I am large, I contain multitudes." Indeed, as Tagore has clearly stated, "human mind is deep and variegated ; swayed by multiple pulls and pressures it has to bend [and adjust]. That is the sign of its life, its humanity, and its protests against sterile immobility. One who does not face this ambivalence and weakness has a very narrow, hard, and dead mind. Our instinct, which we ridicule often, is the motor of life, it elevates us unto the infinite through pain and pleasure, sanctity and sin." Yet, beneath all his contradictions and ambivalence in respect of a number of issues there is a strong undercurrent of Rabindranath's essential humanism that was nurtured by his native culture he inherited and the Western culture of his day he imbibed. Nothing illustrates this problematic of Tagore's "myriad-minded" genius more clearly and wonderfully than his poems dealing with love.

Admittedly, this paper does not pretend to posit an entirely novel interpretation of Tagore's poems and lyrics dealing with love. On the other hand, the following pages bring together insights of several distinguished studies in Bengali to highlight the profile of Rabindranath, the sensitive, sensuous, shy as well as a spiritual human being. Tagore's delicate and refined sensibilities dictated his poetic imagination and public discourse and his entire life was dedicated to celebrate the beautiful and the eternal and proclaim the triumph of human love sublimated in cosmic compassion and agape or divine love.

In fact, the poet himself confessed to his own fluid understanding of love in a letter to Pramatha Chaudhuri, husband of Tagore's beloved niece Indira : "I can't tell for sure whether I am driven by [human] love with all its pleasures and pain deriving from union and separation [of lovers] or by an indefinite but inordinate longing for beauty." As early as 1891, Rabindranath had written a poem on *prem* [love]: *"E ye sakhi, hridayer prem—/Sukhduhkhabedanar adianta nahi yar,/ Chiradainya, chirapurna hem./. . . bujha yai adho prem, adhkhana mon—/Samasta ke bujhechhe kakhan?"* [This love of mine springs from the heart./It has limitless pangs and pleasures, always empty, always filled with pure gold./...It's easy to figure out a little love or a bit of the heart's desires,/ But who could fathom the depth of love in its fullness and entirety?]

Any discussion of Rabindranath's concept of erotic love, that is *prem,* must be prefaced by and predicated on his understanding of human love as well as his outlook on the feminine. Jagadish Bhattacharya has discussed in detail the Hindu cultural influences of the Tagore family (even though Brahmo) and the Western intellectual influences of Renaissance Bengal where Rabindranath was born and brought up. The young poet at once internalized the *parakiya* prem [love without lust or *niskam prem*] of the Vaishnab *sahajiyas* represented by the fourteenth-century poet Chandidas as well as the *eros* of Plato (427-347 B.C.) via the *corpus* of Tagore's predecessor in England the "natural Platonist" Percy B. Shelley (1792-1822), the love of Dante Alighieri (1265-1321) expressed for Beatrice Portinari (1266-90) in *La Vita Nuova,* or that of Francesco Petrarca (1304-74) expressed for Laura de Noves (1308-48) in *Canzoniere.* Rabindranath himself admitted to his attraction for the poet John Keats (1795-1821) in an essay in 1895: "Of all the English poets known to me, I feel an especial intimacy with Keats ... [whose] language is marked by a sincere aesthetic delight."

Buddhadeva Bose argues persuasively that Tagore's collection of poems in *Manasi* constitutes the primary *locus* or an "atomic world" *("anubishwa")* of the poet's lyrical *ouevres* and their *leitmotif* is love. Bose argues further that the object of Tagore's love poems in *Manasi* [Woman of Imagination, 1890] is not a concrete identifiable individual but an indefinite fluid entity. At best, as Bose concludes, "most of [Tagore's] poems beginning with *Manasi* down to *Gitanjali* [Song Offerings, 1906-10] are ambivalent or multivalent in that their subject matter love cannot be said to be love in human or divine sense with any certainty."

According to another distinguished Tagore scholar, Kshudiram Das, Rabindranath's literary genius consists, fundamentally, in his assimilation of visible real life *(jiban)* with the idealized or imagined unseen *(arup)* that transcends the sensate world. This synthesis is a reflection of the poet's successful amalgam of the sensuous Western literary tradition and the introspective meditative tradition of his native culture. While Das perhaps comes closer to truth, he tends to overlook the human experiences that inspired some of the poet's outstanding creations in a major way. In the final analysis we must recognize the vast inclusive expanse of his *Weltanschauung* that comprehends a multiplicity of perspectives and trajectories defying any straitjacketed categories.

It must also be noted that Rabindranath's upbringing in a spartan, though never overly puritan, Brahmo family might have conditioned him against any outward expression of emotional outbursts or sexuality. He never experienced any parental indulgence as a child being neither the eldest nor the youngest. His movements inside as well as outside the home were restricted. Admittedly, he was not neglected but, in keeping with the usual practice of his day, as a child he was kept away from the adult world under the control of the household servants, especially the two redoubtable veterans Brajeshwar and Shyam.

From his boyhood, Rabindranath learnt to live a simple but disciplined life. "It could be said that luxury was conspicuous by its absence in our childhood," Tagore recalled later. He wrote elsewhere: "I was a lonely child, I had no friends to play with. But I had the great big visible world to keep me company." He had been a sparse eater, though he did take part in physical exercise on a daily basis. He, however, disliked attending school as he must have found the atmosphere there boring and choking. At the same time, he was subjected to a strict regimen of studies and musical lessons at home under private tutors.

His evolution into adulthood occurred under such a controlled environment. The Brahmo etiquette of his family permitted free mixing between male and female members under certain parameters that were neither wholly patriarchal nor entirely egalitarian in terms of genders. Even as a mature young man Tagore manifested his uneasiness in female company. Admiring his young England-educated nephew Surendranath's spontaneous socialization with young women *(besh ritimata paka styley alap),* the thirty-two year old poet confessed: "Even at 32 I am unable to converse with women in such an easy, self-assured, and elegant manner. I stumble while walking, fumble while talking, and I am at a loss as to where to place hands or what to do with my long legs; while thus preoccupied with them I fail to continue conversations [with women] satisfactorily. In a crowded room [dimly] lit by three candles it becomes impossible for a clumsy and cowardly creature like me to get myself close to a young woman like iron to a magnet."

No wonder the young Rabindranath failed to summon a typical masculine response to the Maratha belle Anna Tadkhad's unabashed but sincere gesture to get him to hug and kiss her. Many years later, the poet confessed to his timid unromantic indifference to the pretty Anna's (he had nicknamed her "Nalini") overtures. He was similarly unresponsive to the erotic advances of the Scott sisters of Bloomsbury, London where the young poet had been a paying guest. As he told Dilip Ray many years later, he had little doubt that the girls, his "lovers in former life" *(purba janamer priya),* really fell for him and yet we notice his shy behavior at the initial stage of his meeting with them; he could not even summon the courage to look at one of them, Miss J, straight in the eye, lest he should lose his cool beholding her "well-chiseled countenance" *[apurba chhanche dhala mukh].* The poet's experiences with the mature, independent-minded, and intellectual Victoria Ocampo (1891-1979) of Argentina, whom he named Bijaya (a Bengali synonym for Victoria), register a similar episode of unrequited passion. One might reasonably suppose that his intimacy with Kadambari (1858-84), wife of his elder brother Jyotirindranath (1849-1925), was immaculate—it being a romantic communion or (as will be discussed later, *bhalobasa*) because of a tabooed relationship.

Kadambari had possessed the poet's heart by gifting away hers to him. In fact Tagore dedicated a number of poems to her: *Bhagnahriday* (Heartbreak,1881), *Chhabi O Gaan* (Images and Lyrics,1884), *Prakritir Pratishodh* (Nature's Revenge,1884), *Shaishab Sangeet* (Song of Childhood,1884), *Bhanusingha Thakurer Padabali* (Lyrics by Bhanusingha Thakur,1884), and the like. Victoria Ocampo, on the other hand, fell in love hook, line and sinker with a handsome sexagenarian fit to be her father in age, and she did not hide her feelings for her *gurudeb.* "I love you. Nothing can alter that," she confessed candidly in one of her missives to the master and concluded reiterating her feelings for him: "let me tell you, Gurudev, that I love you". The old bard in turn dedicated his anthology *Purabi* (1925) to his Argentine adorer Bijaya.

As he recalled his enchanted encounter: *Bidesher bhalobasa diye/ Ye preyasi petechhe asan/ Chiradin rakhibe bandhiya/ Kane kane tahari bhasan./ Bhasa yar jana chhila nako,/ Ankhi yar kayechhila katha,/ Jagaye rakhibe chiradin/ Sakarun tahari barata* [The lover who has gifted a throne/ with her love from a strange land,/Her whisperings will ring in (my) ears/For all time to come./Her language I did not know/Only her eyes spoke to me./Her melancholy message will endure for all time to come]. Ketaki Kushari Dyson, who has admirably probed into Ocampo's relationship with the aging Rabindranath in 1924-25, maintains that she became a Muse for the poet's creative corpus after 1924.

Dyson's claims for Ocampo's impact on Rabindranath's literary output since the mid 1920s conflict with Bhattacharya's observations on the influence of the precocious child Ranu Adhikari (later Lady Ranu Mukherjee), whose beauty, simplicity, and gloriously freewheeling love and admiration for the handsome old man inspired his creative genius in significant ways. The child Ranu appeared as the messenger of the poet's *Jibandebata* reminding him of the playmate of his early youth Kadambari—"morning star of his life transformed into the evening star [of his old age]" *(bhorer tara elo sanhjher tarar beshe).* Even Tagore's younger relatives wondered about the "new inspiration" and "cause" of the "outpouring of new poems of a fine and noble vintage."

There were other women in the poet's life—less glamorous intellectually—who impacted his psyche and work, women such as his child-bride Mrinalini (though more a spouse than a Muse), his niece Indira, his sister-in-law Jnadanandini, his daughter-in-law Pratima, his granddaughter Nandita, and Rani Mahalanabis, and Rani Chanda.

When we examine the various stages in Tagore's understanding and appreciation of woman's humanity, we cannot fail to notice that while as an adolescent, he saw her as a fairy queen of his dream world; as a young man he saw her as a romantic princess. Naturally, women awakened his unbridled youthful passion; witness his output during 1878-84. For instance, his *Kabikahini* [A Poet's Lore] and *Banaphool* [Wild Flowers], the two novellas in verse, published in 1878 and 1880 respectively, with their theme of an intimate relationship between femininity and the natural world, express the poet's spontaneous lyrical genius but contain a mishmash of wishy-washy sentimental excesses.

Recalling *Bhagnahriday,* Tagore himself observed later that at the time of composing this piece his mind was filled with vaporous bubble and his sentimental gunk was being churned in the whirlpool of fantasies without any purpose. This was sterile stirring—devoid of creativity and beauty. His lack of direction and aimless amorous fantasy yielded to intensely passionate longings especially in pieces such as *Asahay*

Bhalobasa (Unbearable Passion), *Ami Hara* (Loss of 'I'), *Upahar* (Gift), and *Durdin* (Hard Times), all belonging to the collection titled *Sandhya Sangeet* [Evening Song, 1882] .

The young poet's heart was shivering in trepidation having been overcome by an uncontrollable longing for the bliss of a mysterious woman's touch: *"Man mor pagaler hena / Pranpane shudhay se yena, / Praner majhe ki karile tomare go pai, / Ye thnai rayechhe shunya ki karile se shunya purai"* (My ecstatic heart seeks you in daring desperation,/Asking how could I get near you, how [could I] fill the void [in my heart] that you created). As he confided to Pramatha Chaudhuri: "I passed the whole day [during the period of the composition of *Chhabi O Gaan* [Pictures and Songs] like a lunatic—I was overwhelmed by the gushing flood tide of my newly awakened youth."

By the time Rabindranath composed the poems of *Chhabi O Gaan,* he had crossed the boundary of dreamy and idealized romantic longings of adolescence and entered the tumultuous world of youth assailed by an intense feeling of adult erotic urge. Unlike the earlier mood of his adolescence, when he sought the abstract and idealized woman of his fancy, the fully grown young man now set out to construct the image of a realistic female. As he recalled the period of the composition of *Chhabi O Gan* in his old age, his "desire [for a woman's love] was not to be satisfied with mere music, he now wished to savor her physical beauty."

This state of mind is made lyrically manifest in the piece that cries out loud: *Hridaye jagaye basanar shikha / Nayane sajaye maya marichika / Shudhu ghure mari marubhume / Tabu kena, tabu kena michhe e pipasa. / Biswa-charachara lupta haye yay / E ki ghor prem andharahu pray / Jibana-youbana grase / Tabe kena, tabe kena michhe e kuyasa.* [I move about aimlessly with my heart burning in desire/And my eyes beholding an illusive mirage./ What, then, my love is for?/This tremendous passion, like the blinding *Rahu,* consumes my youth and my life./Why, then, is this love of mine?] (*Mayar Khela* [Play of Maya], 1888). Such anxious longings and ecstatic excitement mark his poems, *inter alia,* "Nirjharer Swapnabhanga" [The Awakening of the Waterfall], and "Ananta Jiban" [Eternal Life], all belonging to the anthology titled *Prabhat Sangeet* (1883). It is well known how Rabindranath came to write his profoundly moving long poem "Nirjharer Swapnabhanga" in a fit of sudden illumination that had all the qualities of an epiphany. Sometime in 1881-82 Rabindranath lodged with his brother Jyotirindranath and Kadambari at 10 Sudder Street, Kolkata, just behind the National Museum. Here, as he later recalled in *Jibansmriti* (My Reminiscences): "One morning I happened to be standing on the verandah looking that way. The sun was just rising through the leafy tops of the trees. As I gazed, all of a sudden a lid seemed to fall from my eyes, and I found the world bathed in a wonderful radiance, with waves of beauty and joy swelling on every side. .... That very day the poem 'Nirjharer Swapnabhanga' (The Awakening of the Waterfall), gushed forth and coursed on like a cascade."

Interestingly enough, Rabindranath's ecstatic exclamation *"jagiya uthechhe pran/ore uthali uthechhe bari/ore praner basana praner abeg rudhia rakhite nari"* [My aroused heart is overflowing with uncontrollable passion] was as sensual as it was spiritual, reminiscent of child Ramakrishna's *samadhi* at the sight of flying cranes in the cloudy sky or the sixteenth-century German reformer Martin Luther's wondrous vision of the merciful Christ upon reading St. Paul's letter to the Romans. The poem contains Tagore's paradigm of love and, as many critics agree, heralds the birth of Rabindranath, the future world poet. It is fairly certain that the inspiration behind this literary masterpiece was the poet's sister-in-law and that there developed an intimacy between the two young sensitive and impressionable individuals of almost the same age.

It is noteworthy that the poet's later creations, *Kadi O Komal* (Sharps and Flats, 1886) and *Manasi,* in particular, brought in, to paraphrase his own observations, the fresh fruits of the heady autumn *(sharatkal)* in place of his former sentimental torrents of the rainy season *(barsakal)*. However, the autumnal fruits also generated an ambivalent image of the female—at once passionate mistress and compassionate mother. Thus in his essay *Dui Bon* [Two Sisters], Tagore wrote that women are of two kinds: erotic *(priya)* and motherly *(ma)*. To cite a few lines from the poem "Hriday Asan" (Heart's Throne) in *Kadi O Komal: Komal dukhani bahu sharame lataye/ Bikashita stan duti aguliya ray,/Tari majhkhane ki re rayechhe lukaye/Atishay-sayatan-gopan hriday!/Sei niralay sei komal asane/Duikhani snehasphuta staner chhayay/Kishor premer mridu pradoskirane/Anata ankhir tale rakhibe amay* [(Her) two tender arms cling shyly to cover and protect the two blossoming breasts./In between them lies hidden [her] carefully nurtured heart!/In that secret tender seat under the shade of the two loving breasts and her sunken eyes [she] will keep me ensconced at the faint twilight of youthful love].

In *Purna Milan* [Total Union], the poet's eroticism is acutely clear: *Trisita paran aji kandichhe katare/Tomare sarbanga diye karite darshan/Abar kothao—/Oi dehakhani buke tule neba bala/Panchadash batsarer ek gachhi mala* [My thirsty heart is crying out/To behold you with my every limb./Girl, I shall place your body in my heart like a garland of fifteen.] Other pieces such as "Stan" (Breast), "Chumban" (Kiss), "Bibasana" (Undressed), "Bahu" (Arms), "Charan" (Feet), "Deher Milan" (Physical Union) etc. from *Kadi O Komal* celebrated the charms of the female physique.

In his maturer years Tagore came to view his relationship with women as something deeper and dearer than that of a partner in the game of love. In one of the poems of his *Sonar Tari,* the poet's *kabita kalpanalata* (Muse) or *manassundari* (the beautiful woman of imagination) becomes *jibaner adhisthatri debi* (presiding goddess of life) and *antaralakshmi* (goddess of the innermost recesses of heart). She also becomes what the poet calls *jibandebata* (lord of life).

As he wrote in *Chitra* (1896): *Rate preyasir rup dhari/ Tumi esechha praneswari,/Prate kakhan debir beshe/Tumi samukhe udile hese/Ami sambhrambhare rayechhi dandaye dure abanata shire/Aji nirmalbay shanta ushay nirjan naditire* [You came to me at night in the/Guise of a lover./At dawn you appeared smiling,/Decked as a Goddess./And awestruck, I remain standing on the desolate riverbank yonder/With my head hung low in wonder] ("Rate O Prabhate" [At Night and at Dawn]).

For Tagore, thus, woman is *se yena tufan / yahare chanchal kare se tarike kare khan khan* (she is like a torrent./She pulverizes the boat she shakes); she is a *yadukari bachane chalane* (a charmer in her gait and speech), who is *prasadhan sadhane chatura* (an adept at making herself up), and yet the same woman lights and puts out a small lamp in her room./ After her morning bath she unlocks her hair and meditates her silent prayer *(grihakone chhoto deep jvalay nebay / Snan sanga kari elochule prabhate nirab nibedane stab kare ekmane)* ("Ujjiban," *Mahua*).

This melange of opposite attitudes bears testimony to the poet's unstated albeit undoubted thesis that true human love is more than lust, it is also the channel of receiving the assurance of divine grace. The capstone for such a realization is to be noticed in *Mahua* (1928) which contains, among others, the following piece: "Woman is God's greatest gift descended on earth to bestow dignity and honor upon man" *[Nari se ye mahendrer dan, / esechhe dharitritale purusere sampite sanman,* "Spardha" (Audacity)]. In another piece the poet wrote: *Dibe se khuli / E ghor dhulir / Abaran. / Tahar hate / ankhir pate / jagat-jaga jagaran. / Se hasikhani anibe tani / sabar hasi / Gadibe geha, jagabe sneha / jibanrashi* [She will unveil/this dusty cloak./This world will awaken to her look./Her smile will make everyone smile,/ And nurture a home and evoke affection in every life] ("Shunya Hridayer Akankhya"[Desires of an Empty Heart]). Thus, as the poet proclaims in *Malini*, woman is neither a goddess nor an abstraction but a familiar female of flesh and blood—*debi na re, daya na re, gharer se meye.*

We also need to note that Rabindranath's idealized woman is no mere abstraction even though she is a product of his creative genius. Thus his *manasi* is a mix of sensuous experience as well as poetic imagination. As has been noted above, he did acknowledge *la femme* to be god's gift, and yet he could write: *Shudhu bidhatar sristi naha tumi nari. / Purus gadechhe tore soundarya sanchari / Apan antar hate* [Woman, you're not created by god alone./You're also made of the beauty of man's heart]. In his famous lyric from *Manaspratima* [Idol of Imagination] he sang: *Tumi amara sadhera sadhana / Ami apana manera madhuri mishaye tomare karechhi rachana* [You're the prayers of my desire/ I've created you from my imagination of the sweet and the beautiful]. Thus the poet could announce to his *manasi* with confidence as well as humility: *Aj tumi apanake chinechha/Amar chena diye* [You now know who you are/By my reckoning].

In a number of subsequent poems, Rabindranath celebrated the beauty and beatitude of femininity in nature. His idea of *prem* has now been transmuted or sublimated into *bhalobasa* that is as much spiritual and cerebral *(manomai)* as it is passionate and physical. The poet even resurrects the Hindu cupid Madan, who suffered death by being immolated in Shiva's angry fire, as the deity of love reborn as a hero *(mrityu hate otho Pushpadhanu/Hey Atanu, birer tanute laha tanu).*

Here we must recall Rabindranath's definition of *bhalobasa.* As early as 1881, the young poet had written in an essay in *Bharati* that "*bhalobasa* is more than mere self-surrender. Rather, it is surrendering the very best of one's self. *Bhalobasa* is not just installing the idol of the goddess in the heart. It is, more appropriately, installing the idol in the heart's sanctum." In his "Pashchim Yatrir Diary" (Diary of a Traveler to the West) written on board the vessel "Haruna Maru *en route* to South America in October 1924, Tagore expatiated on the meaning of *prem* in the double import of the word: *bhalolaga* (liking) and *bhalobasa* (love). The former is directed toward the self while the latter toward the other. *Bhalolaga* is gratified in enjoyment, *bhalobasa* achieves fulfillment in sacrifice and surrender. "*Bhalobasa* realizes itself in the spirit, it is the expansion of human personality," Tagore concluded.

In "Upahar" [Gift] Tagore wrote: *Bhule gechhi kabe tumi chhelebela ekdin/Maramer kachhe esechhile/Snehamay chhayamay sandhyasama ankhi meli/Ekbar bujhi hesechhile/Age ke janita balo kata ki lukano chhila/Hriday nibhrite/tomar nayan diya amar nijer hiya/Painu dekhite* [I have forgotten when in my youth you came to my heart/And looked at me with your loving eyes cool as the evening shadows./Who could have known what treasure was hidden in my heart until I could discover it through your gaze] *(Sandhyasangit).* The poet's lover is not just an erotic playmate of youth; she is also his soulmate in life and beyond. His idea of femininity shows a remarkable fusion of Western and Eastern ideas in his reconstruction of the character of Chitrangada in the Hindu epic *Mahabharata.* As he makes her proclaim in the famous lyrical play *Chitrangada: Ami Chitrangada ami rajendranandini/Debi nahi, nahi samanya ramani./Puja kari rakhibe mathay, seo ami/Nai; abahela kari pusiya rakhibe/Pichhe, seo ami nahi. Yadi parshve rakho/More sankater pathe, duruha chintar/Yadi angsha dao, yadi anumati karo/Kathin brater taba sahay haite,/Yadi sukhe duhkhe more karo sahachari,/Amar paibe tabe parichay.* [I am princess Chitrangada,/Not a goddess to be worshiped/On an altar,/Nor a mere woman pushed behind/With indifference./If you let me walk beside you/In weal and woe/And make me your comrade/In difficult venture,/You will know me/For what I am.] "In her," observes Rajat Ray, "the older Indian idea of wife as a partner in the duties of family life *(sahadharmini)* had developed, under Western influence, into the romantic concept of a comrade in perilous action." Clinton Seely further clarifies the term *bhalobasa* by comparing it to the commonly understood terms such as sneha (a kind of filial attraction) and *prem* (amorous romantic love). *Bhalobasa,* Seely concludes, "comprehends both *sneha* and *prem."*

Niharranjan Ray astutely observes that for Tagore "love cannot deny or bypass the reality of the body's desire; but a love which never learns to go beyond the body knows no real fulfillment, no peace, and is, therefore, unreal." Indeed, as the poet himself has written in *Creative Unity,* "in human nature sexual passion is fiercely individual and destructive, but dominated by the ideal of love, it has been made to flower into a perfection of beauty, becoming in its best expression symbolical of the spiritual truth in man which is his kinship of love with the Infinite." In his poem "Nisphal Kamana" [Unrequited Passion] he had admonished: *Bhalobaso, preme hao bali,/Cheona tahare./Akankhar dhan nahe atma manaber/* [Love (her), and be strong in love,/but do not desire her./Human soul is not an object of lust.]

Rabindranath has often been seen as a mystic for whom, in Vaishnavic terms, *atmendriya pritiichha* [self-centered love and desire] or *eros* [*kam*] coalesced in love for God [*prem*], krishnendriya pritiichha [Krishna—or God-centered love and desire]. In other words, the poet's idea of love is tantalizingly comparable to the Christian idea of *agape*. However, I argue that Rabindranath's idea of love cannot be apprehended by regarding him a mystic or regarding his idea of *prem* or *eros* as divine *agape*. Abbé Henri Bremond distinguishes between mystical, that is, religious and poetical activity and considers the latter as an imperfect form of the former. Even if poetry is considered as a kind of prayer in that it employs "some of the resources of the deep-seated soul," it is, according to Bremond, an imitation of mystical prayer, an *ersatz* religious solution to soteriological problems.

Then, *agape* is radically different from *eros*. *Agape* is a noble spiritual love that mimics the love of God for all His creations. In *agape*, all things are loved unconditionally with no consideration of a transactional *quid pro quo*. It is unmotivated or as the Bengali expression has it *ahaituki prem*. *Eros*, on the other hand, is motivated by the acquisition of happiness. Eros recognizes value in the object of love and loves it. *Agape* loves and creates value in its object of love. As the psychologist Erich Fromm has it, eros is based on the proposition "I love you because I need you" while *agape* is predicated on the plea "I need you because I love you." *Eros* is man's way to God, *agape* is God's way to man.

Jagadish Bhattacharya posits, following the definition of the seventeenth-century Bengali aesthetician Kabikarnapura, that Rabindranath's idea of love could be something analogous to suprasensuous eros or *pritirati*, that is a feeling or sentiment which delights *(rati)* the heart but remains *asamproyagabisaya* or devoid of carnality. Rabindranath's idea of *pritirati*, is poignantly expressed in his poem *Banaspati* (The *Dendron*) in which, standing in the sunset hours of life, the tired titan expressed his desire for a final repose and quiet after having struggled with the *Sturm und Drang* of his soul buffeted by the crosscurrents of his unrequited passion and unfulfilled mission in life. In his response of December 28, 1924 to the overture of his Argentine hostess, who had written him to say "I have gone through such joy and such sufferings all these days! Joy because I felt near you; sufferings, because you ignored my nearness," the aging and ailing Rabindranath wrote to that "incomparable one" *[tulanahinare]* he had met "on the verdant bank of the blue ocean" *[sunil sagarer shyamal kinare]: Daya karo, daya karo, aranyak ei tapaswire,/ Dhairya dharo, ogo digangana,/Byartha karibare tay ashanta abege phire phire/ baner angane matiyo na./E ki tibra prem, e ye shilabristi nirmam duhsaha—/Duranta chumban-bege taba/Chhindite jharate chao andha sukhe, kaha more kaha,/kishor korak naba naba?/Asuk tomar prem diptirupe nilambartale,/Shaktirupe eso, digangana./Uthuk spandita hoye sakhe sakhe pallabe balkale/Sughambhir tomar bandana./Dao tare sei tej mahatwe yahar samadhan,/Sarthak hok se banaspati./Biswer anjali yena bhariya karite pare dan/Tapsyar purna parinati.* [Hold back, please, O Goddess of Directions, do not distract this mendicant of the forest with your restless desire./ The hailstorm of your intense passion is merciless and unbearable./ Tell me, do you intend to pluck the new born buds with your violent kisses?/ Let your love descend as the light from the blue sky/ And you, Goddess, come as the primal energy, *Shakti.*/Let the leaves and the bark of this *dendron* pulsate in singing your paean./ Endow it with your power so that it may achieve the final consummation of its prayers by offering all it has to the world at large].

Especially Tagore's last three collections of poems—*Rogshayyay* (In Sickbed), *Arogya,* (Recovery), and *Janmadine* (On My Birthday) written during October 1940-March 1941—reveal an enigmatic convergence of the artist and the ascetic. All the pieces of these collections are characterized by a quiet grandeur: *shanta rasa.* Though, according to Bagbhatta, this particular rasa or aesthetic delight has its marker in *samyakjnan,* that is, awareness of the Absolute Soul *(Paramatman)* or God, in Tagore *shanta rasa* displays the unity of the two divergent consciousness: "the sweet earthy passion" *(martyer madhuratama asakti)* and "the sublime freedom of the heavens" *(akasher nirmalatama mukti).* This consciousness informs his idea of love or *bhalobasa* as it evolved from the impetuous, rebellious, and "delirious cascading waterfall" *(nirjharer pralapkallol)* of his youth to a serene and silent prayer "in cosmic quiescence" *(nikhiler brihat shantite).* In the sunset hours of his life, in a relatively obscure but a truly lyrical piece titled "Sandhyay" [In the Evening], the poet beseeches his beloved to be as beautiful, serene, and quiet as the evening and asks her to come to his life all by herself: *Ogo tumi sandhyar mata hao ...omni sundar shanta ...mata dhire dhire amar jibantire/Barek dandao ekakini.*

Rabindranath was a humanist *par excellence* who loved this beautiful earth and its colorful inhabitants so much that he refused to depart from this world: "I do not want to die in this beautiful world,/ But live in the hearts of men" *[Marite chahina ami, sundar bhubane, /manaber majhe ami banchibare chai] (Kadi O Komal).* He candidly confessed to his commitments to the world at large in his letter to his Argentine hostess and admirer Victoria Ocampo: "My true home is there where from my surroundings comes the call to me to bring out the best that I have, for that inevitably leads me to the touch with the universal." He wrote in his Reminiscences: "I guess my work has only one theme—reconciling the finite with the infinite."

Tagore's quintessential humanism is implicit in his concepts of *dharma* and *debata.* For him *dharma,* loosely translated as religion, is *Manuser Dharma* (Religion of Man, 1931) and *debata* (God) is *Jibandebata* (Lord of Life). As he explained: "That creative energy inside me which is unifying as well as signifying all the pleasures and pain of my life, and my changing self through many rebirths I had called Lord of Life *(Jibandebata).*" The *Jibandebata* is also, as Tagore himself has said borrowing the *Baul* (rustic roving singing minstrels) imagery, "the man or woman of the heart" or *maner manus.* A noteworthy feature of Tagore's God is that He presides over His created world. Tagore has little patience with Shankaracharya's *mayavad* that reduces this world to a mere illusion or a dream. To him, this world, created by God, is intensely real. "Without the world," he declares, "God would be phantasm, without God the world would be chaos." Tagore's conviction that "to know the Supreme Joy through all earthly love, to perceive the visible form of the Exquisite One through the world of beauty is what I call the realisation of freedom" is a telling testament of his pronounced earth-credo or terraphilia.

As early as 1901 Rabindranath wrote: *Bairagya sadhane mukti, se amar nai / Asankhya bandhan-majhe mahanandamai / Labhiba muktir swad* [Deliverance is not for me in renunciation. /I feel the embrace of freedom in a thousand bonds of delight]. About three decades later, he reiterated: *Shudhayo na more tumi mukti kotha, mukti kare kai, / Ami sadhak nai, ami guru nai / Ami kabi, achhi / Dharanir ati kachhakachhi / Eparer kheyar ghatay* [Ask me not what salvation means or where to get it./Sage or mentor I'm not./I am but a poet who stays close to this earth on this side of the bank (of life)]. In another poem, he confessed: "How I wish to quench my thirst by drinking time and again the wine of bliss from all the vessels of this world" *[Ichha kare barbar mitaite sadh / Pan kari biswer sakal patra hate / Anandamadiradhara naba naba srote]*. Sometime later, the poet announced: *Labhiachhi jibaloke manbjanmer adhikar, / Dhanya ei soubhagya amar* [I'm blessed to be born a human in this world living beings] ("Barsashes" [Year End], 1926). In a short poem composed toward the end of his life the poet proclaimed in no uncertain terms: *Shes sparsa niye yaba yabe dharanir bale yabo, 'Tomar dhulir tilak parechhi bhale; dekhechhi nityer jyoti duryoger mayar adale. / Satyer anandarup e dhulite niyechhe murati / Ei jene e dhulay rakhinu pranati* [When I go having touched this earth for the last time, I would say, 'Today I have marked my forehead with your dust;/I have seen the bright eternity behind the mist of danger and turmoil./ I know that the beautiful truth has realized itself and I place my head on the dust (of this world)'].

He had sung: *Amar mukti alloy alloy ei akashe / Amar mukti dhulay dhulay ghase ghase / Amar mukti sarbajaner maner majheDuhkha-bipad tuchha kara kathin kaje* [My deliverance is in the lighted firmament, in every dust particle and in every grass of the earth/ ... My salvation is in the universal mind and in my exertions defying all dangers and disappointments]. The ailing *Bisvakabi* [World Poet] tendered his final offering not to a deity of the distant heavens but to humanity of this world: *Ami bratya, ami mantrahin./Sakal mandirer bahire amar puja aj samapta hala/Deblok theke/ Manabloke,/Akashe jyotirmay puruse/Ar maner manuse amar antartama anande* [I am the uninitiated pariah,/Today I have performed my final worship with profound bliss of the bright God of the skies/And the Man of My Heart on this world away from the temples] (*Patraput* [The Leaves], 1936).

Yet Tagore was far from a naïve starry-eyed philanthropist or a supramundane mystic or prophet. Even though he delighted in his interaction with peoples and ideas, he was also painfully aware of the deceit, deviousness, and iniquity of his world. Some of his contemporaries considered him as a poet of ethereal, even unreal *[bastutantrahin]* fantasies. A one-time friend of the poet, Narendranath Datta (premonastic name of Swami Vivekananda, 1863-1902), who had taken lessons in Brahmo prayer songs from Rabindranath, called him a purveyor of "erotic venom." An influential poet and literary critic in Britian ridiculed Tagore's English translation of his own poems as the product of an illiterate Indian. On October 25, 1930 he wrote to Indira: "By god's grace I was born with a tough physique so that I could take as much abuse as I can from my own country[men]."

On September 14, 1933 Rabindranath wrote: "It is a matter of great regret that for [some people] scandal mongering makes a good living. I thus realize how widespread and deep is the animus against me in my country. How little pain my country people feel by hurting and insulting me! Had this not been the case, scurrilous criticisms against me would not have been so profitable." Tagore's biographer Mukhopadhyay laments: "At what an inauspicious moment did he compose *Sonar Tari!* No other single creation of Rabindranath spewed so much flattery as well as vitriol either earlier or later....Really speaking, the poet was actually the target of attack, his poetry an excuse, because some people sought to belittle those qualities of Rabindranath's multifaceted genius that had been recognized by the majority of the intellectuals of the country."

Although Tagore frankly confessed to being a romantic he did reckon with his personal struggle against the terrifying real world on his own terms. He would deal with it by bringing together the *bhairab* [terrifying reality] and the *sundar* [the ideal and the beautiful]. He wrote: *Yetha oi bastab jagat/ Sekhane anagonar path/Achhe amar chena./Sethakar dena/ Shodh kari—se nahe kathai taha jani/ tahar ahban ami mani./ Shoukhin bastab setha nahi hai./Sethay sundar yena bhairaber sathe/Chale hate hate* [I'm familiar with the road to the real world./I know, too, that I can't pay my debts to it in words/But I respond to its call./...No fancy reality could be found there./ There the terrific and the terrible walk hand in hand./] His *Sheslekha,* composed in the last year of his life contain a couple of poems that reveal his personal struggle: *Rupnaraner kule/ Jege uthilam,/Janilam e jagat svapna nai./Rakter akashe dekhilam/Apanar rup,/Chinilam apanare aghate aghate/ bedanay bedanay;/Satya ye kathin,/Kathinere bhalobasilam,/ Se kakhano kare na banchana./Amrityur duhkher tapasya e jiban,/Satyer darun mulya labh karibare,/Mirtyute sakal dena shodh kare dite* [I awoke on the bank of the Rupnaran/And realized that this world is not a phantasm./I beheld my visage etched in blood,/And recognized myself amidst many hurts and aches;/I fell in love with the relentless reality that knows no deception./

This life of mine is a long painful prayer till I redeem all my debts and receive the terrible price of truth in death]. The very last piece, dictated from deathbed is eloquent, elegant, and evocative: *Tomar sristir path rekhechha akirna kari/ Bichitra chhalanajale/He chhalanamayi./Mithya bisvasher phand petechha nipun hate/Saral jibane./Ei prabanchanadiye mahatvere karechha chinhita./...Satyere se pai/Apan aloke—dhouta antare antare./Kichhute parena tare prabanchite,/Shes puraskar niye yai se ye/Apan bhandare./Anayase ye perechhe chhalana sahite/Se pay tomar hate/Shantir akshay adhikar* [Sorceress, you've strewn the path of/Your creation in a mesh of varied wiles./Cleverly you've laid a snare of false beliefs/In artless lives./You've marked the (honest) and great with deceptions/....Though crooked outside/He's upright within,/And that is his pride./Though all call him disturbed,/He finds truth in the inner recesses of his heart/Washed clean by his inner light./Nothing can fool him;/He carries to his treasure-house/ His final reward./He who could put up with your deceit receives from you the right/To everlasting peace].

Tagore's humanism in its cosmic expanse makes him an aesthete whose experience of beauty and the creative art expressed in it go against the grain of ancient Indian or Vedantic aesthetics which, to quote a sentence from a modern exponent of the subject, "makes us progressively conscious of the illusoriness of the empirical world and ego-life and of the reality of the higher and non-attached spirit within us." However, Tagore did not think that the function of art was to make us realize "the illusoriness of the empirical world" and the hyper-reality of a higher world. By detachment and disinterestedness of aesthetic experience he understood detachment from the exigencies of action and never from the world of humanity and of nature where his every step on the green meadow or in the grove has filled his life with enchanting and exciting delight *(Ghase ghase pa phelechhi baner pathe jete/phuler gandhe bharechhe man uthechhe pran mete)*. As he wrote, "from the dawn of history the poets and artists have been infusing the colours and music of their own soul into the structure of existence.

And from this I have known certainly that the earth and the sky are woven with the fibres of man's mind." He has thus found his niche under the starry firmament and his song springs forth in utter amazement *(Akash-bhara surya-tara, / Bishwa-bhara pran / Tahari majhkhane ami peyechhi, peyechhi mor sthan. / Bismaye jage, jage amar pran)*. One of the most poignant pieces proclaiming the poet's aesthetic amalgam of human and cosmic love may be found in the collection titled *Chaitali* [Late Harvest] (1896): *Amader dujaner pratham chumban. / Ananta nakshatralok uthila shihari/ Amader chakshe ela ashrujal bhari* (Our first kiss./The limitless galaxy shuddered./ Tears filled our eyes). This is what Theodor Lipps had called *Einfühlung* or empathy. This empathy is love in all its forms: love between a man and a woman *(eros)*, man's love for God and God's for man *(agape),* and aesthetic love *(Einfühlung),* that is, love for the world at large through empathy, which means "feeling into" rather than sympathy, which means "feeling with."

We should bear in mind that the poet had expressed such sentiments eloquently earlier in his poem "Ananta Prem" [Love Eternal]: *Nikhiler shukh nikhiler dukh/Nikhil praner priti/ Ekti premer majhare mishechhe/ sakal premer smriti/Sakal kaler sakal premer giti* [The bliss, blight, and love of the world has merged into one love that holds the memory and music of universal love for all times]. Elsewhere he endorsed the sentiment of a woman poet of medieval India and cited her in his own translation: I salute the Life in the house and the Life abroad in the unknown,/The Life full of joy and the Life weary with its pains,/The Life eternally moving, rocking the world into stillness,/The Life deep and silent, breaking out into roaring waves. Nirad Chaudhuri observes that mystical faith in "Rabindranath Tagore's philosophy of life is at once rooted in the faith in earthly existence and in life beyond death." In other words, following Abu Sayeed Ayyub, it may be concluded that for Rabindranath love of woman, nature, and god is a connected concept.

The lover Rabindranath cannot be separated from the aesthetic priest, the worshiper of his *Jibandebata.* As he had declared in a lecture in the United States in 1917: "With the growth of man's spiritual life, our worship has become worship of love." This worship is also accompanied with a gender transformation of the object of love.

Thus the poet's ususal lover, the woman, now becomes a male with a masculine name *Jibandebata, antaratama* (the most intimate one) to whom the male poet now expresses his love as a woman (in Edward Thompson's unkind words expressing a "zenana imagery"): *Ohe anaratama,/mitechhe ki taba sakal tiyas/Asi antare mama?/Duhkhasukher laksa dharay/Patra bharia diyachhi tomay,/Nithur pidane ningadi baksa/Dalita draksa sama./* [My lord, have you drunk enough of me? /I have crushed my breast like vineyards,/ filling your cup with my joys and sorrows/].

This reversal of gender whereby the poet himself becomes a woman supplicating to a male lover must have been facilitated by his Vaishnabic cultural heritage. Interestingly enough, Rabindranath's poetic career began as the precocious Bhanusingha composing erotic lyrics on the Vaishnavic theme of the love between Radha and Krishna. In his advancing years, especially past his middle age, the poet harked back to the same font of his poetic consciousness, the Vaishnava devotional style of feminization of the male devotee.

Thus the poems addressed to his *Jibandebata* are more philosophical versions of his romantic lyrics of adolescence and early youth transforming his erotic consciousness into *prem* (in the true sense of *bhalobasa*): *Sab cheye satya mor, sei mrityunjay,/se amar prem./Tare ami rakhiya elem/ Aparibartan arghya tomar uddeshe* [My love is immortal and it's the highest truth (of my life)./That eternal offering of mine I have dedicated to you].

The unabashed romantic matured into a brooding philosopher who combined in himself the *premik* (lover) and the *pujari* (worshiper). This erotic ascetic, the dendron of the forest *(aranyak banaspati)*, awaited till his dying day, staking all his possessions, the advent of his surreal lover, *Jibandebata,* the darling deity of life, who is also *kautukmayi antaryami* (playful indwelling woman), *antartama jibannath* (lord of life who is inside the innermost), or *priyatama pranesh* (the most beloved lord of life): For the return of the One/ Who has left me on the road,/ I eagerly wait with all my load. / He is never seen but he can see,/ Yet thus unseen he loves me. /My heart is lost in my secret affair/ With that amazing intimate Lover *(Amar sakal niye base achhi/ Sarbanasher ashay /Ami tar lagi path cheye achhi/ Pathe ye jan bhasay/ Ye jan dey na dekha yay ye dekhe/ Bhalobase adal theke/Amar man majechhe sei gabhirer/ Gopan bhalobasay).* Rabindranath Tagore was no world-weary self-abnegating ascetic. He was a seeker of the ultimate freedom and beauty in this life on this planet, and not a beyonder. "Not self-immolation, but self-expression must be our aim," the poet proclaimed—and this should serve as his enduring epitaph.

THE PARROT'S TALE

Once there was a bird. It was an utterly foolish bird. It sang songs, but did not read the scriptures. It flew, it jumped, but did not have the faintest sense of etiquette.

The King said, "Such birds! They are of no use at all. They only eat the fruits in the orchards and the royal fruit-market runs a deficit."

He called the minister, and commanded, "Educate it."

The King's nephew was given the responsibility of educating the bird.

The scholars held long discussions, the subject being — "What is the reason behind the foolishness of this creature?"

The conclusion was: much learning could not be stored in the tiny nest that the bird could make with just chips and twigs. So, first of all, it was necessary to build a good cage for it. The scholars got amply rewarded and went home merrily.

The goldsmith started building the cage. The cage turned out to be so exquisite that everyone under the sun rushed to see it. Some said, "Education indeed!" Others said, "Education or no education, at least the bird has got the cage! What a lucky bird!"

The goldsmith got a bagful of rewards. He set out for home cheerfully. The pundit came to teach the bird. He took a pinch of snuff and said, "A few books won't do."

The nephew summoned the scribes. They copied from the books and copied from those copies and made an enormous mound of such things. Whoever saw it, said, "Bravo! Learning is going to overflow!"

The scribes got cartfuls of rewards. At once they rushed home. None of their descendants faced any poverty ever since.

The nephew was always busy, doing endless number of things regarding the surveillance of the precious cage. Repairs were quite frequent. Apart from that, there was the washing and the cleaning and the polishing of the cage. Everyone admitted, "Sure signs of improvement."

Many people were employed and to supervise them, many more people were employed. Each of them got a handful of coins every month and filled their chests with them.

They, their brothers, sisters and cousins began to live in great luxury and happiness.

The world lacks many things; only fault-finders are there in plenty. They said, "There are improvements of the cage all right, but nobody cares for the bird."

The words reached the King's ears. He called the nephew and said, "What's this I hear, dear nephew?"

The nephew said, "Your Majesty! If you want to know the truth then call the goldsmith, send for the pundits and the scribes, summon the repairmen and their supervisors. The fault-finders cannot make both ends meet and talk nonsense."

The situation became crystal-clear to the King, and a gold necklace adorned the nephew's neck.

The King wished to see for himself the lightening speed at which education was proceeding. So one day he came to the education center with his entire entourage of friends, companions and courtiers.

As soon as he reached the entrance, there arose a chorus of bells and drums and harps and flutes and lyres and lutes and cellos and violins and cymbals and mandolins and trombones and bassoons and harpsichords and clavichords. The pundits swung their pig-tails and started chanting hymns at the top of their voices. The repairmen and the laborers and the goldsmith and the scribes and the supervisors and the cousins greeted the King with a huge uproar.

The Nephew said, "Your Majesty! What do you think?"

The King said, "Amazing! This is a non-trivial amount of sound!"

The Nephew said, "It's not just the sound Your Majesty, there is also a non-trivial amount of money behind it."

The King was extremely pleased. He started back. He came out of the front door and was about to ride his elephant, when a fault-finder, who had been hiding in a bush, yelled, "Your Majesty! Have you looked at the bird?"

The King was startled. He said, "Oh! I forgot. I didn't see the bird after all."

He went in once again and told the pundit, "I want to see your method of educating the bird."

And he saw it. Very pleasing indeed. The method was so overwhelming compared to the bird that one could hardly notice the bird. It seemed it was rather irrelevant to look at the bird. The King understood that the arrangements were faultless.

There was no corn in the cage, no water either. Only heaps of pages had been torn out from heaps of books; and with the tip of a pen, those pages were being stuffed into the bird's mouth. There was no room in the mouth for the bird to squeeze out a cry, let alone a tune. It was really a terribly pleasing sight.

This time, before mounting the elephant, the King ordered the ear-pulling expert to pull the fault-finder's ears severely.

In a rather respectable and predictable way, the bird became half-dead as the days passed. The guardians understood that the situation was hopeful. But still — as its bad habits were — the bird looked at the morning sun and flapped its wings in a very objectionable manner. Some days it was even found to make an attempt to break the rods of the cage with its sickly beak.

The administrator said, "What audacity!"

Immediately, the blacksmith came to the education department with bellows and fire and hammer and chisels. His hits were absolutely spectacular! An iron chain was manufactured and the wings of the bird were cut off.

The King's relatives shook their heads gravely and said, "In this land, you see, the birds are not only stupid, but ungrateful as well."

Then the pundits came with a pen in one hand and a spear in another and did something which one could really call education.

The blacksmith became very well-to-do. His wife got gold ornaments. The administrator gained a title from the King for his alertness.

The bird died — no one knew when. The infamous fault-finder spread the news, "The bird has died."

The King called the nephew and asked, "Dear nephew, what is this that I hear?"

The nephew said, "Your Majesty, the bird's education is now complete."

The King asked, "Does it still jump?"

The nephew said, "God forbid."

"Does it still fly?"

"No."

"Does it sing any more?"

"No."

"Does it scream if it doesn't get food?"

"No."

The King said, "Bring the bird in. I would like to see it."

The bird was brought in. With it came the administrator, the guards, the horsemen. The King felt the bird. It didn't open its mouth and didn't utter a word. Only the pages of books, stuffed inside its stomach, raised a ruffling sound.

Outside, where the gentle south wind and the blossoming woods were heralding spring, the young green leaves filled the sky with a deep and heavy sigh.

The poet's lover gave her parting kiss long ago. He has almost forgotten it in the hiatus of the long separation. But he now remembers her and asks her forgiveness piteously for his lapse of memory. How many leaves of *madhabi* flower wilted, how many noons noisy with dove song, how many evenings have left their golden amnesia, how many nights have written an obscure script and lapsed in oblivion after that last kiss. Even if the poet asks forgiveness of his long lost beloved, he nevertheless is fully aware that his lover, his *Jibandebata*, has already blessed his life with her touch.

Tabu jani. Ekdin tumi dekha diyechhile bale
Ganer phasale mor e jiban uthechhila phale.
Ajo nai shes
... ...
Tomar parash nahi ar
Kintu ki parashmani rekhe gechha antare amar
Bishver amrita chhabi ajio to dekha dey more
Kshane kshane akaran anander sudhapatra bhare
Amare karay pan. (ibid.)
[I know my life blossomed in songs because
You came to me.
It's still not empty yet
... ...
Though I miss your touch
I know I carry your touchstone inside me
I still behold the immortal visage of the world
And drink the cup of gratuitous bliss every moment.]
(Purabi)

...I have tried to unravel the mystery and mystique of Rabindranath's *jibandebata* according to my own understanding. My explanation may not be valid even. Yet, I must conclude by claiming that the font of Tagore's sensibilities enriching his poetic career and filling it with variegated forms and fragrance is, undeniably, his consciousness of universal life. This consciousness colored his childhood, adolescence, and youth, and the same consciousness brings a twilight tinge to fill the sunset hours of his life.

Without daring to take my eyes off him, I climbed onto the verandah and said, "Sit down. I'll get you something to eat." We gave him a few mangoes. I sat down on the deck-chair and wondered what to do next. The man looked harmless, but how would I go to sleep with a madman outside my door? The servants did not sleep in the house, there was nobody around to carry a message. It did not seem that the man intended to depart soon. Having finished the mangoes, he settled down comfortably. I would have been happy to keep him busy with some more food, but there was nothing more in the house. What were we to do now? We decided to wait for the guards to arrive on their nightly rounds around Santiniketan. They should have come, but tonight when we needed them, they were late. The minutes passed; we could see neither their flashlights nor hear their whistles. I sat there. Not far away, Miss Petit slept on peacefully. Jyotirmoybabu tried to rouse her, but she only said, "Oh, he is mad, he won 't hurt us". Then she turned over and went back to sleep.

But our dark night's visitor showed no signs of leaving. Nor did it seem a good idea to let him go without ascertaining his destination. If pleased with our services, how long would it be before his return? Faced with no other option, we decided to enlist Miss Petit's help. This time, Makshirani woke her up and explained the situation. She immediately appeared, dressed in a black kimono. She jumped off the veranda and briskly went up to the intruder,

'You want to meet Rabindranath Thakur? Come with me, I will take you to him.' At first, the man stood silent and motionless. Saying

'Come, come, come with me', the fearless woman almost dragged him away and disappeared with him into the dark fields. We two intrepid knights of Bengal, stood aside and watched.

Ultimately Jyotirmoybabu accompanied Miss Petit, though it served no purpose other than saving face, and I stayed to guard the family. They soon returned, having turned him over to the watchman at Uttarayan. We slept restfully that night, heartened by the presence of a very brave woman next door.

From then on, it was arranged that a gardener would sleep in the house; we also realised that the guards had been instructed to keep a close watch over us. But we did not have to suffer such a night-time intrusion again. Insanity though seemed to be in the air, for another mad person graced Uttarayan with her presence the next day, a woman this time. She came from Burdwan by train, carrying a cat in her arms, covered with her sari like a baby. She sent message, "Go tell Bouthan that Sarala Debi has come fro m Jorasanko." She took Pratima Debi by surprise. Though mad, she was still in possession of some sense, and seemed well-informed; her eyes rested with keenness on many of the articles lying around the house. She did not seem prepared to go away with empty hands, so she was given some money, taken to the Bolpur station and put on the train.

One day we heard that a cobra had its den below a neem tree near the Ratan Kuthi kitchen—the servants saw it all the time; once Kashi had only just missed stepping on it. Almost on cue, we began to be showered with innumerable stories about local snakes. Once, a certain gentleman was staying in the same room that we were in now. He was working at the table one day when something fell from above with a thud. Startled, he looked up to see a snake. When he looked up at the ceiling, he saw another one peeping out. prema-murati hridaye jage, ananda nahi dhare.

(Sinking in a sea of nectar, I forget the world, sun and moon disappear. I see no country, no history, no border -an image of love awakes in my heart, I cannot contain my joy.)

It captures the spirit of the original and at the same time works on its own as a beautiful poem. One could not ask for more

A Foreign Shine and Assumed Gestures: The Ersatz Tagore of the West between the arms of the Beloved, in the ecstasy of love's joy:

Bring the tearful streams of the rainy clouds to your eyes, and cover your heart with the shadow of darkness:

Bring your face nearer to His ear, and speak of the deepest longings of your heart.

Kabir says: "Listen to me, brother! bring the vision of the Beloved in your heart."

Crisis in Civilization, and a Poet's Alternatives: Education as one alternative weapon

Under the present circumstances it may not sound like an old fashioned romantic cliché if someone declares today, that the aim of all education is to seek a world where mankind can co-exist with nature in an atmosphere of fearless warmth, trust and freedom.

A poet may naturally claim that finding joy in the simple things of life, and compassion for our fellow creatures are the basic values upon which small children's education should be founded, as these happen to hold the secret of creative energy. It dose not sound far fetched because joy and compassion are also the ultimate end of civilization.

What we are doing to ourselves today throughout the world, is driving this planet towards the final moment, where all creation ends, and destruction takes over. Creativity is god's gift to mankind, it cannot grow freely when it is used as a tool for hatred, as creativity is by definition contrary to destruction. Awareness of the responsibilities of being human and of our human failures is the foundation upon which creativity rests.

I am trying to examine how far a poet can foresee a crisis that a civilization might *face, of which education is an important component,* and how, as a sensitive, creative, responsible human being he can think of possible alternatives to counteract the dangers. A poet has positive dreams for this universe. He is also practical and pragmatic, because he cares for this universe. With his knowledge rooted in reality and his instinct and imagination flying into the distant future, he has a shrewd understanding of the course that human history is about to take and is pained and worried about the future of mankind that his poet's vision can foresee.

Our poet used his visionary imagination to predict and to solve the dangers that western civilization was creating for itself and for the rest of the world, *because the east was emulating its ways partly by choice, and partly by choice, and partly through values imposed by colonial educational policies.*

The so-called mystic saint could very clearly see the logical, practical conclusions of a dangerous process that had already begun its course. And he tried to offer practical solutions, tried to change the course of history as far as he could by spreading his anxious thoughts far and wide and by actively working with the people. *Rabindranath was very much of an educational activist as we understand the term today.* He saw education as a holistic device which prepared a complete human being for the betterment of the world. It was expected to build a child's values right from the beginning.

An incorrigible pacifist, the poet protested against all war and violence, denounced terrorism even when the young men were risking their lives fighting to free his own country. In those emotionally charged days of nationalist movement he wrote very strongly against the very concept of nationalism, as a divisive element created by western technology that disturbed peaceful coexistence, and encouraged hostility among countries by fanning self-pride. So he talked about connectivity, and internationalism. He wanted his students to imbibe all these values, and possess an inner eye, in order to build a better world based not on separatism and self-pride but on togetherness and mutual trust.

Rabindranath was one of the earliest environmentalists in today's world, who began the act of afforestation to protect the land from erosion, wrote powerful songs about it to spread the message, and had made planting of trees into an annual festival in his school more than seventy five years ago.

A secular educationist per se, he created secular festivities in his school which could be shared by students of all religions. Realising the social and educational significance of sharing rituals and of enjoying festivals together, he invented secular festivals for the old and the young.

There were festivities in his school to celebrate the coming of every season. *Barsho Shesh* and *Naba barsho* for summer, *Barshaa Mangal* for monsoon, *Sharadotsab* for Autumn, *Basantotsab* for Spring. And he encouraged *Paush Mela,* the winter fair introduced by his father Maharshi Debendranath which celebrated the harvest time and brought the rural and the urban together, by making the interchange of culture and commerce possible between the two.

All these were integral parts of Tagore's educational policy, which stretched well beyond the limits of his school, to ways of building future citizens of the world.

Just as introducing the cooperative system in the rural areas was his way of educating the rural poor to function together, in order to earn a livelihood. Taking his lessons from the European farmers, he began a cooperative movement for the *adivasis* in the rural areas, the *samabaayika,* a cooperative banking system for the rural areas.

Disgusted by the flawed colonial education system that was imposed upon Indian children, he offered an alternative schooling system. *The western mode of education, he felt, was more harmful than helpful for us, it steamrolled the children into artificial discipline, taught textbooks that were meant for children of an unfamiliar culture, an unfamiliar climate, forced them to learn too many things by rote without touching base.* It did not reflect the reality of the students' lives. The foreign dress code, for example, was unsuitable for a warm climate, it also kept them away from being in touch with nature and their natural surroundings. So, in his experimental school the students wore comfortable Indian clothes, walked barefoot, to feel the ground beneath their feet, and classes were held in the open air under the shade of trees. The students were encouraged to be creative, to sing, draw, paint, sculpt, dance, act, tell stories, write poetry, cherish open spaces, as well as enjoy a huge playground and a well furnished library. So much for their body and their mind. The prayer meetings in the morning took care of their spirits.

Education could not be complete without knowing your own cultural roots.

Though not a trained anthropologist, but a sensitive and farsighted man, Rabindranath was instinctively aware of the value of preserving tribal culture. Therefore while trying to solve the dire economic needs of the *adivasis,* and educating them in health, agriculture, savings and other modern day practical ways of survival, he encouraged undisturbed preservation of their own tribal culture without interfering with their basic lifestyle.

Tagore wanted a system of education that would bring his people the best of both worlds, the East and the West, the rural and the urban, the ancient and the contemporary. Yes, a poet can cherish such a dream, and take on its responsibilities, and more.

Tagore was rubbishing the concept of the Nation as a selfish product of western technology that harmed peace by promoting difference. Instead of spreading cooperation, communication and consideration, it promoted suspicion, competition and coercion, and instigated violent passions and hostilities. Like nation, the concepts of race, religion and ethnicity, also divide mankind into warring groups and we urgently need a loose, broad state structure, the concept of "No–Nation," to accommodate all in their own space. Any civilization that rests upon dividing up people, carries the seed of its own destruction within itself. Proper education within the right value system would open the inner eye and make people see the truth.

And political power, he wrote, was dependent on economic power and could not be separated from it. Tagore warned us of a world where "the greed to possess more and more things" (the term 'consumerism' was not yet known) and a demand and supply policy that creates artificial demand among people to possess more and more material goods will bring about a day when technology will destroy the earth. He could foresee a time when *western civilization would lead itself and the rest of the world to destruction. If our education had its roots in Indian culture, he genuinely believed, it could teach mankind how to rise above these misleading divisive notions, and peacefully co-exist.*

Rabindranath felt that in India the colonial education system was imposed form above, the strong discipline in the schools was based on fear, not on sympathy. The mechanically imposed system did not take account of the individual students' state of mind or body, it forced its rules upon them, ultimately killing their souls.

Tota kahini "The Parrot's Tale" is a shattering piece on the abuse of student by an inhuman education system. It is a powerful satire expressing his disapproval of the heartless notion of forced formal education as it was applied in India. An alienated system that took a cruel pride in self and did not care for the other's reality.

Instead of liberating and enriching the mind, mindless colonial education chained it, separated it form its natural surroundings, stole its joy of life and killed its soul, thus ultimately defeating the sole purpose of education.

In fact he saw western civilization itself as a civilization based on war and fear and *not* on empathy. Education system was an integral part of it. He predicted in the voice of a seer, about war, long before fascism and ethnic murder appeared in Europe—"Those who are constantly developing their instinct of fight and the intolerance of aliens will be eliminated." he wrote (*Nationalism p. 97*). A situation had been created when "a watchful attitude of animosity against Others was taken as a solution to their problems."

Tagore knew in his heart, that this was no permanent solution to human problems. "We are confronted with two alternatives," he wrote, "it will be interminable competition, or cooperation." (*p. 101*). And competition was what Western education system pampered, not cooperation.

Worried about the connected sources of power in the western civilization, industry, commerce, and military, Tagore called the system "the gigantic organization for hurting others and for warding off their blows" (and poor man had no idea then in 1916 how many billions of dollars would be spent in the world for the purpose of Defense, in another 50 years time.)

"Only those people have survived and achieved civilization", he wrote, "who have the spirit of cooperation strong in them." (*p. 99-100*)

The goal of all education, he felt, was to create this spirit of cooperation in human mind. To connect people, to protect and promote human civilization.

The western notion of education, he was afraid, installed wrong values in children. It fanned their sense of separateness, whereas India, he firmly believed, had a better alternative to offer its students, "the spirit of co-operation." which was at the root of human civilization.

Forever our contemporary, Rabindranath had worried about Globalization as well. Addressed by his countrymen as *Bishwa Kabi,* a World Poet, he had always perceived human consciousness as one. A sense of the wholeness of the world rules his heart as well as his mind.

Tagore had commented (as early as in 1916) that although the western civilization stressed separateness, rather than unity, nevertheless, science and technology were bringing the world together. "The whole world is becoming one country through scientific facility. And the moment is arriving when you also must find a basis of unity which is not political." (*p. 99*).

This basis he felt, had to be *a moral power* which alone could hold the center together for mankind. *By moral power he meant "the higher instincts of sympathy and mutual help." (p. 99) Education was meant to develop this moral power of sympathy in mankind.*

But was western education system achieving this end? The first world war had started, when Tagore wrote, "The people who are lacking in this higher moral power, and who therefore cannot combine in fellowship with one another, must perish or live in a state of degradation" (*p.99*) Nearly a century later, needless to say, we are living upon this planet in a state of perpetual, pitiful degradation, because the world has not succeeded in "combining in fellowship" as the poet wanted.

The keyword to solve the crisis in human civilization, for Rabindranath, perhaps, was transparency. Openness was all. No secret spying outfits, no shutting out of aliens through strict immigration laws, no secret societies for political activists, even if it is for human rights and the independence of a country. Open up your heart, and have an open mind, you'll solve most of your problems. Open up all your doors and windows, in your mind, in your politics, in your trade, in your culture. Let ideas freely flow through the peoples of the world, let us all be in touch, and exchange thoughts. *This was the ultimate aim of education.*

Education should allow us to welcome fresh air into our closed spaces, and break down artificial barriers, because, he felt, real differences among mankind should be recognized not glossed over, nor bulldozed into oneness, yet an overall unity does exist and should be respected.

It needs emotional and intellectual sympathy and cooperation. And this, the poet believed was the whole object of human civilization. Without intellectual sympathy one race can never understand the problems of another. *The British system of education in India, lacked emotional as well as intellectual sympathy. Tota Kahini is a picture of that terrible lacunae that leads to the failure of the system.*

In this context Rabindranath juxtaposed two basic concepts that guide us today, competition and cooperation. One leads to war and the other leads to peace. *The western education system was one that encouraged competition. Tagore wanted to create a fresh education system which will emphasize cooperation.*

The course that human history has taken in the 20th century would have pained Rabindranath no doubt but would not have taken him by surprise. Although he had not heard the words that we live with, like the holocaust, or Hiroshima, the My Lai, or Bosnia, the Green House Effect, or 9/11, and he did not live to see his country divided into three nations, knew neither Khomeini nor Laden, neither Bush nor Modi, — yet he knew exactly which route history was taking, and had tried to warn the world. And to protect this from self-destruction.

Tagore knew the deadly effects of suspicion, fear and hatred among nations, as well as communities, of fundamentalism, and ethnic pride. The heating of the planet through thoughtless deforestation, and poisoning of the earth, water and sky through technology, all this he had known through his visionary's eyes. Imagining the uncertain future of a shortsighted, self-defeating mankind, he had nightmares which were expressed in his last speech, *Crisis in Civilization.*

And all his life Rabindranath had searched for and found a million ways to offer us positive alternatives to counter them. *Creating a new system of education was only one of them.*

In Bangla storytelling formula, a tale begins, *Ek je chhilo raja,* ("There was a king"). In one of his last pieces written in 1941, just before his death, he begins his tale with this formulaic expression *Ek je achhe manush* ("There is a man"). He makes two enormously important changes in the formula, he changes its tense from the past to the present, and changes its subject from a king to a common man. Instead of *"there was"* he writes *"there is"*, and instead of *"a king"* he writes *"a man"*, meaning a *human being.*

These were the alternatives he offered to mankind, to grapple with the crisis our civilization had created for itself, and the world was passing through in 1941. The focus was to be shifted from the past *to the present,* not the *present moment* but the continuous presence, *bartaman,* indicating the eternal presence of mankind upon this planet. And also a shift from the royalty to the common man, from the source of political power, to the source of moral strength.

Not freedom from history, nor submission to it, but continuous adjustment to its needs, trying to *mould* its course, is what we need for the survival of the human spirit.

And that, Tagore believed, was what real education ought to prepare us for. Let him speak in his own voice.

At a time when interest in Rabindranath Tagore, also in the non-English speaking West, may be said to be entering a new phase, with the promise of a wider readership both inside and outside academic circles, all three of Uma Das Gupta's books, published in impressive succession of each other, carry a weighty significance. From the point of view of contemporary global history too, which numerous scholars across the board of humanities have rightly perceived as having entered a new cycle of imperialism, Tagore's idea(l)s offer much scope for important reappraisal. The three books by Uma Das Gupta on Tagore, two of which are biographies and the third an edited collection of letters, are an important contribution in this direction.

Biography is an art in itself. Not unlike literary translation, it requires its author to be able to read as a critic and write as a writer. Uma Das Gupta succeeds on both counts. Her works dealing with the life of the Bengali polymath are an outcome of years of careful research and extensive reading. While in her short biography of Tagore, her voice is clearly in the forefront, in *Rabindranath Tagore: my life in my words*, she is, as it were, a hidden presence. Her style is engaging, achieving a fine balance which satisfies the general reader and specialist alike. Moreover, her longstanding involvement with Santiniketan, going back to her parents' close association with Tagore, gives her writing an intimacy that brings the reader even closer to the subject.

For a Tagore biography to succeed, however, there is yet another requirement. It is suggested by Tagore's own scepticism towards retelling life's events as they supposedly *really* happened. Even in the case of autobiography, they are of necessity artistic recreations, in Tagore's case captivatingly so. A sensitive biographer is therefore urged to adopt an approach that is concerned less with the chronicling of external events than with elaborating ideas which informed the artist's long and creative life. Uma Das Gupta clearly takes this as her guideline in organising the contents of both the biographies, a point she makes in her Introduction to *Rabindranath Tagore: my life in my words*: "In the final analysis, [Tagore's] life history is mainly a biography of ideas and artistic creations." Ideas, in Tagore's world, take precedence over life's happenings, though his life was astoundingly rich in both.

The main ideas explored in *Rabindranath Tagore; A Biography* are those of the poet as an educator and rural reformer and not so much as a writer and poet.

This choice seems in part pragmatic, dictated by the author's own area of expertise (her knowledge of the history of Tagore's institution of Visva-Bharati in Santiniketan). At the same time it is motivated by presenting the lesser covered sides of Tagore and his many concerns. Finally, there were the constraints imposed by the OUP biographies series, with its objective that the life histories of men and women who contributed towards building modern India be short.

Thus in just over a hundred pages of ten concisely written chapters, packed with information (sometimes gleaned also from oral sources), the life of Tagore is portrayed through a series of interrelated themes, such as nationalism, internationalism, lessons from India's history, the need for an alternative, world-encompassing education, a search for self-esteem, to mention the main ones.

What we are presented with, is, in Uma Das Gupta's formulation, "an indefatigable man of action": a founder of a school and a university, a pioneer in rural reconstruction work, an untiring globe-trotter out on a mission, in other words a man struggling every step of the way to make a difference in the lives of his countrymen and "bring change", in what small way he could, "to an unequal and unjust world".

Oftentimes against great odds and little understanding both at home and abroad, Tagore is seen to emerge as what another eminent scholar William Radice has termed a "one-man counter-culture".

If Uma Das Gupta's biography extends the portrayal of Tagore beyond the common perception of him as a poet and writer – and the subject of Tagore's creative writing is dealt within fewer than ten pages – there is certain poetic justice in that she closes the biography with a poem.

The social consciousness in Tagore was never separate from his artistic consciousness; the man of action was never far from the contemplative man.

The ethical source from which both drew was essentially the same: "a universal humanist outlook". This was the imaginative ideal, the biography makes clear, in terms of which Rabindranath was ceaselessly moving, with many twists and turns on the way, from occasionally quite traditionalist beginnings, but over the years through ever-widening sympathies and sensibilities as both a man and poet.

Closing the biography with a poem which bespeaks a strong a sense of remoteness, even failure, in the face of the world's vast impenetrable demands, serves also another point. It shows Tagore at his most vulnerable and human.

The poem's selection seems almost strategic in that it resists the temptation for a larger-than-life portrayal of the poet, as it also importantly suggests a point of contact between him and our own individual lives. "I believe that if we can inwardly relate to this poem", says Uma Das Gupta, "we shall find he is there as a friend in our lives helping us to live with honesty in our weaknesses and our strengths." That is surely the best way to keep Tagore's legacy meaningful and alive.

One of the many strengths of this short biography is the wide assortment of citations, sourced from Tagore's own writings but also from those of others, with which Uma Das Gupta weaves the threads of the main body of her text into a tight and multicoloured fabric. Each and every chapter is preceded by at least two pithy quotations, which help set the tone and drive her point home. It seems she misses no opportunity to give Tagore – or anyone else deserving, for that matter – a chance to speak.

Even her decision to confine herself to selecting letters for the *Appendix* from the body of his letters written in English is guided by her desire "to represent him in his own words". Language too is no barrier: where English translation is unavailable or inadequate, she resorts to her own translation skills and opens another chink for the non-Bengali readers to appreciate Tagore more fully.

All these skills come to bear more fully in her *Rabindranath Tagore: my life in my words*, a book of almost four hundred pages. Although this project was initiated by Penguin books and not the author herself (she was invited to "write" Tagore's autobiography), it feels as though it had grown organically from her shorter biography.

The sources she draws on and translates from are vast and impressive. She had not only plumbed the Rabindra Bhavana archives in Santiniketan but also the Department of Western Manuscripts of the Bodleian Library (University of Oxford) and Senate House Library (London) for the papers of Tagore's various English correspondents. To know that only the Santiniketan archives house close to six thousand letters is to get a sense of the Herculean task she undertook.

There are as many as 117 entries translated by her from the original Bengali, nearly all of which appear here for the first time in English. Only a few of the letters to his wife and children had previously appeared in Krishna Dutta's and Andrew Robinson's translation in their *Selected Letters of Rabindranath Tagore*.

Those who do not read Bengali, but love Tagore and want to access as much of his writing as possible will be extremely pleased by this turnout. In the meantime, another important autobiographical work, *Âtmaparichay*, which Uma Das Gupta draws on and translates from, has also appeared for the first time in a full English translation.

Having more than one translation at hand to draw on is always useful. It gives a fuller, and more contested, picture of what for non-Bengali speakers must remain an unattainable original.

The site of contestation opened up by the two different translations of some of Tagore's letters to his family, particularly to his wife, is indeed interesting. It raises questions that seem to divide opinion among Bengalis to this day. Consider this example from one of the letters Tagore wrote to Mrinalini Devi. In Uma Das Gupta's translation, the passage reads:

Please don't work any harder for my happiness. Your love is enough. But it would be very nice if you and I could work together and think together with one mind.

I know that cannot always happen even if we wish it [...] I don't wish to leave you *out* of anything. Everyone has the right to do things their own way, as they would like to. *It may not be possible for you to agree with my wishes and inclinations every time* – I would not worry about it. It is good enough if you spare me sadness wherever possible, and sweeten my life the way you do with your love (emphasis mine). While in Dutta and Robinson, the same passage is rendered as:

> *To make me happy you need not try very hard – your sincere love is enough. Of course, if you and I could be united in everything we do and think, that would be best– but one cannot will such things [...] I do not want*

> *to leave you* behind *in anything – but at the same time I am afraid of forcing you. Each of us has his own separate taste, inclination and ability.* You do not possess the power to make your own nature correspond with my wishes and inclinations. *Therefore, instead of torturing yourself about it, if you sweeten my life with your love and care, and try to protect me from unnecessary pain, your efforts will be precious to me (my emphasis).*

Every translation is inevitably also an act of interpretation, but the two interpretations emerging from the above passages are pulling in two quite different directions. Telling your wife how much you value her love, hoping to transcend all separation and merge in both thought and action, while realizing that is unattainable, is quite different from telling you wife that she is incapable (*you do not posses the power*) of moulding herself to your expectations, so she need not *torture* herself about it, for inevitably she will be left *behind*, something you deeply regret.

The interpretative thrust that guides Dutta and Robinson rests on their conviction that "while Rabindranath was certainly affectionate towards [Mrinalini], his feelings did not seem to have had the depth of genuine companionship". Elsewhere in their introduction the finality of their verdict is even more disparaging: "Rabindranath's simple affection for his young wife Mrinalini, and her lack of sophistication, are clear from this letter, written on board ship to Europe".

In contrast, Uma Das Gupta's reading evokes an altogether softer, more intimate, at times deeply touching, voice. "His letters tell us how closely he communicated with her, how much he wanted his family near him". If one interpretation places Tagore's young family "at the centre of his life", the other sees his family to have been an increasingly subordinate part of "the greater cause to which he felt his life was dedicated". Inadvertently, as with all translated texts, we find ourselves pondering how much of what we are reading is the actual voice of Tagore and how much the voice of the translator.

Where do the two successfully converge and where do they pull apart? The greatest challenge of any translation is in getting the author's voice to come across as authentically as possible in another language, and to resist the temptation of imposing one's own. It is an exercise in humility as much as in linguistic aptitude. Through his own trials as a translator of his own writings, Tagore came to understand the vital importance, as well as the difficulty, of achieving both.

Translation is clearly a sensitive issue. In the appositely titled *A Difficult Friendship; Letters of Edward Thompson and Rabindranath Tagore 1913 – 1940* it was the very question of translation that first drove a wedge between Tagore and the ex-Methodist missionary, historian, novelist and poet, who was also his first serious Western biographer. With its overt criticism of Tagore, Thompson's second biography brought their friendship to a near breaking point. Whether that criticism was justified is an issue that still animates discussion in "Tagore circles".

Edward Thompson (1886 – 1967) was born of Wesleyan Methodist missionary parents and spent his first six years in India. He was then taken to England by his parents, only to return at the age of 24, taking up a teaching post at Bankura College in southern Bengal. He learned Bengali well enough to be able to read and appreciate Tagore in the original. Entering Tagore's life at the crucial juncture of the poet receiving the Nobel Prize, when having English translations became a matter of increased urgency, Thompson, being a creative writer himself, was drawn into the intricate web of Tagore's many literary collaborators and associates.

He was a zealous participant, sometimes over-zealous, and Tagore, having risen in stature overnight and suddenly pulled into the vortex of public life, did not find it easy to cope with Thompson's eagerness to assist him. "When men thickly surround me and clamour for their dues", he wrote to Thompson in what must have been more than a subtle attempt to ward him off, "they do not get my best".

Indeed, in this exchange Tagore reveals a side to his character that those who desire to see him as superhuman would prefer to ignore. There was certainly something of a prima donna in the way he would engage Thompson when it suited him and dismiss him when it did not.

The ins-and-outs of what came to pass between the poet, the translator-*cum*-proofreader circle of Tagore's English collaborators, and the Macmillan Company of London is minutely recorded and presented in another of Uma Das Gupta's sophisticated and scholarly books.

All the surviving letters between the two men are arranged into eight chronologically arranged chapters and annotated with comprehensive notes. The book also has a substantial introduction covering the wider background to their relationship, as well as separate smaller introductions to the letter sections, providing further context and commentary to their exchange.

At times the commentary seems almost more interesting than the letters, which often deal with the practicalities of their working relationship, and are rather brusque and factual. Certainly they are not as engaging as the letters Tagore wrote to William Rothenstein or C. F. Andrews, his other two lifelong friends and associates. It was only towards the end of their difficult friendship, once they had both managed "to overcome national egoism, personal pain, and mutual annoyance" (Das Gupta's 2003: 2), and were able to share their ideas with understanding that their letters became more full-bodied.

Tagore was able to appreciate more fully Thompson's "interest in international justice" and assimilate his harsh criticism of his own translations in a moment of painful self-realisation: "I have done gross injustice to my original productions partly owing to my incompetence and partly to carelessness". Thompson, on the other hand, gave Tagore all the recognition he deserved: "[Y]ou stand for a new kind of man, neither Eastern nor Western but a reconciler of the best of both".

While the two biographies are clearly aimed at a wide readership across the English-speaking world, *Difficult Friendship* is more specifically a Tagoreophile treat. It complements nicely earlier works dealing with this troublesome but ultimately fulfilling relationship across the colonial divide, especially E. P. Thompson's brilliant study of his father's relationship with the Bengali poet, aptly titled *Alien Homage*.

If there is an air of polemics surrounding this corner of Tagore studies (E. P. Thompson apart, we can mention also William Radice, Harish Trivedi, and Mary Lago), Uma Das Gupta chooses to steer away from these controversies. In her characteristic fashion she prefers to present the facts and let them speak for themselves.

BIBLIOGRAPHY

Andrews, C.F. : *Rabindranath Tagore : Selected Stories*, New Delhi, Srishti, 2004.

Arabinda Poddar : *Tagore : The Political Personality*, Kolkata, Indiana, 2004.

Bakshi, S.R. : *Rabindra Nath Tagore and the Challenges of Today*, New Delhi, Om Publications, 2001.

Barman, Suren Deb : *Rabindranath Tagore and Tripura*, Kolkata, Minerva, 2006.

Bhattacharya, Sabyasachi : *Vande Mataram : The Biography of a Song*, New Delhi, Penguin, 2003.

Bose, Aurobindo : *Later Poems of Rabindranath Tagore*, New Delhi, Rupa & Co., 2002.

Chakrabarti, Mohit : *Rabindranath Tagore : A Miscellany*, New Delhi, Kanishka Pub., 2003.

Chakrabarti, Santosh : *Studies in Tagore : Critical Essays*, New Delhi, Atlantic, 2004.

Chatterjee, Indira : *A Thematic Study of Tagore's Novels*, Gurgaon, Shubhi Pub., 2007.

Chaudhuri, Sukanta : *Rabindranath Tagore : Selected Writings for Children*, New Delhi, Oxford University Press, 2002.

Datta, Asit Kumar : *Aesthetics and the Poetic Image of Rabindranath Tagore*, Delhi, Abhijeet Pub., 2007.

Datta, P.K. : *Rabindranath Tagore's The Home and the World: A Critical Companion*, Delhi, Permanent Black, 2003.

Eunice, De Souza : *Early Indian Poetry in English : An Anthology: 1829-1947*, New Delhi, Oxford University Press, 2005.

Ghatak, Maitreya : *Dust on the Road : The Activist Writings of Mahasweta Devi*, Calcutta, Seagull Books, 2000.

Ghosh, Santidev : *Rabindrasangeet Vichitra : Rabindra Sangeet Miscellany*, New Delhi, Concept, 2006.

Goel, Sandeep : *The Dum Dum Bullet : Adventures of a Corporate Soldier*, New Delhi, Penguin, 2004.

Guha, Sreejata : *Home and the World : Ghare Baire/ Rabindranath Tagore,* New Delhi, Penguin, 2005.

Gupta, Sinjita : *Mystic Moods : Short Stories of Rabindranath Tagore*, New Delhi, UBS Pub., 2005.

Heyman, Michael : *The Tenth Rasa : An Anthology of Indian Nonsense*, New Delhi, Penguin, 2007.

Hussein, Abdullah : *Downfall by Degrees,* New Delhi, Katha, 2004.

Iyer, V.R. Krishna : *Sublime Footprints,* New Delhi, Gyan Publishing House, 2007.

Jha, Gauri Shankar : *Current Perspectives in Indian English Literature*, New Delhi, Atlantic Pub., 2006.

Joseph, T. and S. Francis : *Edmund Spenser : A Critical Study*, New Delhi, Anmol Pub., 2005.

Lal, Ananda : *Rabindranath Tagore : Three Plays*, New Delhi, Oxford University Press, 2001.

Mahapatra, Jayanta : *Door of Paper : Essays and Memoirs*, Delhi, Authors Press, 2007.

Malik, Keshav : *The Echoing Grove : Poems and Paintings*, New Delhi, National Publishing House, 2005.

Mathur, Anurag : *The Department of Denials*, New Delhi, Penguin, 2004.

Mittal, C.R. : *Eliot's Early Poetry in Perspective,* New Delhi, Atlantic, 2001.

Mohit Chakrabarti : *Religion and Rabindranath,* New Delhi, Kalpaz Pub., 2008.

Mukherjee, Aparna : *The Social Philosophy of Rabindranath Tagore*, New Delhi, Classical, 2004.

Mukherji, Rajkumar : *Devadas-Key to Saratchandra*, Kolkata, Bona, 2005.

Nayar, Rana : *Earthy Tones : A Selection of Best Punjabi Short Stories: Gurdial Singh*, Delhi, Fiction House, 2002.

Pandya, Ketki N. : *Tagore's Chitra and Aurobindo's Savitri : A Comparative Study*, New Delhi, Atlantic, 2004.

Paul, S.K. and Amar Nath Prasad : *Recritiquing Rabindranath Tagore*, New Delhi, Sarup and Sons, 2006.

Prasad, Amar Nath and M.B. Gaijan : *Dalit Literature : A Critical Exploration*, New Delhi, Sarup and Sons, 2007.

Rhys, Ernest : *Rabindranath Tagore : A Biography*, Gurgaon, Shubhi Publications, 2004.

Roy, Pabitrakumar : *Rabindranath Tagore*, New Delhi, Munshiram Manoharlal, 2002.

Sanyal, Bandana : *Achalayatan : The Petrified Place, Rabindranath Tagore*, New Delhi, Rupa, 2006.

Sen, Pulinbihari and Kshitis Roy : *Rabindranath Tagore : A Tribute*, New Delhi, Hope India Publications, 2006.

Sil, Rita D. : *Profile of Rabindranath Tagore in World Literature*, New Delhi, Khama, 2002.

Singh, Kh. Kunjo : *Humanism and Nationalism in Tagore's Novels*, New Delhi, Atlantic, 2002.

Smith, R.V. : *The Delhi that No-one Knows*, New Delhi, DC Pub., 2005.

Soule, Arun : *Dimensions of Violence in the Works of Norman Mailer*, Jaipur, RBSA, 2003.

Sukanta, Chaudhuri : *Rabindranath Tagore : Selected Short Stories*, Delhi, Oxford University Press, 2000.

Tagore, Rabindranath : *The Art of Tagore*, New Delhi, Rupa and Co., 2004.

Tiwary, R.S. : *Current Indian Creativity in English*, Jaipur, Book Enclave, 2003.

Yadav, Ajay Singh : *Darkness Before Dawn*, Bhopal, Light House Books, 2000.

INDEX

P

R

S

T

U

V

W

Z

□□□